Waiting for Reform under Putin and Medvedev

Waiting for Reform under Putin and Medvedev

Edited by

Lena Jonson
Head of the Russia Research Programme and Senior Research Fellow,
Swedish Institute of International Affairs, Sweden

and

Stephen White
James Bryce Professor of Politics, University of Glasgow, UK

First published 2012 by
PALGRAVE MACMILLAN

Palgrave Macmillan in the UK is an imprint of Macmillan Publishers Limited, registered in England, company number 785998, of Houndmills, Basingstoke, Hampshire RG21 6XS.

Palgrave Macmillan in the US is a division of St Martin's Press LLC, 175 Fifth Avenue, New York, NY 10010.

Palgrave Macmillan is the global academic imprint of the above companies and has companies and representatives throughout the world.

Palgrave® and Macmillan® are registered trademarks in the United States, the United Kingdom, Europe and other countries

ISBN 978–1–137–01119–0

This book is printed on paper suitable for recycling and made from fully managed and sustained forest sources. Logging, pulping and manufacturing processes are expected to conform to the environmental regulations of the country of origin.

A catalogue record for this book is available from the British Library.

A catalog record for this book is available from the Library of Congress.

10 9 8 7 6 5 4 3 2 1
21 20 19 18 17 16 15 14 13 12

Printed and bound in Great Britain by
CPI Antony Rowe, Chippenham and Eastbourne

Contents

Tables and Figures

Tables

Figures

General Editor's Preface

This is the third world congress organized by the International Council for Central and East European Studies (ICCEES) that has the privilege of seeing congress volumes published by Palgrave Macmillan. That this is happening is an indication not only of the very fruitful relationship that ICCEES has with Palgrave Macmillan, but also of the recognition that the field of Central and East European Studies continues to enjoy not only academic excellence, but also continued pertinence as an area of study.

In their preface to earlier volumes from the 1995 Warsaw and the 2005 Berlin congresses, my two predecessors as general editor, Professor Ronald Hill of Trinity College Dublin and Roger E. Kanet of the University of Miami, outlined the historical conditions that not only brought about the creation of ICCEES, but above all the importance of publishing the research that is presented at ICCEES congresses. All congresses (including the one in Tampere, Finland in 2000) studied Central and Eastern Europe through the lens of various disciplines, but also mirrored the changes that were taking place in the area since Western scholars came together in Banff, Canada in 1974 to organize the research they were engaged in but which lacked an organizational structure that could coordinate their results and offer an opportunity for debate and discussion. This is why the International Committee for Soviet and East European Studies (ICSEES) was created; today it is known as the International Council for Central and East European Studies. The change in name reflected not only the mutations that the area was undergoing, but also the field of study.

After 1989 the societies and states of Central and Eastern Europe began experiencing major political, economic and social change. As a result, no longer were Western scholars engaged in 'Communist Studies,' rather they were focusing on an area that was undergoing redefinition as a geopolitical region. Domestic politics were in flux and interstate relations were experiencing a qualitative change that stressed henceforth cooperation rather than confrontation. ICCEES understood the need to give its congresses thematic direction. The 1990 ICCEES World Congress in Harrogate, England celebrated the end of the Cold War; the 1995 Warsaw congress focused on the democratic development of the former 'Communist states'; the 2000 congress, in Tampere,

Finland, stressed the divergences, convergences and uncertainties in Central and Eastern Europe; the 2005 Berlin congress focused on the European Union; the 2010 Stockholm congress examined the prospects for wider cooperation in Eurasia. This volume in this series reflects this last theme.

Putting together a volume that has thematic unity from the plethora of papers presented at a world congress is a major challenge. There was a time when it was sufficient to bring together high quality papers and publish them as congress proceedings. The list of such publications, found on the ICCEES web page, testifies to the vitality of research in the area. This is no longer the case; fortunately, many journals offer a publishing outlet for high class single presentations. This volume presents more than just excellent individual research results; it offers an important scholarly perspective. It marks a major contribution.

Stanislav J. Kirschbaum
York University, Glendon College, Toronto, Canada

Preface and Acknowledgements

This volume is based on papers presented at the IV World Congress of the International Council for Central and East European Studies. The congress was held in Stockholm in July 2010, when 'modernization' was still a buzzword of Russian official discourse. The term 'political modernization' was not included in the Russian government programme, yet the need for political reforms had been raised and discussed by Russian research institutes and centres. They argued that no modernization programme would be successful if it was not complemented by reforms opening up the closed political system. At some point it seemed that the then President Dmitrii Medvedev shared their view. Discussion of the topic of political reforms, or 'political modernization', at the congress was therefore timely.

As we began to entertain the idea of producing this book, one question seemed natural. What makes the system so resistant to change? We chose 'Modernization, or Waiting for Reform under Putin and Medvedev' as our working title for the book. It underlined the Russian dilemma – on the one hand, a policy of modernization, including political reforms, and on the other hand, a reluctance to introduce reforms, with the concomitant postponement of any tangible results.

By September 2011, when Medvedev announced that he would not stand for a second term as president, it had become clear that modernization had lost its position as an official strategic buzzword. Medvedev's successor in the 2012 elections, Vladimir Putin, emphasized words like 'stability' and 'consolidation'. If political reforms had ever really been on the agenda, they were now removed.

At this point we dropped the word modernization and changed the title of the book to *Waiting for Reform under Putin and Medvedev*. With this new title the topic of the book had become even more important. The election of Putin as president in March 2012 seemed to kill most expectations for reform. Yet the mass protests after the December 2011 parliamentary elections showed that during his new presidential term Putin will have to face the same persistent dilemma – how to develop the country while not reforming its obsolete political structures.

The book analyses different aspects of the Russian system's resistance to reform. This resistance has become so solid that even the piecemeal reforms introduced by Putin and Medvedev evaporated along the way and were not implemented. This resistance of the system and its capacity to reproduce itself in old forms over and over again will constitute a real threat to a future reformer in power. Although it does not provide any definitive solution to the reform dilemma, we believe that this book provides insights that will remain valid for many years to come.

Among the authors are some of the most brilliant Russian and Western sociologists and political scientists. It is interesting to see how they interlink and complement each other in their work. We are grateful to Michael Muravyov, who translated some of the Russian chapters, and to Connie Wall, our copyeditor.

Last but certainly not least we want to thank the Executive Committee of the International Council for Central and East European Studies (ICCEES) for its support and especially the Swedish branch of ICCEES Sällskapet för studier av Ryssland, Central-och Östeuropa samt Centralasien – for the grant that facilitated our work preparing the volume for publication.

Lena Jonson and Stephen White
Stockholm and Glasgow

Contributors

Irina Busygina is Professor in the Department of Comparative Politics at Moscow State Institute of International Relations. Her major research interests are comparative federalism, Russian politics and European integration. Email: ira.busygina@gmail.com

Paul Chaisty is Lecturer in Politics at St Antony's College, Oxford University. He is the author of *Legislative Politics and Economic Power in Russia* as well as other works on Russian legislative and party politics. Email: paul.chaisty@politics.ox.ac.uk

Boris Dubin is a sociologist, translator, Head of the Department of Political and Social Studies at the Levada Analytical Center in Moscow, and Deputy Editor-in-Chief of the magazine *The Russian Public Opinion Herald*. Email: dubinbv@yandex.ru

Clementine Fauconnier is a PhD student in Russian studies at the Institute of Political Sciences and the CERI (Center for International Studies and Research) in Paris. Email: clementine.fauconnier@wanadoo.fr

Mikhail Filippov is Associate Professor in the Department of Political Science, Binghamton University (SUNY), USA. Email: filippov@binghamton.edu

Stephen Fortescue is Associate Professor in Russian Politics at the School of Social Sciences, University of New South Wales, Australia. His research fields include the Russian mining and metals industry, Russian business–government relations, and the Russian policy-making process. Email: s.fortescue@unsw.edu.au

Lev Gudkov is a sociologist, professor, Director of the Levada Center, and Editor-in-Chief of *The Russian Public Opinion Herald*. He is the author of books and articles on the problems of post-Communist society, its transition, and the sociology of culture and literature. Email: gudkov@levada.ru

Nicolas Hayoz is Associate Professor of Political Science and the Director of the Interdisciplinary Institute of Central and Eastern Europe at the University of Fribourg, Switzerland. Email: nicolas.hayoz@uifr.ch

Eugene Huskey is a William R. Kenan Professor of Political Science and Russian Studies at Stetson University in Florida, USA. Email: ehuskey@stetson.edu

Lena Jonson is Senior Research Fellow, Associate Professor, and Head of the Russia Research Program at the Swedish Institute of International Affairs in Stockholm. Email: lena.jonson@ui.se

Emil Pain is General Director of the Centre for Ethno-Political Studies in Moscow and Professor at the National Research University–Higher School of Economics. He was an adviser on nationality policy to the Russian president in 1996–99. Email: painea@mail.ru

Nikolai Petrov is Scholar-in-Residence at the Carnegie Moscow Center, where he chairs the programme 'Society and Regions'. Email: npetrov@carnegie.ru

Stephen White is the James Bryce Professor of Politics and Senior Research Associate of the University's School of Central and East European Studies, University of Glasgow, Scotland, UK. Email: s.white@socsci.gla.ac.uk

Mark Urnov is Professor and Academic Supervisor at the Faculty of Politics, National Research University–Higher School of Economics in Moscow. He was the head of the Analytical Directorate of the Russian president during 1994–96. Email: markurnov@gmail.com

1
Introduction

Lena Jonson and Stephen White

The subject of this book is the problems encountered in the period 2008–11 in efforts to introduce reform in the Russian political system that had developed over the years since Vladimir Putin came to power, in 2000. The key question is: What makes this system so resistant to change?

Modernization and Reform

In September 2009 Dmitrii Medvedev made the term 'modernization' a buzzword in official Russian discourse with his article 'Go, Russia!' a year and a half after he was elected president.[1] He declared that modernization was necessary for the country's survival. By 'modernization' he seemed to mean profound 'change' – far-reaching reform. Emphasizing the need for technological innovations and for boosting the global competitiveness of the stagnant Russian economy, he also noted that to reach that goal Russian governance had to be improved. Observers interpreted his speech as a sign of a new awareness among the Russian leadership arising from the consequences of the 2008 international economic and financial crisis. In the years that followed, Medvedev's criticism of the state of affairs in Russia often seemed as harsh as any criticism of liberal oppositionists: he spoke out against corruption, inefficiency, the absence of democracy, authoritarianism, and the lack of rule of law.[2] And people's expectations heightened to see the reforms he intended to introduce.

Putin actually used the term 'modernization' earlier, in 2008, in what became the government's so-called Strategy 2020.[3] However, he did not include any broader political criticism, as Medvedev later did. Taking into consideration the fact that Medvedev was appointed by Putin

1

as his successor, people soon questioned how much political reform Medvedev had on his agenda.

What was actually meant by 'modernization' in Russian discourse? As pointed out by Mark Urnov in this volume, in the Russian debate the word is usually understood in terms of a kind of 'catching up' with the economically most developed countries. Over the centuries several prominent Russian statesmen, tsars and party general secretaries started large-scale projects for that purpose. Such campaigns were initiated and led from above and were carried out by force or through forceful mobilization of people and at great human cost. Ivan Groznyi, Peter the Great and Stalin are prime examples.

Throughout Russian history there have also been proponents of modernization among so-called benevolent rulers who tried to strengthen the Russian state by opening up a closed and old-fashioned system and improving people's living conditions. Among them are Alexander II in the 1860s, Petr Stolypin in the early twentieth century, Nikita Khrushchev in the early post-Stalin period, and of course the early period of Mikhail Gorbachev's perestroika policy in the late 1980s. Still, these were campaigns directed from above, as were some more modest campaigns to improve the system without touching the institutional structures of society, such as the *'uskorenie'* ('speeding-up' campaign) under Yurii Andropov in the early 1980s. This campaign was later picked up by the newly appointed Party General Secretary Mikhail Gorbachev but it eventually developed into something much more far-reaching than was originally intended.

Russian history demonstrates that efforts to modernize the country with the help of democratic reforms have failed and were replaced by periods of restoration as the pendulum of reaction stroke back, writes the Russian-born American historian Alexander Yanov.[4] This also happened to the reforms of the 1860s, when Alexander II turned authoritarian in the second half of his reign and was succeeded by the even more reactionary Alexander III. According to this logic, the Putin regime can be seen as a restoration and a reaction against the democratic reforms that failed during Boris Yeltsin's term in office. Russian history thus shows that modernization of society and democratic reforms do not necessarily go hand in hand. There are forceful and less forceful modernization campaigns, and usually none of them results in democratization.

Contemporary Western theories about modernization have a different perspective on what modernization of society means, the impending consequences, and how it comes about. Western theories emphasize the integration of socio-economic development, cultural change and democratization.[5] Pointing to the different stages in the process of modernization (industrial and post-industrial), they emphasize the role of socio-cultural values in the process of socio-economic change and the changes these values undergo. To most of these theorists, such as Ronald Inglehart and Christian Welzel, the role of dynamics for change coming from below becomes more important the more developed a society is.

As pointed out by Emil Pain in this volume, successful modernization is linked to measures taken by the authorities to create channels for the demands from below to surface. In Russian history, modernization and reform have not been the results of initiatives from below. Popular uprisings or outbursts of discontent have been either exploited politically by determined groups, like the Bolsheviks who channeled popular discontent into the October 1917 coup, or brutally crushed by the authorities, as in the 1905 demonstration in St Petersburg and the 1962 workers' demonstration in the city of Novocherkassk. Mechanisms and regular channels for political influence from below have been absent, blocked or minimal.

In this study we are mindful of the distinctions and differences in the various understandings of 'modernization', so the term is used differently depending on the context. Nevertheless, a basic assumption in our study is that modernization in contemporary Russia cannot take place without concomitant political modernization, that is, political reforms to democratize the country.

Waiting for Reform

Medvedev's articles and speeches had no immediate effect on government policy, which reflected the resistance from officials within the state apparatus to measures that would 'rock the boat'. Thus, no decisive measures were announced to come to grips with the problems of the country. No holistic or systemic approach was presented to handle problems that were interrelated. While Medvedev took policy initiatives in some important fields, such as a new law on the fight against corruption, reformation of the *militsiya* (the police) renaming it the *politsiya*, support for small and medium-size business, he avoided carrying out structural political reforms. Medvedev's initiatives, criticized for being too modest, nevertheless ran into difficulties and were hard to implement. There seemed to be resistance not only from individual officials, who naturally preferred the status quo, but also from the system, which seemed by definition resistant to change. Thus, the country waited impatiently for reform under Putin and even more so under Medvedev. This volume examines in detail what makes reform in Russia so difficult. The question is discussed from different angles in five parts.

Several of the Russian authors who contributed to this volume describe the present system as not only highly resistant to change but also caught in a vicious circle. The more the system fears independent political activities from below, the more it centralizes decision-making and blocks transparency; the more narrow the circle of the loyal and trusted becomes, the more privileges its members receive; the more corruption grows at the top, the more disillusion spreads at the bottom and popular trust in the authorities wanes; and the more the illnesses and stagnation of society grow, the weaker the authorities become. The general picture drawn by the authors thus shows an urgent need for deep-going structural reform, but this is what the Putin regime has studiously avoided.

Putin's 'model of vertical state power' is at the heart of the vicious circle. The population, says Emil Pain, is highly sceptical of the vertical state, and the widespread corruption among officials contributes to cementing this view. Further concentration of state power therefore foments further corruption, thus undermining the already low level of trust. Putin's vertical power model feeds socio-cultural attitudes of alienation, judicial nihilism and total distrust.

An Outline of the Volume and Authors' Findings

What makes the Russian system continue to revolve in this vicious circle? The first part of this volume introduces the issue of modernization and the Russian debate on a modernization policy. The second part analyses the main characteristics of the political system as it took form under Putin's presidency to elucidate factors that can explain the high degree of system resistance to reform. The third part includes case studies of piecemeal reform introduced by Putin or Medvedev to make the system of policymaking and governance more effective. The fourth part looks at the challenges and risks of modernization, as such a policy influences existing power relations between competing interests at the federal and regional levels. The fifth part reflects on the political development beyond the 'modernization' campaign during Medvedev's presidency.

In the first part of this volume, on the challenges of modernization, Nicolas Hayoz points out the influence from global processes and analyses what he calls the Russian discourse of resistance to globalization. He discusses the concept of 'sovereign democracy' as an element of this discourse and explores the interdependency of ideology and organizational power. He describes the system as weak and resistant to change but still stable enough to not risk a breakdown in the near future. It is a closed authoritarian system with the person at the top symbolizing the hierarchy of centrally controlled bureaucracies. It lacks checks and balances, free media and a functioning civil society. State-driven and state-sponsored organizations have replaced civil society. Yet the top of the system is vulnerable to challenges by rival networks and internal conflicts.

The concept of sovereign democracy was introduced in Russia after the 2004 Orange Revolution in Ukraine as a strategy aimed at legitimizing the Russian authoritarian centralized political system and encouraging vigilance against the West while presenting the symbol of a strong Russia. The concept was used to shield Russia and distance it from the influence of Western political models and experiences. The 2008 international financial crisis accentuated the need to further develop the discursive strategy. A vision for the future was needed, and, he claims, modernization thus became the new discourse. Hayoz thus views modernization in the context of the power vertical.

Mark Urnov analyses the Russian debate on modernization during the late 2000s and finds two major approaches, which he calls the 'conservative' and the 'liberal' doctrine. Reading official government documents, statements and reports of research institutes he identifies these different aproaches with different modernization strategies of President Medvedev and Prime Minister Putin. Urnov compares views on the role of values and motivation for successful modernization of economic policy, the political system and relations with the outside world.

In the second part of the volume, on characteristics of the Russian political system, Lev Gudkov points to the continuity from Soviet times. The current system was created (or rather assembled) from 'pieces', 'structural wrecks' and 'material' of the old system, although the composition and the functions of the social institutions changed, he claims, quoting the well-known Russian sociologist Yurii Levada. The major reason for the break-up of the Soviet system was its inability to change. Lacking mechanisms for change and for the handover of power caused serious tensions within the political elite. The *nomenklatura* system, which enabled the Communist Party leadership to control Russian society, was dysfunctional mainly because it could not adapt to new circumstances. It broke down, yet its major 'components' of key institutions continued into the post-Soviet era, although at that time guided by interests of a departmental, corporate or clan-based character. Among them was the most secretive and powerful institution, the secret police or the KGB (later renamed the Federal Security Service, FSB), which defied change and maintained its structure, and soon became very powerful.

Under Putin, writes Gudkov, the secret police in fact became the political leadership in disguise. As Putin strengthened his grip over the mass media, the judicial system, elections, parliament and non-governmental organizations, the secret police went from being a tool of power to becoming the *actual power* defining political tasks and taking decisions. Its methods thus permeated the system, and a combination of legal and illegal methods became the major resources of the regime. Among these methods, Gudkov says, are provocations and false trials, which the regime covers with a legal facade. As a result, political institutions are only decorative, and the law lost its status.

The logic of power consolidation continues to feed this development and, argues Gudkov, the current regime is unable to stop it. Coercion is therefore on the rise and will continue to escalate, the scope of ballot rigging and court trials is expanding, and the pursuit of complete domination over the public is on the rise. The regime has reached a stage where sheer instincts of self-preservation constitute the main dynamic. Although some in the top leadership may see the danger of this type of stagnation, large segments of the population know about and accept it, seeing no alternative and having no resources or channels to influence the situation.

In the next chapter, Boris Dubin analyses the myths that the Putin regime cultivates, primarily the idea that Russia is radically different from the rest of Europe and is predestined to follow a 'unique' Russian path. In the late 1980s and early 1990s most Russians could imagine that there might be political alternatives, which they saw in the European experience. They understood the need for reform in Russia, says Dubin, referring to opinion surveys conducted by the Moscow Levada Center. Public opinion started to change in the mid-1990s, and in the 2000s Russia emphatically considered the country as different from other European countries. This change in opinion was initially a kind of symbolic compensation for the hardships following from the economic reforms of the early 1990s, explains Dubin. People recalled the years of stability under Brezhnev, but under Putin this myth became a tool for the government to rule the masses.

Analysing the 'special path' as a mythological archetype, Dubin explains that it functions by creating a collective 'we', thereby identifying the norm for 'us' and characterizing any deviance from the norm as the 'other' and 'foreign'. The binary we–them character of the Russian special path excludes references to any universal norms cited in discussion of alternatives to the Russian regime and policy. The special path archetype is static and implies acceptance of the situation because it is defined as 'our way'. It also embraces the perception of the ruler as a superior power beyond the reach of ordinary citizens. It is predicated on not only a distance between rulers and the ruled but also strict secrecy in political decision-making. As a result, Dubin continues, politics degenerates into empty ceremonies with infighting at the top and behind the scenes, while the politically passive and scattered masses wait for their leader to care for and guide them. The mythology of a Russian special path is highly relevant to contemporary discussions of modernization in Russia. It constitutes an effective barrier against any development towards competitiveness, individual initiatives from below, and a search for what is new and different.

Emil Pain continues in Chapter 6 the analysis of the characteristics of the system and disusses the role of socio-cultural values. Although socio-cultural values are said to change only slowly over time, sudden and drastic shifts in socio-economic living conditions may force individuals to adapt to a new situation in a short span of time, thereby influencing both their values and their behaviour. In the four-year period 1991–94, the tough years of economic reform, many Russians demonstrated a surprising capacity for taking initiatives when they were forced to find new ways to earn an income and survive. Pain therefore criticizes the current predominant understanding among leading representatives of the two major schools of modernization since, he claims, they regard inertia and passivity as permanent traits of Russian tradition and culture.

Pain paints an overall picture of contemporary Russian society as highly inertial: the most atomized society in Europe with a minimum of traditional and social bonds, and a population that does not challenge the leadership but refuses to implement its will. Nevertheless, he says, initiatives and activities from below are expanding. In those Russian regions where the local leadership facilitates institutional and administrative regulations for business, economic initiatives from below are stimulated. Thus, Pain claims, when the authorities are willing to facilitate innovation, people are prepared to take advantage of these possibilities. Comparative social research shows, he says, that Russians today have come closer to other European countries in their attitudes towards change and risk taking. Yet, Russian attitudes have a strong anarchic bend, show little respect for rules and norms, and have a very low level of mutual trust (belief, trust and confidence). These attitudes can be changed only in a democratic culture, he argues. To create such a culture, the authorities must provide the necessary institutional framework. The energy from below will then contribute to modernizing society.

The third part, on piecemeal reform under Putin and Medvedev, presents cases of piecemeal administrative reform when the Russian government has tried to improve the system of management in politics and in economics. None of these efforts seems to have been successful.

In Chapter 7, Stephen Fortescue analyses the contemporary Russian policymaking process and asks whether it became more efficient after May 2008, when Vladimir Putin became prime minister. 'Efficiency' is defined as whether an issue 'reached the decision stage reasonable quickly' and after appropriately being 'subject to consultation from a full range of interested parties'. Fortescue starts from the assumption that all issues of contemporary policymaking entail multilateral consultation between different specialized interests represented by various bureaucratic agencies. Effective policymaking requires procedures for decision-making rules within the cabinet but also for pre-meeting consultation and for the signing of documents.

Compromising between rivaling bureaucratic interests was a problem during Putin's presidency. Presidential directives were of limited use in this regard. Therefore, after becoming prime minister, Putin tried to solve the problem by making greater use of the practice of smaller, informal meetings that he had introduced during his last years as president. The purpose of these meetings was to influence the parties until they could reach agreement and the policy deadlocks were resolved. This innovation was not enough, concludes Fortescue, and decision-making deadlocks and delays still prevail. Fortescue comments that, while Putin seemed fairly satisfied with the results of this reform of the policymaking process, President Medvedev increasingly expressed his frustration over the failure of government agencies to deliver. The number of presidential directives therefore increased during Medvedev's term as president. Fortescue here points to a source of tension in the Medvedev–Putin duumvirate.

In a democratic society, parliament would play a crucial role in facilitating modernization, writes Paul Chaisty. The task of creating a dynamic and innovative economy requires decision-makers who are capable of taking decisions that can release the economic forces that drive change. While the Russian Duma (lower chamber of parliament) was reasonably prominent in the decade after the adoption of the 1993 Constitution, it became less important during the Putin regime, and comparative studies suggest that the Russian Duma today is among the world's weakest assemblies. Nonetheless, membership of the assembly is still valued by members of Russia's political and economic estab-lishment. For Russia's business elite in particular, seats in the Duma are sought after, and business candidates make up a growing propor-tion of those elected to the lower house. In the Fifth Duma (2007–11), the share of deputies from a business background was almost 40 per cent, or twice the share of those who were elected to the First Duma (1993–95). Nonetheless, this understates the representation of business interests in both houses of the Russian Parliament. When compared with countries with traditionally high levels of business representation such as the United Kingdom and the United States, the dominance of business in the Russian Duma is notable. In Russia, the phenomenon of business over-representation in legislative politics is a general problem that constrains economic modernization at all levels of government, he claims.

Economic legislation is at the centre of most lobbying campaigns in the Russian Parliament. Much of this activity is concerned with the budget and fiscal policy as well as with general framework legislation that affects all areas of the economy. A significant proportion of the activity is clustered around those economic sectors that have featured predominantly in the career profiles of deputies. Three sectors feature most consistently in lobbying campaigns in the lower house: agricul-ture and related manufacturing in the alcohol and tobacco industries; finance, which includes legislation that regulates the banking and insurance sectors; and energy, that is, legislation affecting the oil, gas and electricity industries. While the number of party and regional rep-resentatives is significant in the occupational backgrounds of Duma deputies, many deputies have also had careers in business.

In December 2008 the Russian Parliament passed one of the most important pieces of legislation in its effort to de-bureaucratize the small business sector. In Chapter 9, Eugene Huskey analyses the intensified state efforts to de-bureaucratize the environment for business since Dmitrii Medvedev assumed the presidency. In order to inject dynamism into the economic system he initiated a campaign to support small and medium-size business. In Russia complicated state regulations and wide-spread corruption have hampered the development of business. In spite of government attempts since 2001 to improve the conditions for small and medium-size companies, the situation did not improve. Medvedev chose to focus on the aspect of inspection of companies by various state agencies because state inspection is one of the most lucrative sources for bribes in return for not reporting actual or claimed violations of rules. The purpose of the 2008 law was to limit the exposure of business to state inspections.

Huskey analyses the implementation of the law in the summer of 2009, in the first year after it entered into effect. He concludes that parts of the law are 'very much in keeping with traditional Russian responses to the pathologies of a Stalinist regime ... [creating] yet another checking mechanism or [strengthening] those already in existence, and then [watching] while those institutions are infected by the disease they are asked to cure'. Nevertheless, he regards the state's intensified efforts as a hopeful sign and 'a countervailing current to the hardening of political relations between state and society'.

Clementine Fauconnier introduces the regional dimension of the problems of Russia's modernization and reform. During Putin's presidency a more centralized decision-making structure was introduced in 2000 to give Moscow a greater say and more effective means of administrative control of the regions. Of these measures, the 2004 law was crucial since it made the governors appointees of the president rather than locally elected officials. For fear of losing control over the regions the Putin-loyal United Russia Party was established as the predominant party in all regional assemblies. New election regulations contributed to giving United Russia this standing since the threshold for political parties to enter parliament was increased from 5 to 7 per cent, and the single-member seats in the new Duma were abandoned in favour of proportional elections based on party lists to the Federal Duma as well as to most regional assemblies.

Her chapter analyses how the 'power vertical' was strengthened at the local level by the political recruitment of United Russia. This is a case study of the United Russia Party and its role in the Novgorod region in Russia's north-west, between Moscow and St Petersburg. The study focuses particularly on the process of candidate selection during the federal elections of 2007–08, when a significant part of the former regional political elite was replaced.

A thorough renewal of the political elite took place in those two years in the Novgorod region with a new governor, two new Duma deputies, a new mayor and a new municipal assembly. This resulted not only in the marginalization of former elected officials but also in the selection of people, often elected for the first time supported by the party and without any previous ties to the region. The introduction of so-called primaries deprived the region of any possibility to choose its own Duma candidates and strengthened centralization of the political recruitment process.

In the fourth part of the volume, on the challenges and risks of modernization, Nikolai Petrov discusses the problems of modernizing

Russia's regions against the background of the shifting power balance between the regions and the stronger Federal centre during the past ten years or more. A considerable but uneven de-modernization process has taken place in the regions in political, social and economic terms, he writes. Policy, decided in Moscow, sometimes has paradoxical and unintended consequences for power relations at the regional level. Thus, he says, there is a trend that, as regions lose power to the centre, the internal consolidation among the regional elite is undermined and replaced by intensified political competition. While the region becomes more subordinated to the centre, its links with the citizens decline, as does its political accountability to the region's population.

Petrov evaluates the potential for modernization in the regions, comparing differences with regard to democratic, technological, and social–political conditions. He argues that technological modernization alone will not be enough to resolve the country's main problems. The regions need to become active and independent players initiating modernization. He concludes that Russian regions are in urgent need of political and administrative reform as are their relations with Moscow. Modernization in such a huge and diversified country as Russia is absolutely impossible without restoring and developing real federalism, he writes.

In Chapter 12 Irina Busygina and Mikhail Filippov focus on the role of the state as the major agent of modernization in Russia and a major arena for the ongoing conflict of interests between groups within the state apparatus. The authors find the major factor explaining resistance to reform in Russia in the way the ruling group perceives serious risks to its own interests in genuinely democratic change.

Busygina and Filippov argue that, if the state is to assume the role of a driving force breaking the raw-material orientation of the economy and initiate innovative processes, radical change is required in the system of governance. From the perspective of private investors, both foreign and domestic, the Russian state in its present form is unpredictable, inefficient, deeply corrupt and, most importantly, not a credible guarantor of private property rights. A more democratic Russian state might therefore provide a stronger and more accountable form of government that could facilitate the process of modernization. Yet any serious attempt to change existing institutions, they argue, involves a redistribution of benefits from some groups to other groups with consequences for the present power status quo. The choice of institutional reform might influence the trajectory of political development by causing realignments of major political coalitions with consequences for their willingness to accept compromises. This makes the Russian leadership reluctant to engage in more than modest administrative reforms.

Not only is the balance between competing interests of crucial significance in any development of this kind, but so, too, is the temporal sequence. In particular, the period immediately after a programme of political modernization has been launched is likely to be 'particularly protracted and volatile', and 'both risks and efficiency' will be adversely affected. Successful reform takes a long time and requires a political commitment that is sustained until the fruits of reform become apparent. In these circumstances, it is more likely either that political reform will not be initiated or, if it is nonetheless initiated, it will not yield the positive economic results that have been promised for a considerable time to come.

The fact that Russia is a multi-ethnic, multicultural and multilayered federal state makes democratic transition and modernization a particularly protracted, difficult and volatile process, the two authors claim. Since political reform is likely to cause instability in its initial stage, the current regimes at the federal centre and in the regions prefer the status quo, even if this means the continuation of an economy distorted by the extraction and export of natural resources and a political system with a highly ineffective state apparatus. The authors find little prospect of successful modernization in the short or medium term.

Finally, in Chapter 13 the editors of the volume return to the discussion of the prospects for reform against the background of the post-election situation in December 2011, when large demonstrations reflected an awakening of civil society.

Initiating Reform

The underlying question in several of the chapters is how reforms could come about. Although rigidity and closeness are described as major characteristics of the system, most of the present authors believe that change will come from above and from within the state apparatus. In this perspective the prospects of an ongoing power struggle at the top between different groupings is discussed. Although during Medvedev's presidency there was no evidence that he was a Gorbachev in disguise, there were signs of disagreement within the state apparatus.

It can be argued that change will never be initiated from above if there is no pressure from below. Were there signs of demands from below during the years when Medvedev was president and Putin the premier? The reactions of the population reflected a preference for *exit* rather than for *voice* as young Russian professionals emigrated, older professionals bought flats in West European capitals and the business elite sent their children to boarding schools in the West.

Nevertheless, the popular uprisings and revolutions in the Arab world in the spring of 2011, which seemed to disprove the conventional wisdom regarding the passivity and parochialism of Arab culture and society, illustrated the unpredictability of political life. The wave of discontent demonstrated a strength that surprised the rest of the world and illustrated how discontent can accumulate over time until it suddenly explodes. Although no one was prepared to draw parallels with Russia, the events were a reminder of how limited our predictions usually are.

The Arab revolts at the same time pointed out a weakness. Popular uprisings can get started from below but to be successful they need both partners with knowledge and experience from within the state apparatus and a political organization capable of taking the lead, guaranteeing a policy towards democracy, and securing popular influence also when the wave of enthusiasm eventually calms down.

Looking back at the era of perestroika, it obviously was the result of a process initiated from above but long awaited by the population. People wanted change. Yet they were mobilized mainly during the August coup of 1991, when they took to the streets to protest against the opponents of the perestroika policy. The popular energy released during the break-up of the Soviet Union soon evaporated as disillusion spread during the hard years of the 1990s. No popular organizations, movements or political parties were created during these years that could take on the task of articulating the demands from below for democratization and political reform. There were no organizations to support, check and constrain the excesses of Yeltsin. There was no one to explain to the masses that democratic transformation is a long and thorny process. Instead, Yeltsin found himself in the position of the lonely reformer, and he soon sold off both the richness of the country and the reform project as such.

In Putin's Russia during the 2000s there were no organizations to put forward popular demands. Moreover, the majority of the Russian population preferred not to get involved in any social upheavals. Instead, the feeling of hopelessness contributed to a general resignation. Yet, in the early 2010s a new political atmosphere seemed to be in the making.

President Medvedev's critique of Russia's administrative and political system helped to make criticism more of a normal and legitimate theme in public discussion. Television remained as loyal as before, but some print newspapers and journals started to publish more critical views.

Together with the free information flow on the Internet, the debate intensified. The international financial crisis of 2008 swept away major illusions about the Russian economy. From 2010 opinion polls showed falling ratings for the president, the prime minister, and the party of power, United Russia. During the spring of 2011 reports were published by Russian research institutes pointing to a crisis in political confidence, especially among the middle class in the large cities. The discontent moved into street action.

Although the number of people participating in protest actions was limited, public meetings and demonstrations frightened the authorities and activated the police and the secret police (the FSB). Human rights demonstrations like 'Strategy 31', initiated by Lyudmila Alekseyeva, were met with police batons and arrests. At the same time, the 10 December meeting in 2010 in Manezh Square in Moscow, when nearly 10,000 angry football fans and a hard core of Russian fascists caused chaos and fright, illustrated how distorted a society becomes when channels for citizens to influence politics are blocked. Russian society was boiling under the surface. The widespread feeling of hopelessness had come to nourish also an upsurge of spontaneous rage.

A sign of the new atmosphere in society was reflected when in April 2011 the state-sponsored contemporary art prize, Innovatsiya, was awarded to the performance group Voina, whose painting of a 65-metre phallus on the bridge outside the FSB building in St Petersburg was seen as a scream of 'fuck you' to the FSB. The same prize, although in a different category, was given to the organizer of the street performance 'Monstratsiya' in Novosibirsk which for almost ten years had puzzled the local police and the FSB with its peaceful carnival-like gatherings under absurd slogans. Something new seemed to be in the air that was not only pressing for a freer atmosphere in society but also demonstrating a new fearlessness of the potential of repression by the FSB. When Medvedev declared in September 2011 that he was stepping down from a second presidential term in favour of Putin's candidacy and then Putin stated that this had been decided several years earlier, they brought a heavy blow to the remaining public confidence in the political system. Medvedev's speech was the final signal that his modernization campaign had definitely come to an end.

The parliamentary elections of December 2011 and presidential election of March 2012 were set far in advance. A new upswing of the world market price of oil improved the Russian economy, although it did not eliminate the structural weaknesses of the raw material-dominated economy. Everything seemed to be under control of the regime, yet the regime felt the fear of losing control. As the elections drew closer, the political situation in Russia became completely deadlocked in the sense that the regime did not want to embark on the kind of structural political reforms that were needed to solve the deep problems of Russia. Instead, the regime postponed decisions on political reform, avoiding anything that could 'rock the boat'. In the meantime, the signs of a new atmosphere of popular impatience were mounting. After the election they erupted into the largest street protests that had been seen since the final days of the Soviet Union.

Demands for modernization and political reforms will intensify in the future. And the capacity of the system to reproduce itself in old forms over and over again will continue to cause problems. The problems discussed in this volume will thus be with us for many years to come. How long does Russia have to wait?

Notes

1. Dmitrii Medvedev (2009), 'Go, Russia!', http://eng.kremlin.ru/news/298.
2. See e.g. Medvedev's video blog of 23 November 2010: 'Nasha demokratiya nesovershenna, my eto prekrasno ponimaem. No my idem vpered' [Our democracy is incomplete, and we fully understand this. But we are going ahead], http://blog.kremlin.ru/post/119/transcript.
3. Putin 8 February (2008), 'Vystuplenie na rasshirennom zasedanii Gosudarstvennogo soveta "O strategii Rossi do 2020 goda"' [Speech at the Enlarged Council "On Russia's Development Strategy to 2020"], http://archive. Kremlin.ru/text/appears/2008/02/159528.shtml; 'The Concept of Long-term Socio-Economic Development of the Russian Federation for the Period up to the Year 2020' (2008), Ministry for Economic Development of the Russian Federation, 17 November, p. 12, available in English on the ERAWATCH website at http://cordis.europa.eu/erawatch/index.cfm?fuseaction=policy. document&uuid=66E60C75-B11F-89C8-5FD91E28F83B1B4D.
4. A. Yanov (2007), *Zagadka nikolaevskoi Rossii 1825–1855* [The Riddle of Russia under Nicolai 1825–1855]; *Kniga vtoraya* (Moscow: Novyi khronograf) is the second volume of the trilogy *Rossiya i Evropa v trekh knigakh 1462–1921* [Russia and Europe in Three Volumes].
5. R. Inglehart and C. Welzel (2005), *Modernization, Cultural Change, and Democracy: The Human Development Sequence* (Cambridge: Cambridge University Press). See also the Russian study based on Western theories of modernization in the Russian case: E. A. Pain and O. D. Volkogonova (eds) (2008), *Rossiiskaya modernizatsiya: razmyshlyaya o samobytnosti* [Russian Modernization: Thinking of Identity] (Moscow: Woodrow Wilson International Center for Scholars/Kennan Institute and Tri kvadrata).

Part I

The Challenge of Modernization in Russia

2
Globalization and Discursive Resistance: Authoritarian Power Structures in Russia and the Challenges of Modernity

Nicolas Hayoz

Introduction

The promises of 1989 are still far from being realized in Eastern Europe. In many regions, particularly in Russia and the other countries of the former Soviet Union, democracy and the idea of freedom are lacking. Instead, different forms of authoritarian or quasi-authoritarian regimes are blocking the democratization process. Obviously, processes such as globalization, Europeanization, modernization and transformation are not just routinely carried out by countries. Countries can attempt to resist global processes or implement only those aspects that suit them – such as global markets and technologies – while avoiding other aspects of modernity such as democracy and the rule of law. This is certainly also a question of the radius of state power at the regional level. State capitalism paired with authoritarian rule seems to be a formula that works rather well in such countries as Russia and China. On the political, economic, scientific and technological levels, these countries are a part of modern world society. They also owe their potential for action, for example in world markets or world politics, and their (new) assertiveness to the existence of global structures that not only increase dependencies and constraints but also create opportunities for states to modernize.

Globalization may present both challenges and risks. Countries that are modernizing can benefit from the advantages of globalization, but they also have to deal with a cultural homogenization that in many cases provokes resistance. In authoritarian regimes such as China's, which is modernizing its cultural past – partially by destroying it – homogenization or Westernization can be prevented more easily than in open societies.[1] On the other hand, globalization can also help keep authoritarian rulers in power. The so-called petro-states, such as Russia, exemplify this trend. Political regimes may also participate in global or European processes and institutions and nourish populist anti-Western rhetoric that differentiates between Western and Russian democracy, for example; this seems to work particularly well in times of crisis. Authoritarian rule and popular expectations are convergent just as authoritarian regimes and anti-Western populist discourse are. The global economic crisis that began in late 2008 appears to have left an impact on the discursive and even the ideological levels in Russia. If the assumption that political discourse needs to be backed by material resources in order to be sustainable is correct, then the Kremlin's notion of 'sovereign democracy' has lost much of its appeal. The financial and economic crisis has shown that the Russian state is not immune to failure. Ideas such as 'sovereign democracy' may thus lose their legitimacy.

The stability of authoritarian regimes such as Russia's is usually guaranteed by a combination of repression and the regime's ability to accommodate different groups and their interests through rent distribution. If the contract 'prosperity against loyalty' loses balance due to a shrinking of the state's resource base (meaning that the state can distribute less rents and accommodate fewer interests), the regime may become more repressive or will need to find an alternative source of legitimacy, possibly an ideological one. The latter has already happened. For the PR specialists of the Russian regime, 'sovereign democracy' has increasingly become the expression of the Russian authoritarian or conservative form of modernization. Putin's 'power vertical' has been presented as 'sovereign democracy', and Medvedev's insistence on modernization may be simply an attempt to say that even quasi-authoritarian regimes need more than sovereignty and have to think about how they want to realize desperately needed socio-economic change. In the regime's own description, modernization is meant to be the continuation of sovereign democracy. It is of course not modernization in the Western sense, including political reforms that should bring the country to the shores of democracy. Putin's 'power vertical' and 'Russia Inc.' controlling the economy indeed involve large-scale modernization and rationalization processes. They certainly aim at increasing Russia's 'competitive power', but they are also meant as strategies to consolidate the power of the socio-political elites. Under that aspect it makes absolute sense to say that sovereign democracy is an attempt to explain the Russian form of modernization: modernization must follow a path whose direction is restricted by the regime's interest in retaining power and its grip on society.

However, a discourse about change is not enough. Change has to be translated into practice and visible signs of improvements in everyday life. If this Russian variant of modernization without democracy is associated with failure and stagnation – this seems increasingly to be the case – then the regime should start thinking about changing its political discourse or PR strategy and reconsider its conception of modernization. It seems that after Russia's process of recovering from the crisis, the discourse of sovereign democracy has been pushed into the background by the discourse on modernization.[2] But it is probably safe to say that both ideas go together as two faces of the same coin. The interesting point here is that modernization remains at the level of rhetoric since under non-democratic conditions it cannot mean serious economic and political reforms. Even more under conditions of a 'petro-state', modernization can only mean 'business as usual': despite the inflationary use of the modernization discourse the regime has no interest or does not seem to be constrained to start reforming the inefficient state structures or establishing a genuine rule of law at all levels of political and economic life.[3] Modernization in a Western sense, involving economic as well as political reforms, would necessarily mean that the regime would have to admit the basic idea of practical democracy – to be accountable and responsible to the citizens.

As all illiberal and authoritarian regimes, Russia needs a discourse to justify its actions and policies, its verbal and often also real wars against its proclaimed internal and external enemies. In a post-ideological era such a discourse may be motivated by specific interests at particular times, the result of contingency. Nevertheless, there is a discourse even if it is composed of bits and pieces navigating among the topics circulating worldwide or in international relations. And this discourse cannot be separated from the power structure that is using it. It may sound strange to affirm that today Russia's power structure is similar to the Communist Party's structure in the former Soviet Union, where the hierarchical power of the party was legitimized by the communist ideology. This is to say ideology does not make sense without control. The 'genetic code' of Soviet communism was always ideology *and* control. This is also the case in today's Russia: Putin's 'system' continues to be primarily about control of a society and a nation with many centrifugal forces. The regime is based on a mix of power networks, organizational power and distribution policies, and it tries to integrate them as elements of a discourse or a doctrine. However, in its non-modern conception of society and politics, it is ill-prepared to handle the challenges and now, increasingly, the multiple challenges (including political opposition) it has to face in the different social spheres. A modern society cannot be steered like a company. And the inadequacy of the government's responses to the multiple crises and challenges may be the beginning of a process of delegitimation of the regime. This would be, so to say, a kind of conning of globalization and Europeanization: a regime can try to immunize itself, but it cannot be sure that it can control the risks of doing so. This chapter examines specific strategies of resistance in the case of Russia, particularly in the political sphere, aiming to explore the interdependency of ideology and organizational power in Russia (of 'Russia Inc.'). And it seeks to show how such immunization strategies, oriented particularly against Western democratic models, are, at the regional level, the organizing and instrumentalizing of society and large systems such as law, economy, politics or education in such a way that the autonomy of these social spheres may be threatened.

The Attractions and Functions of 'Sovereign Democracy'

The discourse on sovereign democracy obviously serves different interests but can only be understood against the background of the centralized quasi-authoritarian power structure that has been established by Putin and his allies in the state bureaucracy. An ideology is not enough to stabilize an authoritarian power structure, and stabilization should not be confused with legitimization. Rather, legitimization may contribute to the stability of power. Under Soviet communism, the party ideology faded away before the party structure disappeared. While the party structure could stabilize itself for a few years through corruption and a system of favours, once the economic basis had eroded the party collapsed. Today's power structure in Russia may not collapse but, since it is not based on a dynamic power that has the potential for change, its stability is continuously challenged by rival networks and conflicts between them. Moreover, even though the personal power of the leaders may be appreciated by a majority of a public who have no concern for the formal features of a modern democracy, personal power is always visible and exposed power that can easily be challenged if it does not produce visible results.

The meanings of sovereign democracy also raise the question to what extent this battle formula contributes to the stability of the regime. This is again a difficult question; it is not clear what stabilization and stability actually mean in a country like Russia. Stability in a democratic regime is fairly easy to measure, for example the stability of a government based on a coalition of parties, which may or may not achieve the necessary majority to form a stable government. In Russia, where power is not based on change through elections, the stability of the supreme power, 'the Kremlin', is probably based on a continuous balancing of interests among rival factions and groups in the state bureaucracy, which are held together by a personalized power structure and its networks at the top of the hierarchy. The discourse on sovereign democracy, with the implicit message 'we have things under control', not only satisfies the expectations and frustrations of the wider public but also can be considered as a useful ideological device contributing to the coherence and discipline of an oversized and over-centralized state bureaucracy. And finally, sovereign democracy is a distinction that informs observers, whether the public, elites, opponents or the international community, how to look at Russia and how the country's 'collective identity' should be understood in terms of political semantics. Stability in Russia probably has as much to do with the reproduction mechanism of power as with the more symbolic and ideological side of power, which has to find convincing illustrations of insecure countries and their identity.

Some argue that the successful model of economic development, combining an open economy with a closed political system, has made regimes such as Russia's and China's more attractive in a political world characterized by the competition between democratic and authoritarian regimes.[4] This may no longer be the case but it is probably safe to say that the attractiveness of a model like sovereign democracy follows a political conjuncture: the fact that the formula no longer circulates in the public space could mean that the regime no longer needs it. But even if it has lost its momentum, the policies behind this catchphrase have not changed. This was not the case a few years ago, when Russia felt the necessity to react against 'Western interference' in Russian affairs, or in what Russia considered to be its 'zones of influence', or against triumphant liberalism in the West. In this regard Ivan Krastev shows the extent to which Moscow's answer to the danger represented by the Orange Revolution in Ukraine became the concept of sovereign democracy, in practice and in discourse.[5] The Orange Revolution brought a popular president to power and thus showed for the first time that regime change through mass revolt was possible in an ex-Soviet country – not least of all due to Western democracy-promotion strategies, which included material and financial aid.

The Russian leadership was clearly not prepared to allow similar scenarios to emerge in other neighbouring countries, let alone on Russian soil. Putin's re-establishment of a 'power vertical' was the beginning of political stability for Russia, but it was also the start of his offensive against Western interference and Western-style democracy and its promoters. The anti-Western element in the formula of sovereign democracy also shows that this discourse was directed against the worldwide 'hegemony' of the Western notion of liberalism.

To understand the real impact of a certain discourse we need to not only relate it to the social and economic basis on which it rests, but also connect it to those actors within the relevant power structures who are responsible for the production and reproduction of a certain discourse. The structures within which those actors operate, that is, the type of regime, are highly relevant to the understanding of a certain political discourse. The following remarks therefore focus on Russia's political regime and the kind of discourse it produces.[6] In any study of Russia's political regime, autocracy is clearly the starting point. It is telling that the representatives of the Russian state do not describe their regime in terms of a 'normal' democracy. The Kremlin knows that its political construction has nothing to do with the institutional set-up of a modern democracy. Its political discourse on sovereign democracy does not hide this fact; rather, it is the semantic correlate of autocracy. In other words, what is of interest here is a specific power configuration that produces specific discourses but has to rely on huge organizational resources and systems in order to control society.[7] The discursive and organizational design of the Russian regime presents many insights into its conception of society and its politics. Russia has more difficulties than other regional societies in accepting the implications of modern society and globalization. But the demonstration effects coming from globalization show inevitably that Russia needs to be modernized. It pretends to represent something different, but in fact this 'difference' is emphasized only to justify a certain type of governance model that mainly suits the interests of a small and powerful ruling elite. The difference is no longer strictly ideological, as was the case with the Soviet Union; after all, Russia is a part of the globalized world economy. But politically, the Russian leadership calls attention to its difference with the West since it does not want Russia to submit to any supranational structure that would endanger its sovereign status as a leading regional power with global ambitions.[8]

All this purports to stabilize the system but is in fact also designed to prevent the loss of the power and privileges of Russia's ruling elite.

The Russian state has organized its society in a way similar to China's; it is based on a specific combination of personal power, organizational power and functional differentiation. 'Kremlin Inc.', 'Russia Inc.' or 'militocracy' are slogans that describe organized forms of societies expressing the obsessions of regimes with administrative resources and the construction of centrally controlled bureaucratic hierarchies in all social spheres. It is no coincidence that this phenomenon is reminiscent of Soviet realities of central control by the Communist Party. Authors such as Robert Kagan have made relevant observations about the fact that the Russian and Chinese leaders believe in autocracy and disdain democracy, since the latter is associated with interference, conflicts, divisions, and of course with the instability of power – a power that is under constant threat from society if society is not firmly controlled.[9] The idea of sovereign democracy can be viewed as an instruction for how to protect against the promotion of Western democracy in Russia as well as Western support for democratic movements in what Russia considers its sphere of influence in the neighbouring states. The meaning of political slogans such as sovereign democracy can be controlled more tightly. Globalization is certainly one of the driving forces behind such a 'protectionist' discourse. On the other hand, such discursive claims at a regional level may be tested against the background of emerging global observers in a globalized world: world opinion with corresponding global protest movements, but also academic observers with their research programmes speaking about progress or regression of democracy in specific countries.

Discourse of the Powerful and the Power of Discourse

The concept of sovereign democracy was elaborated with the intention of justifying Russia's 'own path' vis-à-vis a Western audience. It was thus an elite project. Yet in which way did it also work for a broader domestic audience? That depends on what the public reads into the idea of sovereign democracy. If it is about a 'powerful Russia' then the message appeals to a broader audience, but if the idea is about Russia being a democracy *sui generis*, then the message probably misses its aim. Opinion polls show that Russians know what the basic elements of a democracy are and that they are fully aware that their country does not live up to Western standards of democracy. Elections at national level, as well as at most regional levels, are not about transferring but rather retaining power, and the state is not about protecting rights but rather controlling society. The Russian public is one of the most cynical, distrusting and dissatisfied of all the post-communist countries. Almost 90 per cent of poll respondents believe that their public officials are corrupt. The degree of political distrust of almost all political institutions – with the exception of the presidency – should be seen as alarming.[10] Such facts speak another language than the official one about the different Russian democracy. Of course one may point to similar problems in established democracies. But in the case of Russia there are no checks and balances, no political opposition, no free media and no organized civil society that can mobilize against a corrupt power structure in order to call for accountability or replace the holders of power. The gap between the state and society is large. If people do not trust politicians, one may expect that they also do not take ideological propositions seriously. Yet there are considerable differences when looking at different strata of Russian society, for example the reactions of old versus young people to the 'hegemonic' ideological discourses coming from the regime.

Since one objective of the discourse on sovereign democracy is to achieve national or elite unity, increase the strength of the country and define national interests[11] – but not Western-style democracy – the Russian population could interpret this strange semantic construction as part of the elite's efforts to strengthen Russian power at home and internationally, even though it probably had no clear idea about the meaning of this notion. In other words, if the majority understands 'sovereign democracy' more in terms of sovereignty than democracy, then the hegemonic discourse sponsored by the regime works: for instance, in achieving elite unity and protecting against ideological interference from the West. If, however, people read it as a special form of Russian democracy, the discourse also serves an ideological purpose and points to the misleading interpretation that Russia *wants* to be different from other countries and that a strong executive power that controls untrusted political parties, the parliament and most other institutions of the Russian political system is the only way to guarantee stability.

In that sense sovereign democracy serves interests, demands and expectations at many different levels: from street-level communication to the supreme spheres of power, where the main question is about how to guarantee stability and to ensure the survival of the regime. So, depending on the attitudes of the public towards the regime, sovereign democracy can mean two things: a discourse that adequately describes the political practices and the core features of the current Russian regime, and an ideology or even an 'ideological fantasy'.[12] In the latter case, the regime and parts of the public pretend that Russia is a democracy but at the same time know perfectly well that this is not the case. And this may work, since the other part of the concept of sovereign democracy, the word 'sovereign', is the discursive reality that really matters and expresses the way power works in the country, as an authoritarian regime controlling the self-reproduction of power independently, without and against interference from the 'West', the internal public or political antagonists. The critical part of the public in Russia knows that such a discourse can work only in the context of a quasi-authoritarian regime *and* in a culture where official monologues are suppressing and dominating the culture of dialogue. The regime is able and willing to back its power and its discourse with repression. But it is well known that discourses and repression work only under specific conditions. These conditions may change and a hegemonic discourse suddenly finds itself confronted with a competitor.

All political regimes reproduce and maintain specific discourses about the way they or their underlying political system function and how they want to be perceived by the public, whether domestic or international. In authoritarian regimes the legitimating mechanism is not based on democratic elections. The ruler's discourse and practices are therefore always in line with the principles of the established state doctrine. Democratic accountability is not at stake in such cases. On the other hand, in hybrid regimes it is not clear whether a specific regime comes closer to the democratic pole – in that case one may speak of electoral democracies with deficiencies – or to the pole of authoritarian regimes with no elections. The latter case can no longer be described in terms of even an imperfect democracy. Since there is a consensus today that only a democracy with elections can be a source of legitimacy, such regimes must at least formally declare themselves democratic. This may be considered as a more or less opportunistic adaptation to Western hegemony, at least at the discursive level, which is linked to the dynamic constraints of the political system of world society: it observes the realities of a state system through the question of how an established power regime in a specific country deals with the political opposition. Thus, one has to ask to what extent the distinction of government and opposition is accepted in a given political system. But democracy is first of all a communicative structure in which all government communications have to face a second version in the form of communications from an established opposition. Democracy is about the organized, public and legal interplay between government and opposition. In an authoritarian regime the second version of the 'official truth' would come from the illegal opposition or from protest movements that – particularly in the precise situation of an oppressed political opposition – would attempt to establish a counter-hegemonic discourse.

Discursive Practices and Imitation of Democracy in a Quasi-Authoritarian Regime

Russia is an interesting case since it fulfils all the criteria of a semi- or a quasi-authoritarian regime coming close to the authoritarian pole.[13] Russia is a 'facade democracy': control of the media and important social spheres helps maintain the illusion, or rather give the impression, that democratic differentiation exists when it does not. The ruling elite monopolizes access to positions of power. As Ottaway puts it, 'all semi-authoritarian regimes take steps to preserve their core, namely the power of the central government', and they differ in how they deal with those who challenge that power.[14] In such regimes the difference between the positions of the government and the opposition may be maintained, not in an exchange of positions – the democratic solution – but as fixed positions. The contingency of an election is not accepted and an alternation of power in such regimes is out of the question. Opposition parties, despite their existence, are systematically disadvantaged. The illusion of a differentiated democratic system is maintained, but elections exist only in order to produce the 'right' results. One may ask what political change is good for, if no one is interested in change, if people chiefly want stability and security, as is the case in Russia. One should also not forget that 'facade' or 'Potemkin' democracies find the conditions of their existence not only in the past but also in an extremely inegalitarian social structure with a weak potential for change. On the other hand, there can be no democracy without democrats, without a public that is convinced that political opposition and political change are what democracy is about. If political antagonism is not allowed to be expressed and institutionalized in the public sphere, then indeed democracy remains an ideological or even empty construction. The regime may then invent a specific qualifier, such as 'Russian democracy', to underline the fact that Russia is using its own non-Western definitions.

To preserve its power structure and present its political structure as an expression of real democracy, a facade democracy needs – besides the indispensable material basis – a perspective of prosperity, a political theory, a kind of ideological framework about itself and about its conception of future objectives such as modernization. And it needs a lot of organizational power to realize at least parts of the regime's doctrine. The result can be an organized society, a society controlled by the centre of the political system, for example a hegemonic political party, or the power network of a political leader, such as the 'Putin system'. These were given conditions under Soviet rule. The breakdown of communism implied the bankruptcy of an economic model. It was an event that discourse analysts call the crisis of a hegemonic discourse, its dislocation by new meanings and identities. However, a closer look at what happened in the new post-Soviet order shows how old identities have partly been transferred from the old regime to the new one. The discontinuity expressed in new symbols cannot hide the continuity of the old regime, whose members were able to combine old and new power positions under a new rent-seeking capitalism. The representatives of the old Soviet order quickly learned how to cope with elements of the new order – elections and markets – and to use them for their own interests. And, interestingly enough, the 'new' power elites – Putin and his network of power are a part of them – hold values similar to those of the older Soviet generations: confrontation with the West, a conception of modernization without democracy, a rent-seeking mentality within the class of state officials, and a conception of politics as a zero-sum game.

The new Russian state order, the so-called power vertical created under Putin, reproduces to a certain extent Soviet-like organizational structures and state capitalism in a globalized context. It is an undertaking accompanied by discursive strategies aimed at explaining and reinforcing the existing power structure. The 'system of power' established by Putin is a new attempt to control society, its media, its economy, its civil society and its dynamics by political means, bureaucracy and courts. To be sure, a real Russian democracy would have been a simple ideological product if it had not to a certain extent attempted to be different from 'Western' realities. The idea of a sovereign democracy corresponds to the aims and realities of a semi- or quasi-authoritarian regime pretending to be a democracy but organizing the political process in such a way as to retain its monopoly on power. In his analysis of the rise of 'managed democracy' in Russia, Ivan Krastev shows how the 'doubles' of democracy function. The elites, with the help of so-called political technologists, populist communication strategies, media manipulation and administrative resources, create a 'copy' of democracy, a kind of virtual reality.[15] Such an analysis focusing on the populist rhetoric of elites and their public relations specialists can be usefully combined with the organizational aspects of semi-authoritarian regimes. Controlling the public space and the scope of the politically permissible always implies huge organizational power – for example legal and economic means to control the media. In the past few years we have seen how political parties have been built up in Russia as 'clones' (e.g. 'United Russia') whereas the political opposition has been neutralized.

Figure 2.1 illustrates this marginalization of political opposition both inside and outside the political system. The Kremlin Inc. regime controls key aspects of the functional systems through organizations and highly personalized networks. Representatives of the regime's security forces dominate companies of strategic interest. It is precisely at the economic level that an observer gets the impression that Russia functions like a big bureaucratic corporation, as a 'Russia Inc.', which combines highly personalized leadership structures with organizational power and networks of power (friends, loyalties and clients). This does not mean that independent economic or political activities are not possible. They are possible and even admitted – cases in point are the small opposition parties in Russia. But no organization gets a chance to become a real antagonist and to develop a real political opposition against the regime in the sense of becoming an alternative, a structure ready for replacing the incumbent power in the case of an election. That means that beyond a certain size every organization seems to become a risk for the regime – consider the case of Khodorkovsky.

In the past few years, loyal economic elites have replaced those that represented a risk for the regime. Organizations of civil society lost

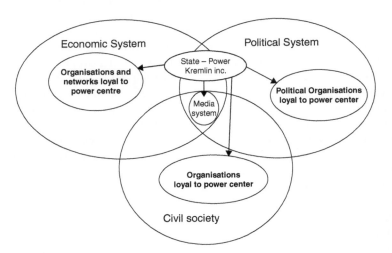

Figure 2.1   Marginalization of opposition inside and outside the political system: 'real' vs 'not real' organizations

their autonomy and new state-driven and state-sponsored organizations were created (such as the youth movement 'Nashi') in order to contain and channel the dynamics of civil society. In general, this can be seen as a strategy of neutralization and de-politicization aimed at reducing the natural checks and balances in society as they are expressed by the pluralism of interests and organizations in politics, economy and society.

The regime maintains a fake model of a liberal regime and creates its own organizations and networks through which it controls the most important social spheres. This regime is presented as the 'real' Russian democracy, as distinguished from false democratic projects in neighbouring states or Western liberal democracies, which are considered to be 'false democracies'.[16] The same logic is at work in relation to the specific organizations of Russian society and politics. 'Real' political parties, created by the regime, are to be distinguished from 'other' parties. 'Real' organizations of civil society have to be distinguished from 'not real others' or false ones. With such a strategy the regime eliminates the pluralism of the political system and interests in society. Despite the fact that the regime also 'sponsors' new political parties, the United Russia Party is so dominant that one may speak of a de-differentiation of the political system.

The Anti-Modern Drive in Russian Politics

The 'us' against 'the others' discourse is in fact an exclusion strategy that cannot be separated from the elite's vision of Russia's power in the world and in the country. An unnerved nation, anxious about retaining its unity and identity, will always attempt to fortify itself behind the shield of its repressive power structure and its own ideology. Metaphorically, 'the Kremlin' stands precisely for that: a power structure that barricades itself behind huge walls to protect itself against 'the others', the public, opponents, 'anti-Russian' movements, foreigners, foreign hostile peoples in the 'near abroad', terrorists and a lot of others. One can only be surprised at the extent to which old-fashioned semantics with the idea of the state as the centre of social order are still at work in Russia. This idea cannot be realized without the mentality of citizens as 'subordinates'. This is certainly also one of the biggest obstacles to building a modern democratic state based on the rule of law. The centre of power lies with the state, more precisely in its executive branch. The unity of the state, of the political top, is what matters in Russia: unity against the differences of a democracy as they are expressed by the presence of an opposition, checks and balances or civil society.

It is a discourse pointing back to the well-administrated paternalist police state of imperial Russia that considered society as something to be kept under control by pedagogic and police means.[17] Transposed into Putin's Russia, the metaphor expresses the idea that a political space for the expression of social autonomy cannot exist. Such a conception tends to eliminate the political, if the latter signifies a continuous conflict between political parties or between different interests in society. It is precisely this imaginary space of the political in which society appears as a nation that is being negated by a bureaucratic and hierarchic conception of society. Unity instead of difference. This could be considered as a return to the pre-modern world of hierarchically conceived societies without the possibility of thinking of themselves in terms of differences. On the other hand, the Soviet Union can be considered one of the last experiments that attempted to return to a unitary conception of power, to an indivisible sovereignty based on the idea or representation of one single people that refused the concept of 'one and the other' (to use Lefort's terms).[18]

A government that cannot accept the institutionalization of 'the other' has to take recourse to the archaic distinction between friends and enemies. And it should be clear that such a regime becomes dangerous particularly for the social environment of politics, where such a conception of the political directly contradicts the autonomous realities of other social spheres, particularly those of the economic system. In any case, any society pretending to be the only 'right' one will always be described as being totalitarian, and it will inevitably provoke opposition: unity necessarily produces differences and new identities based on different distinctions.

Modern politics needs and involves antagonists and opponents. This crucial difference between enemies and opponents points to the core of the political in modern society and also to the problem of morals in politics: as soon as opponents are considered good or bad, an elimination process starts.[19] On the other hand, their acceptance implies competition focused on political victory. The latter can be obtained only by respecting the rules of the game and established procedures. Russia and some other post-communist regimes still have considerable difficulties in 'living' with a political opposition – despite or precisely due to the democratization process. If unity of the political system with its 'elected monarch', or now with its 'double centre' at the top, is the essential feature of the political system, we can expect all official discourses to confirm this unity. It is of course a discourse of the unity of the rulers and the people. As Krastev has put it, if elections are not supposed to change anything, they still accomplish, at the level of political discourse, the function of celebrating unity. This is populism, insisting not on the difference but on the identical nature of the regime and the people. Such thinking is in fact reminiscent of conservative thinking à la Carl Schmitt.[20] It has become fashionable again in Russia to quote Carl Schmitt and in particular his definition of sovereign power based on decision-making in a state of exception. This may be especially useful for Russia and the conflicts on its periphery. But such thinking marks the distance to West European political theory based on how to avoid a state of exception. The identification of sovereignty with unity is, however, problematic – particularly in the context of a quasi-authoritarian regime. In a modern sense sovereignty is, as Luhmann has shown, based on difference, not on unity: it implies the contestation of power. But such a concept of sovereignty is unacceptable for regional autocrats, since it destabilizes authority.[21] A political power unwilling to accept the structural destabilization of the political system that is caused by the difference between government and opposition must necessarily re-moralize politics. It has to explain precisely why this power has the moral (Putin dixit!) right to remain in power. On the other hand the Russian regime – obsessed by stability – opens the door to instability precisely through its unwillingness to institutionalize political change.

All populism needs to mobilize differences between 'us' and 'the others'. The official nationalistic discourse is 'anti-Western', 'anti-orange', 'anti-American', oriented against liberalism or against 'enemies' from within. The distinction between 'friends and enemies' has of course the advantage that it reduces political complexity and helps organize support for a highly personalized power structure in a system based – as several scholars have noted – on 'negative integration'.[22] Moreover, in contemporary Russia, the rhetoric of unity is based on the mobilization of patriotism.[23] It is an appropriate discourse for exceptional times of crisis and war, in a country where the political elite is reproducing elements of the former Soviet 'garrison-state'.

The Changing Meaning of 'Sovereign Democracy'

In a context where the Russian elite presents its quasi-authoritarian system as a 'democratic' alternative to the rejected liberal project of Western Europe and the United States, criticism of Russia's facade democracy misses its point: the regime immunizes itself in asserting that the country has realized its own democratic project. Usually qualifiers of democracy with the addition of an adjective such as 'illiberal' or 'semi-authoritarian' serve to qualify diminished democracies, but in the eyes of Russian elites, qualifiers such as 'sovereign' or 'directed' express the 'Russian way' of thinking. This was certainly true for the times when Putin was president of Russia, and the question is whether this was still true for Medvedev. Interestingly enough, however, the president who succeeded him seemed to be unhappy with such a qualifier and insisted on the fact that Russia is a democracy without any adjective.[24] The reasoning is correct, but presenting Russia as a democracy will only further reveal the huge gap between political reality and rhetoric. Russia will be measured on the basis of a universally accepted theory of democracy, which will not be acceptable for the adepts of 'sovereign democracy': this would definitely show that the emperor is not wearing clothes and sovereign democracy would become a meaningless formula. But the hierarchy, centralization and a powerful repression mechanism would remain. In all quasi- or semi-authoritarian regimes any political opposition has to face huge obstacles in its path to establish itself as an alternative to the incumbent power, which would mean that it had an alternative discourse that it was trying to establish as dominant or even hegemonic.

Nevertheless, the ideological construction created by the Putin regime and its 'technologists of power' seems to work at least for the elites and parts of the Russian public. For them the discourse of sovereign democracy has become a reality. Concepts that circulate in society may change society and the values and thought systems of the people. Political concepts such as 'sovereign democracy' with their strong normative implications may provide keys to a better understanding of a little known political reality. This includes the unverifiable explanations of politicians about causality, about successful political actions, about how to solve big problems or how to overcome the current economic crisis. With globalization penetrating every society and world region, it would be naive to believe that regional political regimes can control the communicative realities of different social contexts beyond a certain extent. An economic crisis can produce new dynamics against which the semantics of 'sovereign democracy' may be useless.

The meanings of 'sovereign democracy' are changing, depending on the expectations of the public that is addressed. For the less educated parts of the Russian public, still oriented towards post-Soviet authoritarianism and towards a highly normative world view, the term sovereign democracy may provide a kind of collective identity anchor. For them, Western democracy is linked with conflict, weakness and inefficiency.

They hesitate to admit that, in democracies, conflict, competition and cooperation can go hand in hand. Power seems to be diluted in democracies, whereas in a so-called sovereign democracy such as Russia power is concentrated in the right place, that is, at the top of society. There are of course people in Russia, such as some representatives of the opposition or of civil society, who understand that sovereign democracy is an empty shell, a 'battle formula', that hides nothing else but an autocratic content. Critical political scientists in Russia know that from a scientific perspective the formula 'sovereign democracy' is meaningless.[25] This is another example of how the meanings of concepts change from one social sphere or system to another. In trying to control the social circulation of such concepts as sovereign democracy, the Kremlin tells us a lot about its conception of power and how it wants to confront the world of the twenty-first century with its rather traditional vision of control, hegemony and domination. Such a conception of power is ill suited to confront the big problems in all social spheres. For ideological reasons and big power concerns it may be reasonable and fashionable to insist on Russia's 'own traditions', but sociologically there is no way in which modernity and its problems, which have obviously also entered into Russia, can be resolved by other means than modern ones, by autonomous knowledge systems and their actors, which cannot be controlled from above.

Conclusion

This brings us back to globalization, to the demonstration effects coming from more successful modernizing nations than Russia, to the simple fact that Russia has not the means to emulate the Chinese way of combining capitalism and authoritarianism or to catch up technologically with the more advanced Western nations. 'Sovereign democracy' may be a Russian answer to globalization and, more specifically, to the challenge of 'Westernization'. But such a discourse does indeed not make much sense if the Russian road to modernity is not successful. A nation may 'import' only those elements of global modernization that correspond to the national interest or the interests of the regime staying in power. But then it also has to make sure that its discursive design and modernization strategy are backed by economic growth, prosperity, promotion prospects, and inclusive welfare programmes and the like. This is far from the case of contemporary Russia. Against this background the concept of 'modernization' became the new catchword after Dmitrii Medvedev became president.

Notes

1. On this aspect of resisting cultural globalization see B. S. Turner and H. H. Khondker (2010), *Globalization East and West* (London: Sage).
2. See in this regard G. P. Herd (2010), *Russia's Strategic Choice: Conservative or Democratic Modernization?*, GCSP Policy Paper No. 2, May, Geneva Center for Security Policy. See also I. Krastev (2011), 'Paradoxes of the New Authoritarianism', *Journal of Democracy*, Vol. 22, No. 2, April.
3. Authors such as Krastev (note 2, p. 15) correctly point to the fact that Russia will 'remain inefficient as long as there is enough oil money to compensate for its inefficiency'. Herd (note 2), referring to A. Orekh, observes that 'real modernization will only begin on the day when the last drop of oil is extracted from swampy Siberia and major gas deposits run out in Russia'.
4. R. Kagan (2008), *The Return of History and the End of Dreams* (London: Atlantic Books), pp. 69 ff.
5. See I. Krastev (2006), 'Democracy's "Doubles"', *Journal of Democracy*, Vol. 7, No. 1, pp. 52–62.
6. See the introductory remarks in A. Galasinska and M. Krzyzanowski (eds) (2009), *Discourse and Transformation in Central and Eastern Europe* (London: Palgrave Macmillan).
7. We refer here to the systems theory of Niklas Luhmann and his distinction between the three types of system level – society, organization and interactions. On organizational systems see e.g. N. Luhmann (1982), *The Differentiation of Society* (New York: Columbia University Press); and N. Luhmann (2000), *Organisation und Entscheidung* [Organization and Decision] (Wiesbaden: Westdeutscher Verlag). See also W. Rasch (2000), *Niklas Luhmann's Modernity* (Stanford: Stanford University Press). For an application of Luhmann's theoretical framework to organized societies like Russia's see N. Hayoz (2007), 'Regionale "organisierte Gesellschaften" und ihre Schwierigkeiten mit der Realität der funktionalen Differenzierung' [Regional 'Organized Societies' and their Difficulties with the Reality of Functional Differentiation], *Soziale Systeme*, Vol. 13, Nos 1 and 2, pp. 160–72.
8. See I. Krastev (2008), 'Russia and the European Order: Sovereign Democracy Explained', *American Interest*, November/December, pp. 16–24.
9. R. Kagan (2008), *The Return of History and the End of Dreams* (London: Atlantic Books), pp. 69 ff.
10. See L. Diamond (2008), *The Spirit of Democracy* (New York: Holt), pp. 198 ff and 64 ff; and R. Rose (2009), *Understanding Post-communist Transformation* (London: Routledge), pp. 60 ff, 153 ff, 173 ff. See also http://www.levada.ru/press/2007040901.html and Freedom House, *Nations in Transit 2009* (see also http://www.unhcr.org/refworld/country,,FREEHOU,,RUS,,4d53f025270.html).
11. See Krastev (note 2).
12. See J. Torfing (1999), *New Theories of Discourse – Laclau, Mouffe and Zizek* (Oxford: Blackwell), pp. 116 f. Following Zizek, the author applies the notion of ideological fantasy to situations in which people act as if the totalizing forms of ideology are true, although they know they are not.

13. On the concept of semi-authoritarianism see M. Ottaway (2003), *Democracy Challenged: The Rise of Semi-Authoritarianism* (Washington, DC: Carnegie Endowment for International Peace).
14. Ottaway (note 13), p. 20. Such a regime may also develop into full authoritarianism. For an evaluation of such risks see L. Shevtsova (2008), *Russia: Lost in Transition* (Washington, DC: Carnegie Endowment for International Peace).
15. Krastev (note 5). In this regard Pierre Hassner has observed that virtual democracy and virtual empire go together. P. Hassner (2008),'Russia's Transition to Autocracy', *Journal of Democracy*, Vol. 19, No. 2, pp. 5–15.
16. See the positions of proponents of the notion of 'sovereign democracy' such as Aleksandr Dugin, for whom Russian sovereign democracy embodies the profound will of the people and national thought. It is opposed to the false and demagogic democracies of dual standards. A. Dugin (2006), 'Suverennaya demokratiya – priznak postanovleniya v Rossii ideologii', 20 September [Sovereign Democracy – Sign of an Evolving Ideology in Russia], http://www.viperson.ru/wind.php?ID=261697&soch=1. See also A. Okara (2007), 'Sovereign Democracy: A New Russian Idea or a PR Project?', *Russia in Global Affairs*, No. 2, pp. 1–8.
17. See M. Raeff (1994), *Political Ideas and Institutions in Imperial Russia* (Boulder: Westview Press), pp. 117 f.
18. See C. Lefort (1981), *L'invention démocratique* (Paris: Seuil), p. 172; C. Lefort (1986), *Essais sur la politique: XIXe–Xxe siècles* (Paris: Seuil), p. 265.
19. See M. Edelman (1991), *Constructing the Political Spectacle* (Chicago: University of Chicago Press), p. 131; and C. Mouffe (2005), *On the Political* (London: Routledge).
20. See I. Krastev (2006), 'Sovereign Democracy – Russian Style', http://www.opendemocracy.net.
21. For a discussion of the differences between Niklas Luhmann and Carl Schmitt with regard to sovereignty see W. Rasch (2000), *Niklas Luhmann's Modernity* (Stanford: Stanford University Press), p. 162.
22. See L. March (2007), 'Russian Nationalism under Putin: A Majority Faith?' in K. Malfliet and R. Laenen (eds), *Elusive Russia: Current Developments in Russian State Identity and Institutional Reform under President Putin* (Leuven: Leuven University Press), pp. 33–52.
23. For this aspect Raviot shows that unity is an integral part of the Russian political culture. It is impressive to note the extent to which elites in post-Soviet countries have used the rhetoric of unity to name the political parties they have created since the breakdown of the Soviet Union. See J. R. Raviot (2008), *Démocratie à la russe: Pouvoir et contre-pouvoir en Russie* (Paris: Elipses).
24. See http://www.expert.ru/printissues/expert/2006/28/interview_medvedev/.
25. For an overview of some of the positions for and against the concept of 'sovereign democracy' see e.g. http://www.gazeta.ru/politics/2007/12/07_a_2398700.shtml.

3
Russian Modernization Doctrines under Debate

Mark Urnov

Introduction

Towards the end of the first decade of the new century, the issue of modernization of the Russian economy, technology base, and society in general became debated more intensely than any other national issue in the country's political, professional and academic communities.[1]

In Russian debates, the term 'modernization' most often stands for a kind of 'catching-up', that is, measures or processes aimed at bridging the gap between Russia and the most developed countries.[2] In 2008 the Russian Government adopted the term 'modernization' in a strategy document, thereby giving it official status – the 'Concept of Long-term Socio-Economic Development of the Russian Federation for the Period up to 2020' (Strategic Concept 2020), a document based on Vladimir Putin's speech at a meeting of the State Council ('On the Development Strategy of Russia up to 2020').[3]

There is no consensus on criteria for the catching-up process or on the appropriate measures to achieve the objectives of modernization. There are many different and sometimes conflicting approaches or ideologies of modernization.[4] They can be roughly categorized as communist, liberal and conservative according to four criteria:

1. *Scope of modernization* – areas in which modernization must take place (from purely technological modernization to modernization of all spheres of social life);
2. *Major institutional agencies of modernization* – state versus non-government agencies with possible state support;
3. *Balance of resources used* – national resources versus a combination of national and foreign resources;

4. *Priorities of state policy* – on the supply side or the demand side of innovation.

The communist doctrine is 'minimalist' in the sense that the key institutional agency is the state, and the resources to be used are exclusively national.[5] The liberal doctrine is 'maximalist', while the conservative one is 'intermediate', located between the other two.

This chapter analyses only the conservative and liberal doctrines. The communist doctrine is not discussed because of its – for present Russian conditions – too far fetched proposals to nationalize natural resources and strategic industries (electricity, transportation, military industry, oil and gas) and restore state control of the national economy. In Russian political and expert circles the 'liberal' and 'conservative' modernization doctrines crystallized as a result of the publication of Dmitrii Medvedev's article 'Go, Russia!' in September 2009 and the report of the Institute of Contemporary Development (ICD) entitled 'Russia in the XXI Century: Vision for the Future' in early 2010.

However, there was a previous debate between 'liberal' and 'conservative' factions, although not in the paradigm 'liberalism versus conservatism'. A most intensive debate took place in 2003, when a report was published by the Council on National Strategy (a non-governmental organization).[6] The report, 'The State and the Oligarchy', which appeared in the press under the title 'Oligarchic Coup under Preparation in Russia', was part of a huge public relations campaign preparing for the seizure of the Yukos Corporation by another oil company, Rossneft, and the trial of Yukos owner Mikhail Khodorkovskii. The report was dedicated to the economic and political threats to Russia stemming from so-called oligarchic modernization.[7] The debate that took place over the following years prepared almost all key positions of the liberal and conservative modernization doctrines that appeared in 2009–10. A majority of these discussions took place in political clubs and at round-tables[8] but were less present in Russia's scholarly journals.

Most Russian academic publications on modernization were written by well-known adherents of the liberal doctrine or by researchers who advocated liberal rather than conservative modernization. Far from being polemical, these papers drew attention to the importance of cultural (value-oriented) change for the success of economic modernization. They emphasized the interdependence of economic modernization and political democratization and the futility of a purely technological modernization.[9] The proponents of conservative modernization focused much more on promoting their concepts within the government and presidential administration. When their ideas appeared in public they were often dressed up in terms such as 'sovereign democracy'[10] or presented as the idea that any cultural modernization had to be prevented, otherwise it would destroy Russian national identity.[11]

One version of the conservative modernization ideology had already been presented in the government's 'Strategic Concept 2020' of 2008 and Putin's speech of the same year, on which it was based. The term 'conservative modernization' was absent from these documents. In this chapter I use the term the way the United Russia Party, led by Putin, uses it. Since November 2009 the party has described itself not as centrist but as a 'conservative force with the aim of conducting modernization and supporting the government programme'.

The ideas of more liberally oriented scholars were incorporated in the ICD report and in Medvedev's article of September 2009, 'Go, Russia!', mentioned above. Some of the basic positions of the ICD report were later confirmed and reinforced in two of Medvedev's speeches in the summer of 2010.[12] These documents provide the most detailed version of the Russian liberal modernization doctrine, formulated as the basis for a political decision-making process.

Medvedev's article generated a surge of publications by proponents of conservative modernization,[13] which emphasized the following:

1. Medvedev's article is only a development and refinement of positions that were formulated by Putin and were contained in the government's 'Strategic Concept 2020'.
2. The key element of modernization is technological; social and sociocultural modernization are only supplementary components.
3. The existing political regime should be maintained.[14]

The last point can be interpreted as relying on the 'Putin majority' to prevent a weakening of the political role of the United Russia Party as the 'framework of Putin's majority and the skeleton of the national modernization coalition', and avoiding a split in the ruling tandem by maintaining Putin as the national and majority leader and Medvedev as the leader of a national coalition for modernization, and of the creative minority of the population. In other words, the supporters of conservative modernization tried to incorporate Medvedev's concept into their own concept of how the Russian political system should function.

The publication of the ICD report provoked strong (not to say furious) negative reactions. Conservatives described it as a set of empty abstractions, out of touch with reality,[15] as a call for 'the day before yesterday',[16] and not reflecting the positions of Medvedev himself.[17]

For their part, the authors of the ICD report suggested that it represented an alternative to the government's 'Strategic Concept 2020'. According to Evgenii Gontmakher, one of its principal drafters and a member of the ICD Board, 'everybody understands that such documents as the "Strategy 2020" are out of date and do not contain clear principles, that they are conceived "for us and for you" (*i nashim, i vashim*)'.[18]

The next section analyses the similarities and differences between the conservative and liberal modernization doctrines.

Conservative and Liberal Modernization Doctrines: The Similarities

The arguments of the two modernization doctrines are similar in many respects:

1. the idea that modernization is necessary,
2. the objectives of modernization,
3. the areas in which it is necessary to act to achieve the main goals of modernization,
4. criticism of the inefficiency of the Russian economy,
5. the emphasis on social and political stability,
6. the negative evaluation of some key aspects of Russian public administration.

In both doctrines the necessity of modernization is defined explicitly: it must be carried out because Russia is a great power and a member of the club of the most advanced countries; therefore, any degradation of the country has to be arrested and the emergence of threats to its position prevented.[19] In the ICD report this dichotomy – *all or nothing, intermediate options are not available* – is explained as follows: 'It is possible that Russia is just doomed to struggle for leadership and a special position in the world because of its size, unique natural resources and human capacities'.[20] The dichotomy contains one of the key elements of Russian/Soviet national identity as a great, leading power playing a decisive role in global political processes.

In the twentieth century there were only two relatively short periods when this kind of great-power mentality did not dominate: from 1917 to the late 1920s, and from the late 1980s to the late 1990s. These two 'atypical' periods had their own specific causes and preconditions. In both cases, Russian political and intellectual elites tended to view the country as a patient to be cured of a grave disease rather than as an example for other countries. Both periods were overtaken by a strongly opposite trend: the pathos of the Great Power.

The main objectives of modernization set out in both doctrines can be summarized in the following five points.

1. *A high standard of living*: a standard close to or comparable with that of the most developed countries[21]
2. *Social justice, law and order*: equal opportunities, social protection of vulnerable groups, guarantees of constitutional rights, etc.
3. *Economic leadership*: a world leader in the energy and commodity sectors, and one of the leading industrial nations with a high potential for innovation
4. Significant improvement of the country's ecological conditions
5. Securing the country from external threats.

Both doctrines emphasize the importance of political and social stability: Putin stated that the major parties must be mindful of 'their immense responsibility for the unity of the nation',[22] and Medvedev pointed to 'maintaining cross-party consensus on strategic issues of foreign policy, social stability' and other aspects of social life.[23]

They both evaluate the existing system of public administration similarly. The conservative doctrine notes that 'today the public administration apparatus is largely a bureaucratic, corrupt system, not motivated towards positive changes, still less for dynamic development', suffering from over-centralization (Putin) and low efficiency.[24] The liberal doctrine refers to the 'authoritarianism' of public administration.[25] Both doctrines highlight the need for profound reforms in public administration and have some proposals in common.

Key areas that both doctrines claim are in need of modernization are: values and motivations (human capital), economics, the political system, public administration, and relations with the outside world.

The next section turns to the differences between the doctrines with regard to these key areas, thereby suggesting that the doctrines should be treated as alternatives rather than complementary.

Conservative and Liberal Modernization Doctrines: The Main Differences

The differences are best seen in the approaches to modernization in the five key areas that are listed above.

Values and Motivation

With regard to values and motivations, the conservative doctrine proposes extremely cautious measures (as befits conservative doctrines). It reduces 'the problem of changing values and motivations' to 'an increase in work motivation' and to the need for 'civic education, patriotic upbringing of youth, [and] the promotion of legal, cultural and moral values among young people'.[26] The latter refers to 'popularization' of the following set of 'community values': health, labour, family, patriotism, service to the country, responsibility, an active civic position, environmental protection, toleration and human rights. This set of values differs from the standard values propagated by the communist regime in only two aspects: toleration and human rights. And this innovation is not at all accentuated. Otherwise, new values are listed modestly in much the same way as the traditional set of Soviet values.[27]

The logic behind the conservative doctrine's ideas for modernization of human capital can be summarized as follows.

1. No radical transformation of dominant values in Russian society of today is required in order to start the modernization process
2. Some correction of values – with the help 'of civil associations' programmes and social advertising' – is however needed.[28]
3. Further changes in values will come with changes in the institutional environment.[29]

In other words, the conservative doctrine treats changes in the value system as a function of changes in formal institutions. The liberal doctrine proposes a much more radical version of human capital modernization, based on the assumption that changing institutions is a function of changing the culture (values).

According to Medvedev, one of the major ills of Russian society is the 'prevalence of paternalistic attitudes', which generate 'inertia, lack of new ideas', etc.[30] The 2010 ICD report considered 'the humanitarian component' as crucial to the modernization process: 'Modernization begins with the right mood. Of particular importance is the humanitarian component: values and principles, morals and motivation, attitudes and system of prohibitions'.[31]

Creating 'the right mood' entails destroying the deep-rooted authoritarian complex of Russian mass consciousness. A 'strategic objective of any modern government' is to 'cultivate' in society a classic set of characteristics of *homo liberalis*, that is citizens who are fully adapted to a competitive economic and political environment and reject paternalism; have independent opinions; are capable of reflection and rationality; are autonomous, dynamic and flexible in their actions; and who take initiative and responsibility. The promotion of these qualities is a necessary condition for replacing the 'parasitical–distributive set of values' with a set of 'creative–productive' values and the model of 'citizens in the service of the state' with the principle 'the state in the service of citizens'.[32]

Mikhail Fedotov, the chairman of the Presidential Human Rights Council under the Russian president and an adviser to the president, also points out the need for modernizing the popular consciousness (while stressing that he is quoting the president): 'What we need is a modernization of social relations and of stereotypes of social behavior. A modernization of consciousness. This is, if you want, an ideological priority. After all, we are thinking archaically'.[33]

Economic Policy

The differences between the two doctrines in the field of economic policy pertain primarily to the relative importance of two ways of promoting innovative development of the economy: creating a *supply* of innovations and their implementation in the economy; or creating a *demand* for innovation on the part of the economy.

According to the conservative doctrine the first type of policy clearly dominates over the second. Here key problems of the Russian economy are reduced mainly to poor technical and technological conditions and the obstacles to improving them. Putin talks about extreme economic inefficiency, unacceptably low productivity, the inertia of the 'energy and raw materials' scenario of development, and 'fragmented economic modernization'.[34] The government's 'Concept up to the year 2020' emphasizes the underdeveloped transport and energy infrastructure; the shortage of qualified engineers and skilled workers; high levels of social inequality and regional differentiation; the poor development of self-organization and regulation of business and society; the low level of confidence and low efficiency of public administration; the slow development of the national innovation system; the poor coordination of education, science and business; the low level of competition in some markets; the high risks involved in conducting business because of corruption, excessive administrative barriers, poor protection of property rights, and so on.[35]

Putin's speech and the government's 'Concept' document contain a concrete, detailed description of the structural and technical aspects of an innovative development of production. The solutions for the demand for innovations, on the other hand, remain in the realm of general 'textbook style' declarations. Putin says that 'it is necessary to develop market institutions and a competitive environment that will motivate companies to cut costs, modernize production and respond flexibly to consumer demand'; that 'a comfortable environment should be established in Russia to attract investment, especially in high-tech industries, and to do business'; and that 'it is necessary *to continue efforts* [italics added] to establish an independent and effective judiciary that unquestionably guarantees protection of entrepreneurial rights, including protection from bureaucratic arbitrary action'.[36]

The document laying out the government's concept for development up to the year 2020 states that the transition from a 'raw materials export model of economic growth to an innovation model requires creating a highly competitive institutional environment that encourages entrepreneurial activity and attracts capital into the economy, presupposes the creation and development of competitive markets, and consistent de-monopolization'.[37]

But in spite of these declarations the conservative doctrine does not contain any plans to de-monopolize the leading and most monopolized industries – at least not until 2020. The government's Concept document contains a special section on the development of the Russian oil and gas industry, aviation, shipbuilding and banking system, but does not mention de-monopolization of these branches. The only economic sectors mentioned in the Concept document as the objects of future de-monopolization are 'the engineering infrastructure (roads, airfields, etc.), and the sphere of limited natural resources, including aquatic biological resources and subsoil'.[38]

To be fair, it should be noted that in his article 'A Miracle is Possible' (on the prospects for developing an innovative economy) Vladislav Surkov, at that time the Kremlin's chief ideologist, highlights the key role of the demand for innovation in the modernization process. However, for him the demand comes primarily from the government and large public and private corporations. The state is a means for forcing innovation. According to Surkov, the value of competition should not be exaggerated: 'the liberal hope for the invisible hand of the market itself is not justified', and 'an excessive number of competing systems degrades the quality of competition'.[39]

The liberal doctrine, on the other hand, stresses the importance of the demand side of innovation. The ICD report states that 'the challenge is to create an economy generating innovation, not to generate innovations to be painfully imposed on the economy' and that 'the main change needed by the innovation economy is to create an environment in which corporations are chasing bearers of knowledge and intangible assets, and not bearers of knowledge chasing corporations'.[40]

The Political System

The differences between the doctrines' approaches to modernization of the political system begin with their evaluations of its current condition. It is therefore useful to start by recalling that, according to Freedom House's 'Nations in Transit', Russia now belongs to the group of 'unfree' countries.

Russia has an authoritarian system of government that gives its citizens few tools to hold their leaders accountable. In 2001–10 Russia's rating for national democratic governance rose from 4.88 to 6.50; for the electoral process from 4.22 to 6.75; and for the independent media from 5.25 to 6.25.[41]

The conservative doctrine avoids estimating the current state of the political system. The liberal doctrine, however, evaluates it negatively: in the Medvedev texts rather gently, but in the ICD report very sharply.

> *Medvedev*: Democratic institutions in general are formed and stabilized, but their quality is far from ideal.[42] We must make better use of our foreign policy tools in solving domestic problems, for the purpose of modernization of our country, its economic, social and – in some measures – political system.[43]
>
> *ICD report*: Business and social activity of citizens has to be released from bureaucratic "vertical pressure", otherwise a "technological" modernization simply will not have any positive results.[44]

The impression that the conservative doctrine regards the existing political system as adaptable for its purposes, while the liberal doctrine considers it a barrier, is supported by an analysis of their respective approaches to political modernization.

The changes proposed by the conservative doctrine do not refer to such concepts as 'political competition', 'opposition', 'political pluralism' or 'free media'. The government's 'Concept' document of 2010 contains only vague statements such as the 'transition to an innovative socially oriented type of development is impossible' without 'developed democratic institutions'; the country needs 'an effectively operating democratic system' that could provide 'effective mechanisms for protecting the rights and freedoms of citizens', and with 'the use of procedures and rules ensuring the identification and consideration of the interests of each social group in decision making at all levels...of power', etc.[45] Such vague formulations are dictated by the genre of the document: government programmes are focused primarily on socio-economic rather than political issues.

Putin refers more explicitly to the political system. Along with a general characteristic of political modernization (which he defines as a transformation of the 'democratic state' into 'an effective instrument of the self-organization of civil society'[46]), Putin offers his vision of a future (i.e. modernized) party system. For him Russia will have several big political parties, which 'must remember their immense responsibility for...national unity' and in any case must not allow society to become fragmented. 'Attempts to split up the society' are equated with 'irresponsible demagogy' and with 'the use of foreign aid and intervention in domestic political struggles', and are regarded as 'immoral' and 'illegal'.[47] Thus, the conservative doctrine does not propose any significant liberalization of the political system.

The liberal doctrine, on the other hand, puts forth a comprehensive programme of political reforms aimed at creating a competitive political environment. In 'Go, Russia!' Medvedev wrote about 'political competition', which provides periodic changes in the power of different parties.[48] The ICD report's section on 'The political future of the country: back to the constitution' states that political modernization of the country is 'a necessary component of modernization' and that the modernized state must be 'the arbiter and manager of all conflicts among pluralistic interests'. This arbitration 'necessarily implies political pluralism...competition in politics, including a change in power of different political forces, independent courts, [and] a general willingness to resolve conflicts within existing institutions'.[49]

Public Administration

In some respects the positions of the two doctrines on the modernization of Russia's public administration are quite close. Nevertheless, there is a fundamental difference. The liberal doctrine contains a draft programme for deep reform of the current power structures, whereas the conservative doctrine makes no mention of this.

The ICD report proposes, in particular, a transition to a professional army; transformation of the *militsiya* into a Federal Service of Criminal Police and municipal police; conversion of interior troops into a National Guard; reorganization of the Federal Security Service (FSB), and so forth.[50] It is obvious that implementation of this package of reforms would fundamentally change the state system and represent the complete rejection of key elements of the Soviet state legacy. It is also clear that, without these reforms, the modernization of public administration would be only partial and unlikely to provide the required level of flexibility for the modernization of other aspects of social life.

Relations with the Outside World

The contrast between the two doctrines is most striking with regard to Russia's foreign relations. They differ in such key areas as: the assessment of the sources and levels of external threats, the view of priority areas of cooperation, and the permissible extent of economic and political cooperation with possible allies.

The conservative doctrine is based on the assumption of a serious military threat, especially from the West, and of a worsening of the geopolitical struggle for control over natural resources. Putin claims that the world has entered a new arms race; that the most developed countries spend ten times more on defence than Russia does; and that the North Atlantic Treaty Organization (NATO) wants Russia to unilaterally implement agreements all the while the alliance is moving geographically closer to Russia's borders. There is no constructive response to Russia's concerns, he says, and Russia is therefore forced to make its own appropriate response: 'in the coming years Russia will start to produce new weapons, not inferior in quality characteristics to weapons at the disposal of other states, and in some cases – exceeding those specifications'.[51] The government's 'Concept' document notes that the development of global economic competition is accompanied by increased geopolitical rivalry, including a struggle for control over raw materials, energy, water and food resources.[52]

On the basis of this paradigm, the conservative doctrine targets the 11-member Commonwealth of Independent States (CIS), China and India as the first three priority areas of political and economic cooperation for Russia; the European Union and the United States are fourth and fifth, respectively. This replicates Soviet foreign policy priorities, which were (1) the community of the former Soviet Union, (2) China and (3) India.

As regards foreign investments in Russia, the conservative doctrine is extremely cautious. In his 'Strategy 2020' speech Putin said nothing about foreign investment in the Russian economy. According to the government's 'Concept', in 2007–20 the share of direct foreign investments in Russia's GDP will remain almost unchanged (3.5% in 2020 as against 3% in 2007). The Concept strategy is not predicated on any special measures to promote foreign investments in basic industries (oil and gas, raw materials, etc.). Putin's document proposes only clarification of the rules of the game; adjustment of the 'conditions of competition of Russian and foreign manufacturers in Russia',[53] and the 'establishment of clear and understandable restrictions on foreign investors in respect of strategic areas'.[54] On high-technology industries the Concept states that their modernization 'is impossible without the involvement of foreign strategic partners, foreign technology and skills', but also that in these sectors 'Russia wishes to establish independent national companies, which could play an active role not only in the domestic but also in the world market'.[55] In other words, the conservative doctrine does not envisage a significant increase in the openness of the country to foreign capital – in this version modernization is supposed to take place primarily on its own.

The liberal doctrine offers a fundamentally different view of Russia's relations with the outside world, although neither Medvedev's speeches nor the ICD report mention any threats to Russia from the West. On the contrary, the European Union and the United States are regarded as important cooperation partners. The ICD report portrays the European Union as a potential strategic Russian ally and even advocates Russia's eventual full membership. Relations with the United States are predicted to develop in the direction of strategic partnership.[56] In both cases 'cooperation' stands for collaboration in both the economic and military–political spheres.

In the economic field the liberal doctrine advocates not only a broad involvement of Western capital in the Russian economy, including basic industries, but also integration of the Russian economy with those of the leading European countries. Thus, according to the ICD report, the framework for a strategic alliance between Russia and the European Union can be created by the 'gradual formation of a united European energy sector, based on cross-ownership of business entities and joint management of production and redistribution of gas and other energy sources'.[57]

In his July 2010 speech to Russian ambassadors, President Medvedev supported economic integration with the West as outlined in the ICD report. He said that Russia 'really needs special modernization alliances with international partners... First of all, with countries such as Germany, France, Italy, the European Union as a whole, [and] with the United States of America'.[58]

In the military field the liberal doctrine advocates close cooperation with the United States in a joint missile defence programme and in

WMD (Weapons of Mass Destruction) non-proliferation measures, particularly as regards the programmes of Iran and North Korea.[59] Another strategic Russian objective is membership of NATO.[60] China is seen rather as a potential danger. The ICD report regards the 'rapid rise of China' as one of the key arguments for building 'a new model of relations with elements of cooperation and competition, especially in the quadrangle USA–Japan–Russia–China'.[61]

The next section of this chapter assesses the extent to which these two modernization doctrines can be put into practice and the possible consequences of their implementation.

Conservative and Liberal Modernization Doctrines: Feasibility and Implications

The Conservative Doctrine

Implementation of the conservative doctrine would run into some very significant institutional and resource constraints. The most significant institutional constraint is a lack of demand for innovation in the economy and in government institutions.

As shown above, the conservative doctrine does not propose either de-monopolization or a smaller government presence in key sectors of the economy, or the termination of 'friendly relations' between the state and a few big private corporations. This is particularly striking since the monopolization of the Russian economy that has taken place in recent years. In 2006–09 five big public companies appeared as monopolies in their respective sectors: the United Aircraft-Engineering Company (2006), the United Ship-building Company (founded in 2007; by 2009 it controlled another 19 companies), Rosnano (2007), RosTechnologies (2008) and RosAuto (2009).

In 2010 the World Economic Forum reported that Russia occupied 'a very low 114th position in this year's ETI' (Enabling Trade Index) and had 'fallen to the last place in the entire sample on the market access subindex'.[62] It now holds 101st place (out of 125) for the quality of domestic competition (the intensity of competition, level of monopolization, size of entry barriers, etc.) and 115th place in terms of its openness to foreign participation.[63]

It is difficult to support the contention that an economy in which the dominant positions are occupied by non-transparent monopolies that are supported by the state budget and protected from foreign competition will have a strong demand for innovations. For these corporations an innovative process would hardly support their survival, but rather would be a source of problems. Putin's evaluation of the current situation in Russian public administration was quoted above. General declarations aside, the conservative doctrine does not contain any significant measures to change this situation. This means that in the foreseeable future the state apparatus will look the same as it does today.

On the World Economic Forum's indices for 2010, the Russian state apparatus is rated as follows: in the Corruption Perceptions Index, 112th place out of 125; ethics and corruption (diversion of public funds, public trust of politicians), 91st place; undue influence (judicial dependence, favouritism in decisions of government officials), 103rd place; and government efficiency (wastefulness of government spending, burden of government regulation, efficiency of the legal framework, transparency of government policymaking), 103rd place.[64] Given this, it would be naive to suggest that there will be any demand in Russia for innovations in the field of public administration.

The state also needs to invest in technological modernization, but the resource constraints are no less serious there. According to various estimates, the share of outdated, physically obsolete equipment in Russian production assets now varies from about 45 to 75 per cent.[65] The average age of production equipment in Russian industries is approximately 13 years, as compared with 7 years in the United States.[66] Putin has a valid point when he says that modernization of the country would require it to change 'almost all … technology, almost all machines and equipment'. And this would require enormous financial resources.

Russia must invest even more resources in its human capital – not only to raise the quality of education, but also to alleviate the severe demographic crisis, that is to slow down the population decline and to improve public health. Today, Russia's population is shrinking at one of the highest rates of all countries in the world (by about 750,000 people annually), primarily due to the decreasing birth rate. If this situation does not improve, by the middle of the twenty-first century the population of Russia will have declined by about a third, to around 100 million people. Leading Russian demographers claim that it is impossible to halt this trend, but it is possible to slow down the process – not the part that depends on the fertility rate (this a cultural factor), but the part determined by the health of the population. The health situation is extremely bad. Natalya Rimashevskaya, one of the most authoritative Russian demographers, says that over the past few decades every succeeding generation was less healthy than the previous one,[67] leading to a mental and physical degradation.

The mortality rate for Russians of working age is seven times higher than the rate in the developed countries. In recent years Russia has rated around 172nd place (of 193 countries) for the occurrence of tuberculosis.[68] In the past century alcoholism in Russia reached catastrophic proportions. In 1914 Russians consumed about 2.5–4 litres of alcohol per capita. According to the World Health Organization, alcohol consumption of more than 8 litres per capita a year poses a threat to the very survival of a population. Meanwhile, the figure for Russia today is 18 litres per capita a year. This terrifying increase is mostly attributed to increased beer consumption. It is clear that unless the demographic crisis is overcome (or at least significantly alleviated) and technological renovation is implemented, any dream of successful modernization will remain a pipe dream.

There are other serious problems that have to be financed and solved. One of these problems is national defence. The conservative doctrine's vision of the world, which notes the increasing geopolitical competition over natural resources and an arms race involving countries that invest ten times more than Russia in defence, dictates the necessity for large military budgets. Because the conservative doctrine does not suggest that the share of foreign investment in the Russian economy should be increased, the country will have to solve the 'guns or butter' dilemma on its own.

This means that civilian and military spending – in accordance with Soviet tradition – will be a zero-sum game, and again in accordance with Soviet tradition 'guns' will win. The results can be predicted by examining some of the allocations in the national budget for 2011: defence, security and law enforcement, 16 per cent; medical care, 4 per cent; education, 3.7 per cent; science, 1.9 per cent; and culture, 0.9 per cent.[69] The problem of the scarcity of domestic resources for modernization is exacerbated by corruption. The impact of this factor can be evaluated by the size of kickbacks, which make up about 50 per cent of the total value of all contracts between the state and private contractors.

All this points to the doubtful feasibility of the conservative modernization doctrine, which would probably result in a waste of time and a devastating dissipation of resources. In my view this project would not contribute to alleviating the demographic crisis, nor to modernizing the civilian sectors of the economy; nor would it create military forces that are comparable in effectiveness with the armed forces of the countries that the conservative doctrine project considers the main source of threats (NATO). Given the fact that this project involves alienation from the West and cooperation with China (a country with territorial claims against Russia, which actively finances the emigration of its male population to the Russian Far East, and whose military spending – according to the Stockholm International Peace Research Institute – already exceeds Russia's by four times), such a strategy is likely to lead to the spread of Chinese influence in the Russian Far East. In the longer run this scenario could result in Russia's becoming the 'little brother' of a Great China.

The Liberal Doctrine

It is easier to see the feasibility of the liberal modernization doctrine. As the authors of the ICD report wrote: 'It is a dangerous illusion to think that Russia – as it is formed today – can be transformed into an innovative country, communicating on equal terms with the leaders of the world's innovative development and competing for the opportunity to manage the future. A truly innovative development (and by and large, even the start of such a development) requires another country – with a different set of values and relations, with different politics and social environment, with a different public administration, with a different mood of business'.[70] In other words, Russia is not equipped to achieve full modernization and cannot therefore be transformed into a leading world power in the twenty-first century.

Conclusion

Of the doctrines of modernization discussed in Russian academic and political communities, the liberal-oriented one, here represented by the ICD report, seems the most profound and honest one. It opens the prospect of a future Russia as part of the European, or rather Euro-Atlantic, civilization – not as a great power but simply as a participant country with a per capita income that is below the European and US average but much higher than the world average. However, in some spheres Russia could be counted as a significant member of the community; as one of the key countries in the collective security system; as a good partner in major space and oceanic research programmes; as a supplier of energy and processed raw materials; as a source of scientific and technological innovations (if integration with the West limits or stops the 'brain drain' from Russia); and as a tourist attraction because of its unique natural areas. The sooner Russia starts to implement a liberal doctrine – that is, the faster it opens up key sectors of its economy to Western investors and fully cooperates militarily with the United States and NATO – the less threatening the 'Chinese factor' will be and the greater the probability that Russia will be able to survive within its current borders.

If Russia is not caught up in trying to achieve a neurotic, unrealistic goal but rather calmly examines its options, it will realize that between the visions of Russia as a superpower and the possible disintegration of the country there are many development trajectories that can provide a quality of life that is better than that in most other parts of the world.

Notes

1. In the 18-year period 1992–2009 the number of publications devoted to this subject in Russian newspapers, magazines and news agency releases nationwide multiplied approximately 1200 times. By the end of the first decade of the twenty-first century, however, there were four times more Russian publications on security issues. Calculated with the services of Integrum World Wide databases; see http://www.integrumworld.com.
2. It is impossible to list all the many publications confirming this statement, but among the most interesting are A. A. Auzan and A. Zolotov (2008), 'Koalitsii za modernizatsiyu: analiz vozmozhnosti vozniknoveniya' [Coalition for Modernization: An Analysis of the Potential], *Voprosy ekonomiki* [Problems of Economy], No. 1, pp. 97–107; S. Dubinin (2010), 'Alternativy modernizatsii' [Alternatives of Modernization], *Svobodnaya mysl* [Free Thought], No. 2, pp. 5–14; L. Grigoriev and V. Tambovtsev (2008), 'Modernizatsiya cherez koalitsii' [Modernization through Coalition], *Voprosy ekonomiki*, No. 1, pp. 59–70; V. Inozemtsev (ed.) (2009), *Modernizatsiya Rossii: usloviya, predposylki, shansy. Vyp. 1,2.* [Modernization of Russia: Terms, Conditions, Chances] (Moscow: Tsentr issledovaniya postindustrialnogo obshchestva [Centre for Studies of Post-industrial Society]); E. Jasin (2007), 'Modernizatsiya i obshchestvo' [Modernization and Society], *Voprosy ekonomiki*, No. 5, pp. 4–29; and V. Polterovich (2008), 'Strategii modernizatsii, instituty i koalitsii' [Strategy for Modernization, Institutions, and Coalitions], *Voprosy ekonomiki*, No. 4, pp. 4–24.
3. 'The Concept of Long-term Socio-Economic Development of the Russian Federation for the Period up to 2010' (see note 3 in 'Introduction', p. 12); V. Putin (2008) (see note 3 in Chapter 1, 'Introduction').
4. By 'ideology' I mean 'any wide-ranging system of beliefs, ways of thought, and categories that provide the foundation of programmes of political and social action', according to the definition in *The Oxford Dictionary of Philosophy*, 2nd edn (2005), (Oxford: Oxford University Press), p. 178.
5. A good example of a communist version of modernization can be found in the report of Gennady Zyuganov, the leader of the Communist Party of the Russian Federation (CPRF), at the 5th CPRF plenum, 3 April 2010. See 'Socialist Modernization – The Way to a Revival of Russia', http://kprf.ru/rus_soc/78111.html.
6. The Council on National Strategy was headed at that time by Stanislav Belkovsky and Iosif Diskin. On the council document see e.g. http://www.Russiajournal.com/nodee16277.
7. See the text of the ICD report at http://www.utro.ru/articles/2003/05/26/201631. shtml. In some publications, including that one, I was mentioned as one of the authors of the report. The present author was a member of the council but did not participate in the preparation of this report. Its publication was the reason for my withdrawal from the council. A few others left the council at the same time: A. Salmin, B. Makarenko and L. Shevtsova.

Salmin died in 2005. As for Makarenko and Shevtsova, they are now two of the consistent supporters of liberal modernization. E.g., Makarenko is one of the authors of the ICD report that is analysed in this chapter.

8. See e.g. transcripts of several meetings of the Open Forum Club:
    1. 8th meeting (10 July 2003): Political coercive tools in Russian Economy: Contexts and consequences, available at http://www.open-forum.ru/meeting.php?fullsten&sten_id=23.
    2. 11th meeting (30 September 2003): Economic Growth and Politics in Russia today, http://www.open-forum.ru/meeting.php?fullsten&sten_id=20.
    3. 13th meeting (28 October 2003): The Yukos affair and scenarios of Russia's development for the next 10 years: A situational analysis, http://www.open-forum.ru/meeting.php?fullsten&sten_id=18.
    4. 17th meeting (3 February 2004): Modernization of Russia: Conflicts and dangers on the road to post-industrial society, http://www.open-forum.ru/meeting.php?fullsten&sten_id=14.

9. See A. G. Vishnevsky (2004), 'Obshchestvo i reformy: Modernizatsiya i kontrmodernizatsiya: chya vozmet?' [Society and Reforms: Modernization and Counter-modernization: Who Would Win?], *Obshchestvennye nauki i sovremennost*¨ [Social Sciences and Modernity], No. 1, pp. 17–25; V. V. Lapkin and V. I. Pantin (2005), 'Ritmy mezhdunarodnogo razvitiya kak faktor politicheskoi modernizatsii Rossii' [Rhythms of the International Development as a Factor for Russia's Modernization], *POLIS*, No. 3, pp. 44–58; Jasin (note 31); A. A. Auzan (2007), 'Koleya rossiiskoi modernizatsii' [Track of Russian Modernization], *Obshchestvennye nauki i sovremennost*, No. 6, pp. 54–60; Auzan and Zolotov (note 31); K. S. Gadgiev (2008), 'Vesternizatsiya ili osobyi put modernizatsii?' [Westernization or Special Path of Modernization?], *POLIS*, No. 4, pp. 148–62.

10. L. V. Poliakov (ed.) (2007), *PRO suverennuyu demokratiyu* [On Sovereign Democracy] (Moscow: Evropa).

11. A. Dugin (2009), 'Chto takoe modernizatsiya' [What is Modernization?], *Politicheskii klass* [Political Class], No. 1, pp. 60–5.

12. Dmitri Medvedev (2009), 'Go, Russia!', http://eng.kremlin.ru/news/298; D. Medvedev (2010), 'Vystuplenie na plenarnom zasedanii Peterburgskogo mezhdunarodnogo ekonomicheskogo foruma, 18 June [Speech at the Plenary Meeting of the International Economic Forum in Petersburg], http://news.kremlin.ru/news/8093; D. Medvedev (2010), 'Vystuplenie na soveshchanii s rossiiskimi poslami i postoyannymi predstavitelyami v mezhdunarodnykh organizatsiyakh' [Speech at the Meeting of Russian Ambassadors and Permanent Representatives to International Organizations], 12 June, http://www.kremlin.ru/transcripts/8325; *Rossiya XXI veka: Obraz zhelaemogo zavtra* [Russia in the XXI Century: Vision for the Future], Institut sovremennogo razvitiya ICD [Institute of Contemporary Development] (2010) (Moscow: Ekon-Inform). For documents in English see the ICD website at http://www.riocenter.ru/en.

13. V. Ivanov (2009), 'Konservativnaya modernizatsiya [Conservative Modernization], *Izvestiya*, 30 November; D. Orlov, D. Badovsky and M. Vinogradov (2010), 'Konservativnaya modernizatsiya – 2010: konfiguratsiya vlasti i novaya politicheskaya povestka dnya. Analiticheskii doklad' [Conservative Modernization 2010: Configuration of Power and the New

Political Agenda. An Analytical Report], *REGNUM*, 3 January, http://www.regnum.ru/news/1241073.html; V. Surkov (2010), 'Chudo vozmozhno' [A Miracle is Possible], *Vedomosti*, 15 February.

14. Various conservative authors write about the need to preserve the existing political regime in different ways. V. Ivanov, a supporter of the 'consensual oligarchy', regards democratization as a dismantling of the regime and believes that it is unacceptable. V. Ivanov (2009), 'Konservativnaya modernizatsiya' [Conservative Modernization], *Izvestiya*, 30 November. The more flexible author Vladislav Surkov writes about the need to start political modernization immediately, 'but not dramatically', and adds that the United Russia Party is likely to win the elections of 2011. V. Surkov (2010), 'Chudo vozmozhno' [A Miracle Is Possible], *Vedomosti*, 15 February.

15. I. Diskin, http://www.politonline.ru/comments/2250.html.

16. L. Polyakov and A. Chesnakov, http://actualcomment.ru/done/456/, or even as state treason: A. Kuchin, http://www.nakanune.ru/articles/14481.

17. D. Orlov and A. Chesnakov, http://actualcomment.ru/done/456/.

18. See http://www.gazeta.ru/politics/2010/02/02_a_3319216.shtml.

19. The conservative version is 'the most attractive country for living', 'leader in socio-economic development and in national security'. V. Putin (2008), 'Vystuplenie na rasshirennom zasedanii Gosudarstvennogo soveta "O strategii razvitiya Rossii do 2020"', 8 February [Speech at the Enlarged Meeting of the State Council 'On Russia's Development Strategy to 2020'] http://archive.kremlin.ru/text/appears/2008/02/159528.shtml: 'our level of economic and social development is in keeping with the status of Russia as one of the world's leading powers of the XXI century'. See Concept (note 3), p. 7, versus 'the loss of positions in the economy, security, and ultimately the loss of sovereignty (Putin).The liberal version: 'an attractive country where people from all over the world will strive to come in search of realization of their dreams, in search of better opportunities for success and self-actualization': D. Medvedev (2010), 'Vystuplenie na plenarnom zasedanii Peterburgskogo mezhdunarodnogo ekonomicheskogo foruma, 18 June [Speech at the Plenary Meeting of the International Economic Forum in Petersburg], http://news.kremlin.ru/news/8093), 'a modern, prosperous and strong Russia', 'a co-founder of a new world economic order and a full-fledged member of the collective political leadership in the post-crisis world"' versus 'the degradation of a Great Power', 'final calming down at a back seat of the world civilization'. *Rossiya XXI veka: Obraz zhelaemogo zavtra* [Russia in the 21st Century, Institut sovremennogo razvitiya (ICD, Institute of Contemporary Development)]. For documents in English see the ICD website at http://www.riocenter.ru/en, p. 4.

20. ICD (note 19), p. 15.

21. In the conservative doctrine this goal is stated as: 'In 2020 the income and quality of life in Russia will reach a level typical of developed economies – in 2020 the per capita GDP should be about 70% of the average of OECD member countries, against approximately 40% in 2007, and the share of the middle class in the population should exceed 50%. Concept (note 3) p. 8. According to the liberal doctrine, the objective of modernization is to achieve a quality of life that is in all respects comparable with the most advanced countries of the world. ICD (note 48), p. 21.

22. Putin (note 3).
23. Medvedev (note 12) .
24. Concept (note 3), p. 9.
25. ICD (note 19), p. 8.
26. Concept (note 3), pp. 55, 73.
27. 'The third task – a civic and patriotic education of youth, a fostering of elaboration of legal, cultural and moral values among young people. The problem can be solved: ... by a popularization ... of social values, such as health; work; family; tolerance; human rights; patriotism, service to the motherland; responsibility, active civil position; by a support of programs aiming to create a unified Russian civil nation, national-state identity; by fostering tolerance toward different ethnic groups; by international cooperation, by stimulating the interest of the youth in the historical and cultural heritage of Russia, in environmental protection ... '. Concept (note 3), pp. 73–4.
28. Concept (note 3), p. 74.
29. The project presupposes that there are a lot of resources to create an institutional environment 'to ensure the development of human capital'. Concept (note 3), p. 85: improving education, expanding opportunities for the realization of individual initiatives, entrepreneurship, etc.
30. Medvedev (note 12).
31. ICD (note 19), p. 8.
32. ICD ibid., pp. 8–9.
33. M. Fedotov (2010), 'Ne bit dubinoi, a obsuzhdat' [Do not Bludgeon but Discuss], *Russkii Newsweek*, No. 43, pp. 24–5.
34. Putin (note 3).
35. Concept (note 3), p. 7.
36. Putin: 'Taking into account that the Yukos affair in general, and the trial of Khodorkovsky and Lebedev in particular, led to the degradation of the Russian judicial system, the appeal "to continue efforts to establish an independent and effective judiciary" sounds a bit strange. According to the World Economic Forum, Russia – in terms of judicial independence – occupied 109th place out of 134 in 2008–2009, and 116th place out of 133 in 2009–2010.' See http://www.weforum.org/documents/gcr0809/index.html and http://www.weforum.org/documents/GCR09/index.html. 'Judges remain beholden to their superiors and are pressured to produce convictions. Security services are increasing their ability to monitor private correspondence. Russia's penitentiaries remain unreformed with torture a common practice. Russia's rating for judicial framework and independence remains unchanged at 5.50'. *Nations in Transit 2010*, see note 15.
37. Concept (note 3), pp. 13–14.
38. Concept (note 3), pp. 126, 143.
39. Surkov (note 14).
40. ICD (note 19), pp. 17, 18.
41. *Nations in Transit 2010*, see Chapter 2 by Hayoz, note 10.
42. Medvedev (note 12).
43. Medvedev (2010) 'Vystuplenie na soveshanii s rossiiskimi poslami i postayannymi predstavitelyami v mezhdunarodnykh organizatsiyakh' [Speech at a Meeting with Russian Ambassadors and Permanent Representatives to International Organisations], 12 June, http://kremlin.ru/transcripts/8325.

44. ICD (note 19), p. 10.
45. Concept (note 3), p. 18.
46. Putin sees this transformation as a process that 'takes years and is carried out' with the help of education and the formation of civil culture by enhancing the role of non-governmental organizations, ombudsmen, and civic chambers as well as, of course, through the development of the Russian multiparty system. Speech by Putin, 8 February 2008 (note 3).
47. Putin ibid.
48. Medvedev (note 12).
49. ICD (note 19), pp. 10, 11.
50. ICD ibid., pp. 38–42, 63–4.
51. Putin (note 3).
52. Concept (note 3), p. 5.
53. Ibid., p. 124.
54. Ibid., p. 150.
55. Ibid., p. 114.
56. ICD (note 19), pp. 44, 45.
57. ICD ibid., p. 44.
58. Medvedev (note 43).
59. ICD (note 19), p. 45.
60. ICD ibid., p. 42.
61. ICD ibid., p. 47.
62. GETR (2010), The Global Enabling Trade Report 2010, World Economic Forum, p. 25, http://www.weforum.org/pdf/GETR10/Global-Enabling-Trade-Report-2010.pdf.
63. Ibid., p. 233.
64. Ibid., p. 233.
65. E. V. Balatsky and A. B. Gusev (2008), 'Proizvodstvennyi park yurskogo perioda [A Non/Productive Park of the Yura Period], *Nezavisimaya gazeta*, 23 April, http://www.ng.ru/science/2008–04–23/20_logics.html; Inozemtsev (note 31); *ROSSTAT* (2008, 2009), *Rossiiskii statisticheskii ezhegodnik* [ROSSTAT. Statistical Yearbook of Russia] (Moscow: Goskomstat Rossii); N. Savelyev (2004), Speech at the meeting of the Open Forum Club on the topic 'The European Union and the CIS. Prospects of Interaction', 27 October, http://www.open-forum.ru.
66. IWEIR, Institute of World Economy and International Relations (2010), *Modernization of Russian Economy: Structural Capacity* (Moscow), http://www.imemo.ru/ru/publ/2010/10004.pdf.
67. Rimashevskaya's speech at the Nikitsky Club, 16 March 2005, unpublished (author's transcript).
68. Human Resource (2004). 'Chelovecheskii resurs i konkurentnosposobnost Rossii v XXI veke: Sovmestnoe zasedanie Kluba "Otkrytyi forum" i Assotsiatsii menedzherov [The Human Resource and Russia's Competitiveness in the XXI Century: Joint Meeting of the Club 'Open Forum' and the Association of Managers] (Moscow).
69. *Vedomosti*, 24 September 2010, http://www.vedomosti.ru/newspaper/print/2010/09/24/246414.
70. ICD (note 19), p. 20.

Part II

Characteristics of the Russian System

4
The Nature and Function of 'Putinism'

Lev Gudkov

Introduction

Since the autumn of 2009, when President Dmitrii Medvedev announced that Russia needed to modernize, the term 'modernization' has constantly appeared in the Russian media. The term had previously been used mainly by academics but now became a mantra that was reiterated in countless speeches by Kremlin politicians and political commentators. The ruling party promoted the campaign slogan 'conservative modernization', the Russian Orthodox Church opened discussion of 'modernization and morality', the police authorities debated 'modernization of the Ministry of the Interior', the generals advocated 'modernization of the military' and the Ministry of Education chanted 'modernization of the educational system'. In other words, modernization became the new fashionable term of officials.

Slogans had changed. 'Modernization' replaced the previous top priority of national projects to combat corruption, legal nihilism and oligarchs. Political analysts started pondering over what President Medvedev had meant, what kind of modernization Russia needed (or what should be modernized), how it should be carried out and by whom, and whether this is at all possible. Western analysts started to talk about the differences between the 'liberal' Medvedev and the 'authoritarian' Putin, about the 'reset' in Russian–US relations, and about new opportunities for Russia to cooperate with the European Union.

The Russian authorities' current modernization rhetoric is reminiscent of campaigns in the relatively recent Soviet past, such as the programme to accelerate the scientific–technical progress of the early Gorbachev years; the optimization of socialist planning and management through new economic and mathematical methods under

Brezhnev; Khrushchev's and Kosygin's reforms of the 1960s; and the many 'catch up and outdo America' campaigns that were initiated in periods of economic stagnation, inefficient production and management, military failures or administration crisis during a change of leadership. Medvedev's modernization programme was announced only after the grave consequences of the 2008 recession put an end to Putin's seven years of 'political stability'. However, many in Russia and the West bought the promise of a 'new course', with its liberalism and critical assessment of the state of affairs in Russia and its policy of non-confrontation with the West. Politicians in the West assumed that words stood for action and overlooked the fact that President Medvedev maintains Putin's policy of a concentration of power: the increasing dependency of the judicial system on the executive branch, the broader responsibilities of the security police (KGB/FSB), the extension of terms in office for the president and Duma deputies, and so on.

It soon became clear, however, that by 'modernization' President Medvedev meant a purely technological upgrade. He wanted to reverse Russia's technological backwardness and bridge the growing gap between Russia and other developed countries. He did not have in mind institutional changes – either to bring society and the state up to European standards or to create favourable conditions for Western investment and technology, such as state support for business, the creation of special tax zones where Western and Russian companies could set up joint ventures, and so on. However, foreign investors did not rush to Russia because they lacked trust in the legal and financial institutions there. The recession after 2008 brought a 15 per cent economic downturn and clearly showed that the Russian political system, as it had developed during the first decade of the 2000s, is not simply conservative (resisting change and incapable of innovations). It primarily functions to curb, block and even paralyse other social subsystems, including the economy, science, education, telecommunications, civil society and public life, all for the sake of preserving the current power structure.

The extremely contradictory views that political analysts have of modern Russia – from unwarranted optimism regarding Russia's future and the inclusion of Russia in the camp of 'normal countries' to scepticism regarding the prospects for democratic change in Russia – reflect analysts' inadequate understanding of the nature of processes on post-Soviet territory. The current Russian regime and its future prospects have not been studied thoroughly. Further research and analysis are needed.

The challenges enumerated above are compounded by the difficulty of establishing a theoretical framework for analysing post-totalitarian social development. Transition theories, which offer a more or less adequate description of the transient processes in Central and Eastern Europe, do not fully apply to the state of affairs on post-Soviet territory. The theoretical debate on totalitarianism of the 1960s and 1970s was cut off shortly before the collapse of communism because it failed to answer the critical question: Is there a way out of a totalitarian regime and what would be its logic? In 1945, the issue was taken off the agenda by the defeat of Nazism and Fascism. In 1989 in Eastern and Central Europe there were other factors at play, yet mainly external forces determined the collapse of the socialist camp. Analysis of the current political regime in Russia (and of other regimes in the former Soviet Union, such as those in Central Asia, Belarus, Azerbaijan and Georgia) can therefore certainly contribute additional material for the discussion of these issues.

Building on the Heritage of the Past

According to the late Russian sociologist Yurii Levada, the current Russian regime was created (or rather assembled) from 'pieces', 'structural wrecks' and 'material' of the old system, although the composition and most importantly the functions of the social institutions changed. From a sociological point of view, the collapse of the Soviet totalitarian system was caused by internal defects. The lack of well-structured mechanisms for renewal of the system and for the handover of power was a cause of major tension in the late Soviet era. After the end of mass terror one of the most crucial mechanisms of the totalitarian society, the *nomenklatura* or ruling class, became the source of many social dysfunctions. The essence of the *nomenklatura*'s organization of power – the merging of party and state authority in support of the totalitarian order – was based on a centralized selection from among top cadres for key positions in various areas of government and finance. They were chosen for their loyalty to the party rather than their skills and knowledge. Such a system ensured the Central Committee of the Soviet Communist Party total control of the social structure, vertical and horizontal social mobility and, consequently, of all political and economic processes in Soviet society.

The term of office for a *nomenklatura* position was on average three years in the late Stalinist era of mass terror. It was extended to six years following Khrushchev's policy of de-stalinization and was 21 years at the end of Brezhnev's period of stagnation. This meant that there was no rotation of the ruling elite, and thus no innovative social change, which caused muted protest in the middle and lowest tiers of the party bureaucracy as well as a drive to renew the leadership as the need for reform was recognized. Gorbachev's effort to reorganize the Communist Party led to a schism in the *nomenklatura* and the collapse of the party-state. The brief rule of Boris Yeltsin, commonly (and mistakenly) characterized as a democratic revolution or democratic transition, was driven by the need to reorganize the political system with the concomitant need for a new balance of interests between factions of the split Soviet bureaucracy, at the time engaged in fierce infighting for power. The possibility of creating a consensus between clans and factions came with the idea of converting part of the political power into property and creating more complex structures for sharing influence and authority.

The Soviet totalitarian system finally collapsed over the three years 1992–94, almost immediately after the first free elections were held and the abolition of the most important *nomenklatura* institutes such as the Soviet Communist Party, the State Planning Committee and the All-Union ministries. However, this did not mean that 'it was all over'. The system had the integrity of its components, but they continued to function, guided by their own interests, whether departmental, corporate or clan-based. The composition of the most secretive institutes of the Soviet state was maintained and managed to resist change: defence and law enforcement structures (the state security agencies, the judiciary, the prosecutor's office, the military and the Ministry of Internal Affairs). However, they were working in an entirely different environment.

Since Russian society was then and still is in a state of political apathy, depression and alienation, the outcome of the competition for supremacy was determined by those who could use illegal resources for the use of force – either direct force (the military, and the Ministry of Internal Affairs in the early years) or later camouflaged force via the secret, illegal resources of the police and secret service.

The Yeltsin government declared that its key objective was to change Russia's historical paradigm – to dismantle the authoritarian and totalitarian power structure and create a new democratic state governed by the rule of law. Yeltsin pursued this objective until the 1995 State Duma parliamentary elections and the 1996 presidential election revealed his low popularity ratings and weakened position. He then faced a difficult dilemma: to seek the support of the unsteady and unpredictable constituency of the party in power or the remnant resources and staff of the state security agencies. By 1997 he had carried out a sharp reversal in domestic policy and, to a lesser extent, in foreign policy, moving towards the *siloviki* – the secret police (former KGB, renamed FSB), other security agencies, the military, and armed units of the Ministry of Internal Affairs – whom he deemed to provide more solid support for his personal power than the new institutions and pro-presidential parties.

The facade of political pluralism – a multi-party system – was created in the early 1990s by the fierce competition between a vast array of fragments and factions of the old *nomenklatura*, which used the mass media, now free from censorship and ideological monopoly, for their own purposes. The objectives of these factions, formed around former secretaries of regional party committees who had become 'presidents' of autonomous republics, 'red directors' of the defence industry, and top-ranking officials of federal ministries, were far from the ideals of democracy and the rule of law. However, their brutal infighting opened opportunities to carry out reforms and adopt laws that could facilitate political compromise. The new political groupings were not parties in the classical sense of Western political theory, that is, they did not originate from any democratic grassroots movement or represent the interests of particular social groups. Over time, these political machines, which had been created by the authorities to mobilize the electorate, increasingly promoted public acceptance of those who *already held* power. They became the 'party of power', the 'party of officials'.[1] They did not compete against democrats or liberals, but rather against similar parties composed of second- or third-tier Soviet officials. This explains why ideological diversity and political pluralism deteriorated and the party programmes lost their distinctive features with each election cycle.[2]

Yeltsin's choice to name as his successor a person from the KGB/FSB[3] determined Russia's future path by opening the doors to power for Soviet secret police staff, whose corporate mentality was alien to liberal ideas, the constitutional state and the policy of Westernization. Let me emphasize this: Putin's regime came to power not as the result of a successful election of a political party with a clear programme and ideology, nor as an outcome of social protest.[4] The Putin regime was not set up as the result of either a collapse of the old system, as had been the case with the Yeltsin administration, or a military defeat.[5] Quite the opposite, with all its apparent deficiencies Yeltsin's institutional system had had a certain safety margin and a potential for development. This helped it to survive the first and most difficult transition period and the crises of those early post-Soviet years, including the 1998 default, and ensure rapid economic recovery in the early years of the 2000s, for which Putin took the credit.

During the government crisis of the 1990s the political leadership regarded the KGB/FSB, which retained its monopoly on state violence, as *the only organized force* capable of providing the solid support that was so badly needed. However, after staking its reliance on the security agency, the Yeltsin administration soon found that it had become a hostage of the political police. The latter used its special resources – the authority to act beyond legal limits and rules – to subordinate the national government, and the FSB became an extraordinary part of the social and political order in the country. As of 2001–02, former staff of the secret police held three quarters of the positions in the top tier of the Russian government and a third of the positions in intermediate levels of government.[6]

However, the relative number of these people in government is not as significant as the change in government practices. By ensuring forced and illegitimate, or inadequately legitimate, redistribution of property, cash flows and administrative influence, figures from a defence or security background became the shadow part of the political leadership. With Putin in power, these people took on a function that was similar to the *nomenklatura*: it was a staff pool (*kadrovyi rezerv*) for recruitment to positions of power. Additionally, by enforcing a vague policy of reprivatization (property takeovers and redistribution of cash flows) and, later, renationalization (by buying the controlling stake in joint stock companies or creating gigantic state corporations), the secret police became a substitute for the regulators of the former planned economy and an instrument for control over the economy.

Putin's regime started off by tightening its grip on the Russian mass media and enforcing political censorship. The next step was making the judges hugely dependent on the president's administration, which ensured that he could 'manage' both national and local elections and redistribute property. It took one and a half, or two, election cycles to form a completely controlled parliament, which effectively stalled the process of separating society from government, a process initiated by the reforms of the 1990s. It was intended both to emasculate the principle of separation of powers that was enshrined in the 1993 Constitution and to restrict the independence (autonomy) of social institutions (including the economy, education and civil society) from the state, in other words, from the executive branch of government. After Putin had dealt with big business, the oligarchs, and regional and municipal authorities, the time had come for non-governmental associations and organizations with no direct link to politics to admit their dependence on the Kremlin. The Kremlin's growing control over the electoral system and NGOs and state intervention in the running of the economy were not counteracted by any public resistance or even the increasing corruption, which is often regarded as public compensation for the state's abuse of power.

According to the logic of power consolidation, the current regime cannot stop this development. Coercion is on the rise and will continue to escalate, there will be more ballot rigging and political trials, and the pursuit of complete supremacy over the Russian population (campaigns against espionage, extremism, falsifiers of history, abuse of the Internet, tax evasion, etc.) will not subside. The regime may have reached a stage when sheer self-preservation compels it to continue on this course, although the political leaders may realize the danger of letting this happen. The scale of the abuse of power or even outright crimes (a plethora of examples appear daily in the Russian media) makes it impossible for them to step down and hand over power to others because this would inevitably result in their being tried and sentenced. The public knows this. They know about the widespread corruption and abuse of power by government officials. However, Russians accept the current situation as a non-alternative case and put up with it since they believe that they cannot change or even influence the political system. Hence, it is crucial to understand the nature of the regime and how it develops and be aware of any scenarios for change.

'Putinism' and Social Science Theory

Political scientists have devoted a great deal of attention to the Russian political system under Putin.[7] However, regardless of the increasing interest and a growing number of publications, there is no single accepted characterization or definition. The very fact that researchers apply different, even though structurally similar, definitions to describe the type of supremacy (such as 'simulated' or 'imitation' democracy, a 'hybrid', 'chimerical' or 'centaur' regime) points to the insufficient analytical tools available. Some political scientists include putinism in the category of authoritarian regimes in transitional processes, where Russia is compared to Mexico or Latin American countries,[8] or Asian states like Indonesia, Malaysia and Singapore. Other scholars, among them Dmitri Furman, see Russia's political system as a normal dictatorship on the same scale as the authoritarian regimes emerging after the collapse of the USSR and preoccupied with adapting to change, which was forced upon them, such as those of Belarus, Azerbaijan, Kazakhstan and other Central Asian states.[9]

The definition that is chosen to characterize the current regime, whether it is 'putinism',[10] a 'controlling regime', a 'corporation of the *siloviki*', a 'police state'[11] or 'state monopoly capitalism', determines the analysis of the regime's sustainability (efficiency of institutions and resources for public support) and potential for evolution or transformation. Our understanding of the nature of the contemporary Russian regime is impeded by our own thought inertia, when we try to place new phenomena in old political classifications. Let me outline a few such features.

There are two views of the current Russian government.

1. The current regime is reverting to the ideals of the USSR, or represents a type of fascist corporate state (analogies between Putin's regime and the early years of Mussolini's rule);[12]
2. The current regime is based entirely on the personal authoritarian rule of Putin.

I believe that both these characterizations are faulty because they stem from the disillusion caused by the gap between liberal expectations, which proved to be mere illusions, and reality. They also stem from the unidimensionality of the political categories of transition theories (transitology) applied to the Russian political system. I believe that putinism is a unique, if not entirely new, phenomenon. I consider this new phenomenon to be primarily a system of *legitimizing supremacy* (authority) and a *technology of power* (a system for controlling the masses).

Proper analysis of the Putin regime is hindered by the fact that Russian political scientists often use Western democratic models as the norm for evaluating Russian reality and by reference to the Soviet totalitarian past. Scholars who use these approaches either compare the Russian reality with normative ideals of democracy and politics (the way it should be),[13] or relate the current situation to a vague conception of the Soviet system. Neither approach offers an adequate explanation for current developments in Russia.

If we try to compare ideal–typical models of totalitarian and authoritarian regimes with 'putinism' we find the following distinctive patterns.

1. There is no old party-state monopoly or system of state and ideological control that permeates all areas of social life and controls vertical and horizontal mobility. The structure, function and efficiency of the United Russia party are not the same as those of the Soviet Communist Party. The role of the ruling party, as well as of other pro-Kremlin parties, is limited to electoral manifestations of loyalty and competition for seats in the State Duma and in regional legislative assemblies. It is not the same type of government or terror infrastructure as the Soviet Communist Party was, nor has it the right to form the government, as democratic countries can.

Putin is not a 'Führer', a charismatic leader, demagogue or orator who has earned the population's confidence in times of extreme crisis. In terms of his psychology and mentality he is an average official from the intelligence and law enforcement agency who came to power after a series of bargains within the establishment and who was not regarded as a charismatic leader until he was in power. His popularity and public support do not stem from any personality cult or identification by the public with him as a symbol of success. His origins lie rather in the more mundane and obvious illusions of the masses that his rule will guarantee prosperity as well as stability and predictability. On the other hand, people generally believe that he is trying to eliminate any other influential, reputable political figures from the political arena, neutralize semi-official sources of information and criticism, and promote the idea that there is no viable alternative to his rule. Vulgar social and political and nationalistic populism add to this image. Public opinion polls do not show that people idolize Vladimir Putin. The basis for his credibility is fairly conservative. He has no pretensions of aiming to contribute to a 'new world order', as totalitarian leaders normally do.

2. There is no messianic ideology, no large-scale preaching of any 'universal explanation' or 'political religion' that could mobilize the Russian people to build a 'new world' and a 'new human being'. As early as under Brezhnev's rule, the role of ideology was limited to guarding the policy of state coercion, constraint and discipline (forced austerity in people's daily life) and substituting communism's missionary outreach with superpower nationalism. The lack of ideology indicates that putinism cannot offer any political roadmap or vision for social development that is so important for the masses (except the promise that they can keep what they have today). It does not hold up any enticing image of tomorrow.[14] The authorities' rhetoric about the need to 'move forward', about innovations, investments and modernization,

are worth about as much as the former plans for 'doubling the Russian GDP' or 'national projects', which had no noticeable effect on society or the economy. This is a typical Soviet-style practice of reporting future plans rather than actual progress. Such calls by Medvedev and Putin are efforts to legitimize their power rather than to create a political platform – and this is why they neglect organizational improvements. They cannot compensate for the lack of public mechanisms for setting political objectives based on the consensus of public interest and ambitions. The effect on the population is insignificant, as indicated by public opinion polls.

3. The objectives of the current Russian regime's foreign policy do not include the expansion or establishment of any second 'Eastern bloc' or other bloc of allied states. The most it aims at is the creation of a buffer or defence against Western influence and the Westernization that is so crucial for modernization, by suppressing attempts to promote political or economic integration with the West. The geopolitical doublespeak is primarily designed to maintain the regime's self-image and serves to consolidate the elite around the authorities and defend the country against the hostile environment and the 'fifth column' of liberals as agents of the West. Russia's foreign policy has an exclusively isolationist or compensatory nature: the focus is on external powers, which they believe must recognize Russia's national interests in its neighbouring states, and major players must show their respect for Russia on the global political stage.

4. Russia does not use terror, massive repression and propaganda, all of which are characteristic of totalitarian regimes that create an environment of paralysing fear in society, to sever the links between morality and society. Control of the mass media varies greatly: it is most severe for television broadcasting, more relaxed in the case of the print media, but still absent on the Internet. Current Kremlin propaganda is not widespread. It influences only a portion of the media programmes – primarily news broadcasts that present public perceptions and interpretations of events, but also topical material such as the fight against terrorism, anti-Western material, and material discrediting the opposition or competitors in politics or business. However, this does not mean that the manipulation of public opinion is weaker. It has simply been transformed as the technology for manipulating public consciousness has changed. Today, the link that was extremely efficient in the 1990s between party activities, non-governmental organizations and the mass media has disappeared. This has stymied attempts to inform the public about current affairs as well as critical public reflection on what

is happening in the Kremlin and otherwise in Russian political life. It has become virtually impossible to hold the authorities accountable for their political actions or decisions. The purpose of the major media outlets (TV and large-circulation newspapers such as *Komsomolskaya pravda*, *Moskovskii komsomolets* and *Argumenty i fakty*), in addition to propaganda for the regime, has been reduced to parody, entertainment and consumer hedonism, which has numbed popular consciousness and public attention to social issues.[15]

5. Russia does not have a state-run, centralized, planned distribution economy that serves the regime's purposes, as it did during the policy of accelerated militaristic modernization and later in the stagnation era of maintaining the status and authority of a superpower. Today the priority is not state property or any system of forced labour. State property has been preserved in the form of state corporations or sectors excluded from the market economy largely due to the selfish interest of clans in concentrating power in their hands through corrupt budget 'sharing' between pro-government businessmen and the management of state corporations. The remaining military-industrial establishment cannot re-arm the Russian military and is primarily export-oriented. In other words, it operates like any other state corporation for the purpose of making profit (the same is true of the other sectors of the state-run economy). The modern Russian economy has been largely decentralized and has a much more complex structure than the Soviet economy had.

6. The mental and psychological support of Russia's regime comes from the periphery, the conservative and depressed environment, which has no means of cushioning the effects of the collapse of the Soviet social infrastructure. The elite is opportunistic and prepared to sell out the current government as soon as it sees signs of the regime's decline. Institutionally, the regime relies on the law enforcement agencies, including the judiciary.

The only ideology the Putin regime can offer the Russian population is a conservative resistance to system change. It focuses on self-preservation and lacks the resources, ideas or leaders to initiate modernization. The regime might realize that there is a need to modernize, but it fears that this could result in the end of state control of many critical areas and would jeopardize its present absolute executive authority. In domestic politics, the regime focuses exclusively on preserving its power in any way it can: discrediting or displacing the opposition from the public sphere in combination with suppressing or restricting alternative sources of influence, using the tactics of demobilization, and keeping people in a state of apathy and alienation, thereby accelerating social fragmentation and individualism. The conditions for massive (negative) regime consolidation are the promotion of Russian great-power nationalism and grassroots xenophobia as well as anti-Western sentiment, nourished by the perverted sense of collective national honour and of 'being selected', 'special' and 'superior'. All this is intended to compensate for the humiliation experienced during the long period of Soviet poverty, the failed aspirations of the 1990s, the enduring sense of inferiority and a collective trauma from the loss of Soviet identity.

It is more difficult to compare putinism with authoritarianism, because authoritarianism is defined far more vaguely than the general model of totalitarianism proposed by Carl Friedrich and Zbigniew Brzezinski.[16] Putinism also has little in common with either forms of traditional authoritarianism (paternalism or sultanism) or authoritarian transition regimes (non-democratic regimes that consistently pursue social and economic modernization, such as those of South Korea, Singapore and Taiwan).[17] It is significantly different from known types of 'abortive modernization' (such as postcolonial despotism in African states and military regimes, or juntas established after the seizure of power by a group of military officers, or various types of repressive government established due to a one-party dictatorship or a political police terror, such as in Haiti).

It is nonetheless possible to discern certain similarities between Putin's regime and classic authoritarianism, such as those listed below.

1. The quasi-personalistic nature of the regime (the idea that 'Putin will fix it all'); constriction or degradation of the political sphere (no public discussion of political objectives or the cost of and resources for pursuing such objectives); and transformation of the government into a tool for enforcing the 'will of the autocrat'. Most ministers in the Russian government are purely technical specialists and executors, not party officials who have won seats in parliamentary elections. Consequently, they are not accountable to the electorate or society in general for policies pursued by the national leader.
2. The increasing reference to 'Russian traditions', reinforcing the significance of conservative interests and anti-modernization orientations.
3. The rapid growth of corruption, permeating all the major areas of the Russian state structure. Corruption is a reaction to the primitive administration structure, inefficiency of the state, administrative abuse of power, and power that merges legislative and executive

functions without any system of checks and balances. The government openly admits that the system is corrupt, signifying that it is unable to manage state functions and is making a veiled appeal to the public to accept the clan system and the private corporate nature of government power as a current reality. Corruption is one of the most powerful means of integrating society with the state: the public bribes government officials, and the state bribes the public with various petty benefits and allowances.

4. The deteriorating quality of Russian management skills, varying from sector to sector, caused by the specific procedures for selecting high-level personnel according to personal loyalty rather than skills as criteria for positions in the administrative apparatuses of departments, the judiciary, the State Duma and other bodies.

'Personalism'

The 'personalism' of the present regime hides an important condition: Vladimir Putin simply represents the existing balance of forces in the very limited group of people who make the most important decisions with regard to the economy, outline the general political direction, and set the tone of politics. Putin is in fact more dependent on this group than they are dependent on him. He hardly has the power to determine the composition of this small group of decision-makers and cannot restrict access to it. One may assume that his power is a function of this shadow government: he can lead the activities of the group, while manipulating the top echelons' competition for power and acting as an arbitrator between factions. His political strategy is determined by the adaptation of power to domestic challenges or external changes. Various surrogate forms of pseudo-institutional innovations originate here, such as the establishment of the Public Chamber (and similar chambers in the regions) as substitute forms of civil society. However, unlike civil society, members of the chambers are appointed by the president (or governors). Similarly, the paramilitary youth movements like Nashi and Molodaya gvardiya perform this function.

Personalism is a strong sign of the weakness and lack of balance in the Russian system. Old institutions have been partially dismantled, while new ones are only declaratory or simply inefficient. Political scientists and journalists confuse this particular *'undifferentiatedness'* of the system with personal power or consolidation of power in the hands of one person. However, this 'personalistic' power requires some decorative democratic institutions: an 'independent' parliament, an 'independent' judiciary and 'electoral democracy'. In other words, this is not a situation in which the federal authorities regard themselves as the only source of law and justice. There are no resources for establishing a real authoritarian or traditionalist system.[18]

The Russian power structure (unlike the South Asian tigers Hong Kong, Singapore, South Korea and Taiwan) *does not include* relations with proper traditional institutions such as *chaebol* (the South Korean form of business conglomerates), other semi-feudal organizations, or ethnic communities (like the Chinese diaspora in Asia) because Russia has not retained any traditional organizations of this kind. Russia simply does not have the conditions to form a traditional authoritarianism. No one in Russia wants to share power with the Orthodox Church or the Islamic muftis. Traditionalist institutions do not supply the authorities with personnel to hire (if anything, the KGB/FSB continues to use the Church for its own purposes).

There is little real interest in preserving authoritarian Russian traditions. The authorities' propaganda appeals to ethno-national 'fundamental moral values', and they for example establish state holidays that they artificially link to some date or fictitious historical event. In any case, this is not the efficient traditionalism of the Iranian ayatollahs or President Ahmadinejad, nor of aggressive Islam in Malaysia or the Middle East. The Russian Orthodox Church does not carry any political weight; it is used exclusively either to reject Western liberal ideas or as a symbolic ethno-confessional resource of national entity, the grand past, the former empire, as well as a barrier against the outside world (glorifying the 'unique Russian way' and the 'unique Russian civilization'). This is an instrumental, not a value-rational, approach to traditionalism, which is meant at least partially to compensate for the authorities' lack of legitimacy in an environment in which the legality of the system is absent. And it is also used to strengthen the foundation of conservatism in society and inhibit modernization.

The regime exploits two ideological keystones: imitative traditionalism and modernization rhetoric (that of both Putin and Medvedev). The latter includes calls for development, state-sponsored technological innovations, the expansion of human capital assets, and combating corruption and 'legal nihilism', but is nonetheless purely verbal rhetoric.

The FSB as an Actual Power Actor

Power in Russia is characterized by a duality: the external, public image, which is portrayed as a legal system, and the real, illegal, informal, operative side. The functions of the security police have changed dramatically: it is no longer the 'armed wing of the Soviet Communist Party' or protectors of the partocracy's interests, the regime or the ideological order. Nor is its major function surveillance of powerful cadres, the channels of mass vertical or horizontal mobility, or channels of information. It is no longer an instrument of intimidation, discipline or coercion to embrace a consensus vision and loyalty, nor a tool of terror or repression of dissidence. Russia's political police is not so much a *tool* of power as *power itself.*

After engaging in a fight for property and influence, the security police inevitably lost its original functionality. From being the tool for enforcing the policy of other powerful bodies (the Politbureau and the Central Committee of the Communist Party, the party *nomenklatura,* and the new Russian authorities after the collapse of the USSR), it became an integral part of the political power apparatus, participating in high-level decision-making and defining objectives. Having taken up crucial positions in the state administration, the leadership of the FSB not only appropriated key positions in the market economy in quasi state-owned and state-owned corporations but also entered the very top echelon of the political elite – the body responsible for national strategic planning and domestic and foreign policy. The FSB thereby defines and decides political tasks, which is a duty that is not *typically assigned to military or security agencies* and for which they are not designed.

Under these circumstances, the executive bureaucracy starts formulating targets for state rule, which contradicts the character of the authority of the highest leadership. The authority of the country's top leadership (recognition of the right to rule) should be based on other sources of legitimacy, other forms of competence, and another history of making one's way into the positions of power than the security police or other executive structures of government have. A bureaucracy that has no checks and balances and no external instance formulating the goals starts working for its own interests. This is exactly what we have in putinism: the purpose of national policy under Putin's rule is to preserve those in power. Putin's discreditation of the 1990s as a time of 'rampant democracy', 'wild capitalism', 'chaos' and 'anti-popular reforms', and the cause of a decline in living standards, targets not only the government of the young reformers but also the very idea of transforming the Soviet system and modernizing the state and society.

The combination of legal and illegal (secret) methods appears to be one of the major resources of the current regime. The practices and illegal activities of the secret police – provocations, false trials, sensitive and illegal information sources, undercover agents and so forth – take place in a situation in which the same agency is in power, so its methods are extraordinarily well protected from the law.

The dependence of the judiciary and legislative branches of government, which not only ignore the interests of the population but also protect the authorities from public oversight, means that the individual is vulnerable to a veiled tyranny. The law loses its status and legal power under these circumstances. This also applies to political procedures: important political and government decisions are made privately and secretly, and are only later officially formulated, passed by the State Duma, and made public through the mass media, politicians and law enforcement agencies. The state violence that permeates the capillary structure of Soviet society is today confined to the preservation of the authorities' power.

The non-transparent nature of authority brings with it an absence of mechanisms for public debate on consistent and publicly formulated objectives that have been worked out and approved by parliamentarians. Such conditions make it impossible to have any coordinated formulation of goals, which requires public participation, ideas and interests: a free mass media, an independent parliament and a multi-party system. The personalization of power is yet another expression of the illegal politics of modern Russia and the degeneration of an entire representative political system. The fact that the motives and interests of those in power are not declared or discussed publicly reflects the non-institutionalized character of politics and the law, and this is a major obstacle to modernization.

The current regime is characterized by fundamentally weak legal institutions and the executive authority's tight grip on the parliament, the judiciary and law enforcement bodies. The lack of transparency in political decision-making is promoted by government institutions with poorly defined functions, which in turn feeds internal tensions. For example, the appearance of economic interests of the FSB provokes other internal conflicts. In turn, this fragmentation of power induces a reinforcement of the police regime and the use of force to manage conflict and tension.

The FSB determines the functioning of Russia's entire political system: previously public or semi-open mechanisms of competition and representation of vested and institutional interests have been suppressed and replaced by various forms of loyalty, a community of corporate interests, power centralization and predetermined objectives. Instead of sustainable, efficient administrative institutions with proper paths for staff career mobility (with corresponding qualifying criteria for officials and applicants to civil service positions, differentiated by zones and spheres of competence, recognition of achievements, etc.) there are clan- or corruption-based relationships.

However, after taking over the most strategic positions of authority and key economic and administrative positions, the FSB came into conflict with its own corporate standards. They no longer work towards a common goal. The functions of the FSB, other security agencies, and various types of police (of the Ministry of Internal Affairs, Federal Drug Control Service, Customs, etc.), as well as, but to a lesser degree, the military have been radically altered. Today, they do not work to benefit the system as a whole, but rather serve the interests of individual clans. Whenever access to property and economic resources is at stake, there is a conflict of interests over the consolidation of private and group positions and the transfer of power resources into private capital, which of course creates conflicts between various clans and corporations. The decentralization processes of power allocation and the emergence of competing interest groups (corporate, regional, financial and administrative) determine the *content* of both domestic and foreign policy of Russia. These powerful groups control budget allocations, facilitate illegal corporate business and offer special favourable terms to certain businesses, including some outside Russia. Bitter turf wars between various bureaucracy and business groups have become the functional equivalent of the former terror organizations.

The growing monopolization of the political space by the United Russia Party, which also absorbs new bureaucratic groups, has not eliminated competition between other groups for power and resources. After the democratic, pro-Western opposition was nullified, the blatant use of administrative resources for the ruling party in recent regional elections also marked the displacement of recently created pro-Kremlin political parties. Parties such as the Just Russia Party (Spravedlivaya Rossiya), Zhirinovsky's Liberal Democratic Party, and recently Dmitry Rogozin's Motherland Party (Rodina) served to absorb public discontent and control protest but subsequently found they no longer served this purpose. Controversial election results due to voting fraud, ballot box stuffing or alteration of the minutes of election commissions do not affect the formal legality of the procedure or the legitimacy of the resulting power constellation. Rather, the purpose of such manipulations is to ensure the current administration's total control of the 2011 and 2012 elections, which will in effect mean that the present power structure may remain dominant until 2024.

The functions of the party machine are limited exclusively to ensuring the demonstration and staging of mass public support. However, both the public and the authorities lack visions for the future. Thus there are no inspiring ideals or any strong state policy. Putin's or Medvedev's modernization rhetoric is not a political strategy but rather serves to cover up the deficit of legitimacy. In reality, there is an anti-modernization orientation of state functions and a systematic simplification of administrative structures in line with the task of maintaining power rather than for any declared objectives.

Conclusion

I define 'putinism' as a system of decentralized use of the institutional resources of violence preserved by the structures of *siloviki*. These structures, inherited from the Soviet totalitarian regime, have been appropriated by people in power pursuing their private, group- or clan-based interests. This environment has transformed the Russian parliamentary parties, the mass media, and the political institutions and organizations into a form of political entrepreneurship with an overwhelmingly powerful role in the economy. Nevertheless, the legitimacy of the authorities remains problematic, and legal only in a strictly formal sense as long as there are no mass protests. This makes the regime unsteady and the prospects for the regime to engage in renewal or peaceful handover of power in the future are remote. The effects of putinism have shown that it is based essentially on a consistent policy of resisting processes of democratization and modernization. It is a policy that uses new techniques of domination to ensure the preservation of a regime that is not accountable to society.

Notes

1. Gaidar's Russia's Democratic Choice Party, after reforming the government, was replaced by the Our Home–Russia Party, led by the new Prime Minister Chernomyrdin, and then, after Chernomyrdin had resigned, by the Fatherland–United Russia Party, led by Evgeny Primakov, Sergei Shoigu, Shaimiev, Luzhkov and Boris Gryzlov, and including in its ranks as conservative leaders former KGB servicemen, communists, regional administrators and high-ranking nomenklatura functionaries.
2. After Putin's accession to power and complete displacement of the opposition, the remaining parties of the 'approved opposition' were transformed into electoral facilities or political broker companies, offering any paying candidate a seat in the legislative assembly, regardless of the candidate's ideology or programme. See A. Kynev (2009), 'Osobennosti mezhpartiinoi

borby v rossiiskikh regionakh: borba grupp vliyaniya i imitatsiya partii-nosti' [Specifics of Party Competition in Russian Regions: Competition of Interest Groups and Imitation of Party Status], *Vestnik obshchestvennogo mneniya* [The Russian Public Opinion Herald], no. 4, pp. 24–37.

3. Putin was not the first or the only candidate for the position.

4. On the contrary, both the party and electoral bases, which ensure public support to the new government system, were formed after the accession to power of Putin and his team.

5. This is especially true regarding the effects of Russia's military defeat in the first Chechen war and the extreme financial and economic crisis of 1998, suspending the trend towards Russian economic recovery from the transitional recession caused by the collapse of the centralized planned economic control system. This crisis caused the transitional period to last a few more years (up to 2003) and stirred extreme public discontent and disappointment in reforms.

6. O. Kryshtanovskaya (2005), *Anatomiya rossiiskoi elity* [Anatomy of the Russian Elite] (Moscow: Zakharov).

7. A. Motyl (2009), 'Russland: Volk, Staat und Führer: Elemente eines faschistischen Systems' [Russia: State and Leader: Elements of a Fascist System], *Osteuropa*, Vol. 59, No. 1, pp. 109–24; Ph. Casula and J. Perovic (eds) (2009), *Identities and Politics During the Putin Presidency. The Foundations of Russia's Stability* (Stuttgart: Ibidem); A. Heinemann-Grüder (2009), 'Kontrollregime: Russland unter Putin & Medvedev' [Control Regime: Russia under Putin and Medvedev], *Osteuropa*, Vol. 59, No. 9, pp. 27–48. The latter research makes numerous references to recent publications regarding the classification and identification of the Putin–Medvedev regime.

8. See e.g. T. Vorozheikina (2009), 'Avtoritarnye rezhimy XX veka i sovremennaya Rossiya: skhodstva i otlichiya' [Authoritarian Regimes of 20th Century and Modern Russia: Similarities and Differences], *Vestnik obshchestvennogo mneniya*, No. 4, pp. 50–68.

9. D. E. Furman (2009), *Politicheskaya sistema Rossii v ryadu drugikh postsovetskikh system* [The Political System of Russia and Other Post-Soviet Systems] (Moscow: Institut Evropy RAN).

10. The nominative term 'putinism', recently coined by political researchers from various countries and independently of each other, does not reflect the specific character or structure of the phenomenon because it links the term to Vladimir Putin's personality. It only points to instinctively sensed novelty and self-sufficiency (or 'normality' of this type of government for former Soviet Union states as per D. E. Furman), as well as specific distinctions of this regime in a comparison with other forms of repressive or totalitarian governments. As far as I can establish, the American researcher and Gulag historian Anne Applebaum was the first to use this term: see 'Putinism: Democracy, the Russian Way', *Berliner Journal*, 2008, no. 16, pp. 43–7.

11. L. Nikitinsky, 'Mentovskoe gosudarstvo kak vid: Nepravitelstvennyi doklad' [Police State as an Individual Type: Non-governmental Report], http://www.ruj.ru//authors/nikitinskiy/090319–1.htm.

12. Z. Brzezinski (2008), 'Putin's Choice', *Washington Quarterly*, Vol. 31, No. 2 (Spring), pp. 95–116; A. Motyl (2009), Russland: Volk, Staat und Führer:

Elemente eines faschistischen Systems [Russia: People, State, and Leader Elements of a Fascist System], *Osteuropa*, Vol. 59, No. 1, pp. 109–24.

13. This also implicitly assumes that the political sphere in 'normal cases' consists of a clear separation of powers, competition between political parties with political programmes to be implemented by the executive branch, and strategies to reach the goals. These normal cases also include governments formed by parties in elections, a competent parliament where the ruling power and the opposition ensure policy implementation through budgetary control, parliamentary enquiries and other instruments for defining objectives and responsibility by the government for its policy. Here I refer not only to a certain 'dogmatism' of an underdeveloped democracy, but also to a failure to see the real political and social relationships in politics and the society, common among the Russian intelligentsia, with its utopianism and uncompromisingly critical view of the authority.

14. However, the opposition does not have a clear vision for the future either; just as the ruling power reports 'future plans', its opponents can operate exclusively with 'yesterday's' ideas.

15. The role of the few remaining relatively independent print periodicals (*Vedomosti, Novaya gazeta, The New Times, Kommersant* and others) is more complicated. Due to their limited circulation (each has 180,000–200,000, i.e. they reach approximately 600,000–800,000 readers including overlaps), they cannot compete with the major mass propaganda outlets. Their role is therefore more communication within the elite and groups around the elite. They function as 'letting off steam', reflecting on current events, criticizing power abuse and thereby identifying the 'legitimate' limits of criticism, i.e. they function as a feedback, although in a distorted way.

16. Carl Friedrich and Zbignew Brzezinski (1956), *Totalitarian Dictatorship and Autocracy* (Cambridge, MA: Harvard University Press).

17. Authoritarian transition regimes cannot be considered self-sufficient, and, consequently, we cannot draw any parallels with Russia, as they relied heavily on the institutional structures created either by the old colonial administration (e.g. civil society or the personnel educated in Hong Kong or Singapore), or occupational administration, receiving the help and comprehensive support of the United States (Taiwan, South Korea and Japan). Russia has very grim prospects in this respect.

18. This is confirmed by the declarative appeal of leading politicians and the general propaganda to promote traditions, the need for the authority of traditional institutions – the Russian Orthodox Church above all, but also regular references to artificial insignia of new military and state rituals, a special 'Day of the City' – indicating a lack of legitimacy of the current regime, the need for an additional authority justification ideology and low credibility of the holders of power.

5
The Myth of the Russian 'Unique Path' and Public Opinion

Boris Dubin

Introduction

How to understand the concept of the 'Unique Russian path', that is, the belief in a special Russian destiny which today constitutes a fundamental part of Russian official rhetoric and is widespread in Russian society? This chapter analyses the symbolic policy of the Russian authorities and the symbolic practices of the Russian public. They are connected through the institutional channels of school, press, and above all television. The analysis is based on Russian nationwide polls of the adult (over 18 years of age) population that were conducted over more than two decades by the Levada Analytical Center.[1] The analytical approach is a form of sociological hermeneutics. It separates the semantic layers of various symbolic formations in public use, in particular the mythologeme (ideologeme) of a 'Russian special path'– my current subject of interest – and interprets them as elements of orientation and identification in various groups of Russian society. In addition, the semantic actions of other collective actors and the operation of communication channels between the participants are taken into consideration.

The Shift Towards 'Being Different'

Three out of five Russian adults consistently agreed during the past decade with the idea that Russia needs to follow a 'special path' different from that of other countries. Meanwhile, in the late 1980s and the early 1990s (until about 1992) identifying with the country, still Soviet at the time, was marked for a relative but clear majority of Russians with negative emotions from the global irrelevance of the Soviet experience, the marginalized status of the country, an acute awareness of commodity shortages, poverty and backwardness. These estimates were broadcast and supported by the print media as well as television at that time, above all by the new and independent outlets. The latter supported a keen discussion of the alternatives to the Soviet regime and its way of life (the image of the 'West', the 'Chinese way', 'Swedish socialism', etc.). The country was offered new national roadmaps for development, where 'those at the top' and the 'grassroots' seemed to express a growing appeal to large-scale changes. The response of the popular conscious-ness was expressed in the public opinion polls of the time.[2]

There was an increasing interest in a 'special path' mythologeme on the part of both the authorities and the masses from the mid-1990s and the eve of the crucial national parliamentary and presidential elections of 1995–96. At this time Boris Yeltsin commissioned a team of experts to formulate a 'national idea'. In other words, whereas opinion polls taken in 1994 indicated that a relative majority (41%of 3000 respond-ents) still considered that Russia lagged far behind the majority of devel-oped countries, 32 per cent already agreed that Russia followed a special and unique path of development and could not be compared with other countries (8% supported the idea that Russia had always been one of the leaders and would never give it up). Later polls showed an ever-growing share of the respondents supporting the second and the third statement, and these two groups made up two-thirds of Russians who participated in the 2008 opinion polls (Table 5.1).

Table 5.1 Opinions on Russia's international status. Which of the following statements do you most agree with? (% respondents in each survey)

	1994 N=3000	2000 N=1600	2008 N=1600
Russia is far behind the majority of developed countries	41	50	28
Russia has always been among the leaders and will never give up this role	8	10	20
Russia follows a special and unique path of development and it cannot be compared to any other countries	32	34	46
Don't know/No answer	19	6	7

Source: Levada Center surveys, various dates.

Behind the early stages of this process one may discern a symbolic compensation for the hardships of a majority of Russians stemming from 'domestic' circumstances – in particular, the painful social consequences of the economic reforms launched in 1992 (after the common euphoria and hopes for a general miracle in late 1980s). Among the 'external' factors one should note the increasingly assertive role of the law enforcement, secret and defence agencies (*siloviki*) in the Russian leadership as the result of the Chechen war, the increasing 'uncontrollability' of the president and the isolation of Russia in international opinion. At the same time, a majority of Russians gravitated towards a symbolic reunion with the Soviet past in a new way with images and figures (Stalin, Brezhnev, Andropov, etc.), selected and represented due to the current situation but in sharp contrast with it. Simultaneously, in the collective consciousness an 'enemy image' and the mythology of Russia as a 'besieged fortress' were again reanimated with the help of mass communication.

In this context it is also worth mentioning the radical reorganization of television starting from 1992 to 1993 with the emergence of new and mostly private owners and the struggle that followed for the government to win back control. This resulted in a restructuring of programmes and line-ups, strengthening Soviet positions on TV (with such new programmes and topics as the 'Russian project', 'Favourite tunes about the great issue' and 'Old cinema').[3] These changes not only affected political shows per se (news and talk-shows), but also had a crucial effect on non-political broadcasting – themes and styles of gala concerts, broadcasting of Soviet movies about spies and secret services, patriotic coverage of Russian sporting wins, and the strengthening of such motifs on the music scene, in comic shows, and so on.

A summary of answers by Russian respondents to questions concerning the character of Russian (and Soviet) uniqueness shows the following major, recurrent and popular perceptions.

1. a difference between Western and Russian *values and traditions* (dividing line, barrier and gap);
2. a special role of the Russian government in public relations (authority and power as constituting the social world and collective identity);
3. the *mass-type character of Russian society, of a collective 'we' as the entity* (the habit of 'sameness', rejection of differences as tools of social equalization, and the blocking of individual initiatives). In this context a 'special path' can be interpreted as the projection of an archaic, or rather archaized intrinsic oneness, which does not distinguish

anything individual or outstanding. Rejecting everything special and individual *inside* society is a condition of its uniqueness in relation to the *external* world;

4. a unique *human character*, as a result first of all of 'historical' circumstances.

Consequently, an understanding of 'our past and our history' becomes something separating us from others. History is presented as a tautology, a circling in a closed circuit, a confirmation of the identity, of 'the same', and most often in the semantics of suffering and patiently enduring common tribulations. From this follows the significance of such self-descriptive characteristics of Russians as 'simple', 'open', 'not driven by success or wealth', 'pooling common resources to make decisions' and so forth (Table 5.2).

The responses and the listed specific features of both the Soviet regime and people reveal a symbolic transcription of some fundamental characteristics of Soviet existence and collective life in Soviet society.

On the one hand, perceptions of the *country* (Russia or the USSR) *as a whole* are distinctive due to the sustainable significance attributed to an external threat or, at any rate, an unfriendly environment, consisting primarily of imagined rejection and hostility on the part of the West. On the other hand, the symbolic 'centre of the world' in this picture is located 'there', behind an impenetrable border. In other words, in the concept of Russian uniqueness is also included – with the exception of the organized and reproduced ignorance of the majority of Russians regarding life abroad – an awareness that Russia is 'peripheral', or even backward. In this sense, there is a notion of Russia being 'secondary', a 'derivative', and a belated reaction to the 'big wide world' outside.

Table 5.2 Opinions on Russia's character and culture. Do you agree or disagree with the statement that Russia has a unique character and a spiritual culture surpassing all other countries? (% respondents in each survey)

	2000	2008
Definitely and rather yes	72	80
Definitely and rather no	20	15
Don't know/No answer	8	5

N=1600 respondents.

Source: as Table 5.1.

The outside world, accordingly, is endowed with the concepts of initiative, activeness and dynamism (generally speaking, independence). However, these concepts – and that is the way mechanisms of collective displacement and projection work! – are coded exclusively in categories of hostility towards 'us'. Sometimes they are coded as an apparent danger, but sometimes as a subtly concealed threat (Table 5.3).

Furthermore, the *unique character* of Russian/Soviet *citizens* transposes the long-term experience of life in a closed society – closed not only from the outside world, as mentioned above, but forcibly and normatively divided from within. The most mundane and common becomes inaccessible and can be accessed only through special means (contacts, favours, bribes, etc.) or in extraordinary circumstances, although again in a forcibly regulated and equalitarian way (war, allowances, coupons or other similar systems).

The reverse side of this existence is the individual's feeling of dependency. Consequently, the restraining dependence on others, which collectively controls the individual, is the characteristic of an equalitarian consciousness. Under these circumstances the hardships are compensated by the feeling that *everyone* is paternalized by a government that is symbolically transformed into the image of a superior and omnipotent authority, and in the idealized expectations of the majority as the caring father or boss (i.e. 'our own authorities').

Metaphor of Uniqueness

The metaphor or mythologeme of the unique *path* is sometimes, when placed in the context of modernization discussions, interpreted, on the

Table 5.3 Opinions on relations between Russia and the West. In your opinion Russia and the West ... (% respondents in each survey)

	1994	1999	2002	2003	2004	2005	2006	2008
Can be truly friendly	60	52	39	39	44	44	35	34
Will always be based on distrust	38	38	51	47	42	42	54	52
Don't know/ No answer	2	10	10	14	14	14	11	14
Number of respondents	3000	3000	1600	1600	1600	1600	1600	1600

one hand, as an indication of a unique Russian national development trajectory, and on the other hand as something culturally universal and common to all countries moving towards a 'modern' and 'developed' society.[4] Meanwhile, there is absolutely no semantics of a goal-oriented movement in the Russian metaphor.

Completely missing from the 'unique path' metaphor are all the dynamic characteristics of an expected goal, a tempo of approaching the goal and a direction, parameters of the initiative and activity level of the participants, consistency of action, progress assessment, route adjustment tools, and other similar characteristics. The vague potency of the changes ('path') without any option of choice (since the path has been set as unique and not subject to any reasoning, comparison or adjustment), without any identified agents for change, without resources, goals, programmes or mechanisms, is in effect also a kind of adaptation. This adaptation, which is common to groups and individuals, has been forced upon them and degrades their status and needs (stigmatization).

The aforementioned circumstance is not a defect in structure but the very design and functional purpose of the 'unique path' metaphor. It is designed to separate 'us' from 'them', so the 'path' has already been set. Moreover, it has been set once and for all, preset as our integral feature. It is another identification of 'us', which is directed towards us and only understood by us, whereas the others ('they') cannot identify, understand or comprehend it.

As regards the subject of the *function* of the metaphor, the observer and the researcher are dealing here with a basic strategy of production/reproduction of the most primary socio-cultural differences and contrasts according to a binary 'we–they' model. Such an asymmetric separation by an impenetrable and for both sides forbidden barrier, 'wall' or 'curtain' is a basic feature of an archaic consciousness and its modern archaizing varieties (ceremonial draws, collective memories, pastiches, etc.). For analytical purposes it is important to note the modal duality of such semantic formations. A 'unique path', as expressed by propaganda and the mass media, various 'hotlines', talk shows, and the like, is represented (offered to be viewed) either as a *reality*, as a given, that is, the norm, or as a *desirability*, a goal, that is, a value. Such a structure – with its fundamental absoluteness and statements 'beyond subjectivity' (*vnesubektivnost*), and hence indivisibility of the semantic category and semantic integrity as though including also its opposite – is logically speaking a negation that blocks in a most serious way all rational discussion of symbolic bonds and patches. On the contrary, they are supposed to invest the area of 'ours' with an inseparable unity, which as a monolith opposes everything different as 'foreign'.

One can assume that a rationalization of another semantic entity (metaphor, ideologeme or mythologeme) could not be produced within a binary particularistic logic, which locks the definition of the situation and excludes a reflexive position. Rationalization requires the instance of a generalized third party (i.e. disengaged and not a stakeholder) or, in other words, access to universal values and symbols. Whereas in the Russian case the maximum level of semantics can only be determined with the use of the closed binary model of 'we–they', with its constant switching of meanings between both these elements and isolation from any external views, control, interpretation or adjustment. Any horizontal relationships between equals are subjugated to vertical, hierarchic and authoritative relationships. The role of the generalized third party – the arbiter – is here replaced by the figure of a superior authority, in the image of a leader.

Since this duality (duality of the collective self-determination) does not assume access to universal values and symbols and rules out any choice based on such references, it does not create any value gap or any constructive conflict between what is given, everyday life and an ideal reality. In the meanwhile, such a semantic gap, such tension and conflict are at the heart of the concept of the autonomous individual ('infinite subjectivity', in the terminology of the German romantics) and its infinite achievement in daily routine activities.[5] Historically, this is a cornerstone of the ideology and culture of modernism. In the Russian context duality does not cause tension or conflict in an individual or a group and does not become an incentive for change. Instead it is reduced to a conflict-free co-existence of seemingly incompatible references and assessment criteria – that is, to doublethink, guile, a means of avoiding responsibility and providing a personal alibi (of non-involvement and innocence). Thus, for instance, the majority of Russians, as evident from public polls, seem to accept Western consumer benefits and certain elements of a Western lifestyle, but defiantly reject the fundamental values of choice, individualism and competition that lie behind them.

In order to continue this line of analysis of the key metaphor, I will point out the importance of uniqueness as an assumed, postulated, but not discussed *exclusion* of Russia from the general order of things and general rules but also as (or by virtue of) its *exclusiveness* with regard to topography, history, and 'our' national and individual character. The appeal to extraordinariness is extremely popular in Russian history. I will not refer to the remote past, suffice to mention how the Soviet authorities used extraordinary measures and the symbolism of extraordinariness at various stages: at the 'heroic' stage, up to the early 1930s when mass propaganda did everything to promote the concept of the global mission of the revolution after its victory in one country; later, during the years of 'exacerbated class struggle' and growing international tensions when the 'Great Terror' was justified; during the large-scale preparation for war from the early 1930s; and during the Second World War and the post-war years of devastation and recovery.

The notations of 'regime', 'order', 'department' and 'meeting' as 'special' in Soviet official language also referred to mythologized notions of secrecy. It is an important aspect of semantics, which is worth reviewing in more detail. All the aforementioned examples refer to figures and derivatives of the authorities. The secrecy (and the stealthiness) of the authorities and the secrets they keep forever sealed mark them as authority per se – or to be more precise, as a traditionalistic authority presenting itself as a supernatural hierarchy, a power beyond common concepts and standards, and therefore empowered and authorized to repeal normal rules and institutions of collective life. The general inaccessibility and incomprehensibility of such an authority is symbolized by its invisibility or, at any rate, as the known limitation of the 'human' to embody such a scale of power. Let me note that this feature – as all semantics of the uniqueness described above – is ambiguous and even paradoxical. Its *secrecy* is continuously *demonstrated*, and without such an obtrusive demonstration its general demonstrativeness would definitely lose much of its meaning. In other words, besides the fact of secrecy, we again deal with its mythology and visual, personified, mythological representations that are clearly and compulsorily separated from everyday life.

Mechanism of Social Adaptation

Secrecy is a way for the government to control the public, and authority, accordingly, is always non-transparent to the public and one could even say invisible. For this very reason power is omnipresent. It is everywhere and nowhere at the same time: everywhere in its full presence and power, but nowhere specifically or particularly (such modes would have diminished its totality and power). If, following the analysis, one removes the enduring mythological taint, the described 'invisibility' of the authorities could be sociologically interpreted as an absence of connection between the authority and the public against extremely weak 'intermediate' institutions in Russia and, consequently, as the irresponsibility of the authorities – in spite of the fact that they are formally elected – before voters and the general public.

It should be noted that acceptance of this situation is part of the common and standard view in society of the authorities, at least of the highest authorities. In public imagination and public political culture, chief executives are empowered with a sort of superior power, but without being responsible for the use of this extraordinary power. They cannot and should not be made responsible. At best, they are responsible only for the 'good' they have done and for certain improvements in the quality of life, but never for the shortcomings and failures of the system (this has been especially true in recent years in relation to Vladimir Putin).

It is important in this context to note that the tendency towards 'invisibility', that is uncontrollability, can refer to both the authorities and the public. The irresponsibility of the authorities is matched by the irresponsibility of the public. An unwillingness to get involved or be responsible and an escape from supervision and control are behavioural tactics that are available to a Russian individual wherever he is, but especially in the closed subsystems of army and jail, forced labour or therapy treatment, and the like (in Lewis Coser's categories, 'greedy institutions').[6] This can safely be called alibi tactics, and, as noted above, this tactic is common in Russian society at both the 'top' and the 'grassroots'.

This means that a worldview based on the mythologemes of uniqueness and isolation, an identification of the mass as a single entity acting for all and everyone being responsible for all, and extraordinariness does not contradict norms and routines as such, but rather correlates and intertwines with it. These modes of collective existence support each other. *Extraordinariness* acts as a way of controlling the masses, who are mobilized and consolidated 'from above' by the authorities. The *habitualness* (as guided by the familiar, and habit as a leveller of differences) is a way of controlling individual initiatives and responsibility from 'below', on the part of the masses.

It is exactly in the relatedness and mutual semantic induction of these two categories – the general, the everyday *norm* observed according to habits, *and the* implied, admissible and unofficially approved *divergence* from the norm as the exception – that I suggest we find the content of the uniqueness category. It captures the distinctive condition and construction of the system of collective life in Russia, recognized and acknowledged here as 'our' (*nash*). The closed nature of both these regimes – the norms and excesses collectively accepted and sanctioned by habit – from external observation and control, blocks any chance of clarification, lucidity or rationalization by any 'private' consciousness. It thereby blocks any independent stance of the individual, legitimacy of any subjective opinion, and any basis for self-regulation. The lack of control of the semantic structure and the rationalization of its inaccessibility allow the *ideological content* to arbitrarily change while keeping the *basic structure away* from universal values and norms. Let me emphasize that what is most important here is not any particular ideology, but rather the modal and alternative-free construction of social life.

This mechanism operates as a protection against a reality that is not recognized, and against generalized and idealized ideas of possibilities. In my opinion, it is a mechanism that protects primarily against an awareness of the gap that arises from the semantic tension between the following schemes.

1. A normative-regulating scheme of everyday life of the individual as of any other individual under the same conditions of 'downgrading adaptation', according to Yury A. Levada's terminology (*ponizhayush-chaya adaptatsiya*);
2. A generalized and idealized scheme of an existence of the collective 'we' under the conditions of mobilization or virtual integration 'from above'; and
3. A universal scheme of values correlating with those of the 'others', the conditional 'all' (conditioned in the sense that they had joined voluntarily and by individual recognition of these common values).

Thus, the ideologeme or mythologeme of a unique path provides an opportunity to mitigate and compensate the conflict between the ideal (declaratory) level of reference points and assessments referring to an indefinite future or a projected image of the compensatory past and actual behaviour in the here and now. This is in other words a gap between an ideal centre (such as the West) and the periphery (Russia). The 'unique path' is far from being any real 'path' or even reference point, but is rather a sort of switch in the collective identification system. It enables switching in the correlative features of 'us' and 'them' from an institutional level of *specific* requirements or *universal* norms – through the image of the authorities as a level legitimizing 'our' social order – to a *diffuse* code of particularistic relations between 'our own'.

It is important to note the repetitive and derivative character and, in these terms, the weakness and deficiency of the common and universal in the structure and current social order in Russia, as we have stated them. I mean the extreme particularistic relations dominating Russian society in the form of closed, personal and immediate contacts between relatives. The monodimensional (horizontal) links between 'people of the same kind as I' are *standard* here. Russians see these links as the only part of social life of which they still feel they are in control, where relations of trust prevail, and where the individual can make a difference and influence something.

Barriers and partitions carry a particular significance in such a segregated, closed society, as they uphold behavioural orientations and motifs of what is attainable and a socially constructed passivity. This condition (it would be wrong to call it support or approval) is a form of authority that the Russian government regards as a technology of rule and an indefinite resource to ensure its own existence. However, the Russian public also refers to this condition as a fundamental characteristic of the Russian character and of Russian collective life, and views it as 'special' and 'ours'. There is a good reason why the term 'patience' has been a consistent leader in public surveys on matters of Russian national character. According to Levada Center opinion surveys, 53 per cent of respondents chose it in 1998 and 2008 to characterize Russian traits. This exceeded by 1.5 times the citation of other important traits of the self-image such as 'soulful', 'able to survive in basic conditions', and 'spiritual values prevalent over material ones'.

The emphasis on and approval of the similarities and horizontal links in collective images of 'us' assume a rejection of social and cultural differences. The latter are not viewed as symptoms of diversity and consequently not as an indication of the resources that might be available for diverse opportunities and as any guarantee of a dynamic society. On the contrary, they are interpreted as indications of inequality and injustice, as covers for aspirations to superiority, which is unjustified by those who are like us (such supremacy is allowed – although with a fair share of suspicion and a continuing grudge – only for those in power). The force of habit usually functions as a social levelling tool. Hence, the obsession in Russian collective consciousness (both 'at the top' and 'at the grassroots') with partitions that collapse, horrible images of chaos, the ghost of 'total permissiveness', and so on. This is yet another 'internal' inhibitor blocking any change, integrated in the social structure and collective consciousness. It helps to ensure that both those 'at the top' and the 'grassroots' preserve the state of atomization in society in the sense that all individuals are identical and passive – a condition one could describe as a 'scattered mass' (*rasseyanaya massa*). The 'common' is understood under these circumstances either as a general collective and equalizing stigma in the *present*, or as an idealized image (again devoid of any specific features or references to individual roles, procedures, etc.) projected into the indefinite and unattainable *future*. Concepts of the 'unique' tend to gravitate towards a compensational image of *the past*. As mentioned above, semantics of the past like 'our past is our history' have gained more significance among Russians and become more strongly identified with the image of the collective 'us'.

Our Collective Past

The empirical data analysis allows the conclusion that over the past 15 years the collective self-identification of the Russian majority reoriented towards the past. This past has over the past ten years become increasingly presented as a 'Soviet' past (the standard here is the image of Brezhnev's era retrospectively reconstructed to contrast with the 'wild' 1990s). Therefore, the structure of the unique path receives an ever more Soviet content. The unique path today is the Soviet path, including the great power notions of the Soviet Union as something vast and formidable. The preferred orientation among the majority of the Russian public can be determined by the late 2000s with a fair level of confidence (see Table 5.4).

The historical 'switch' (shift) of public concern from a hypothetical alternative (choice) and an imagined partnership to uniqueness (exclusivity and isolation, at least symbolically), which we have already considered, is a way of confirming and reinforcing the collective identity among the majority of Russians in space and time. It is a way of establishing continuity in relation to the Soviet past and to confirm its particular set of features (a special type of power, etc., as described above) as 'ours'. The majority of Russians saw the comeback of continuity (identity) as a sign of stability and order associated with the feeling of a return to normalcy, and recognized today as the norm. Along with that, opinion polls give a fair indication that a majority of Russians

Table 5.4 Opinions on where is best to live. Would you like to live in a vast country, respected and feared among other countries, or a small, comfortable and safe country? (February 2008)

First	75
Second	19
Don't know/No answer	6

N=1600 respondents, in % of respondents).

Source: As Table 5.1.

understand the poor quality of this social order (an extreme concentration of power, red tape, inefficient management, corruption, etc.), which, however, does not prevent them from recognizing these conditions as 'ours' and normal for 'us'. An awareness of the real quality of the social order does not undermine the status quo but, incredible as it may seem, the completely opposite – it maintains and reinforces it.

Our second important conclusion is that over the past 15 years maintaining a symbolic collective identity has become more important and useful for various groups in society and for the authorities than any differentiation and competitiveness, any setting of goals and achieving them. Therefore, under these circumstances, politics degenerates into an open staged ceremony with a backstage of infighting within the nomenklatura along special internal and always unwritten rules.

The 'unique path' metaphor, in other words, hides an unwillingness to accept competitiveness, the universal encouragement of success and positive solidarity – the very principles that create modern society. Whereas the government's paternalism and its enhanced role in public life are considered to be key features of the Russian path, the importance of collective control of the individual and the emphasis on 'uniqueness' indicate an unpreparedness for freedom, and above all personal freedom – in other words, an unwillingness to take responsibility for one's own life. Freedom is yet another universal value in the foundation of all modern societies.

In this sense the 'unique path' mythologeme can be interpreted as a systemic obstacle to modernization as it transforms and adapts 'symbolic' elements in accordance with the authorities' requirements of self-preservation, on the one hand, and the habits of the masses and the public's unwillingness to change, on the other. It is important to identify here the inhibitor or stabilizer, that is, a 'soft' adaptation mechanism, rather than any 'severe' barrier or obstacle.

One of the most significant functional features of the mechanism is that the 'unique path' features in public opinion and opinion polls as a meaningful attribute – a certain set of characteristics – although a fairly indefinite one. The answers of respondents are just the beginning of new questions for social scientists to examine; they are not the reporting deliverables but rather a new subject of analysis. It would therefore be more accurate to consider the 'unique path' category as a value operator, a switcher to modal categories of assessments and interpretations of the social environment. It ensures the integration of self-images and images of others, and acts as a mechanism of coordination and relative consent between assessments of the ideal and actual, between the authorities and the masses. It is hard to interpret the complex of uniqueness due to the fact that it acts sometimes as a meaningful and sometimes as a modal factor (regulating and setting the mode of perception) for its carrier. I need to point out that this is the same duality that social scientists identify as Russian (Soviet) 'doublethink' or 'wiliness'. The dual nature of such ideas ensures the carrier a cover in a situation of social uncertainty but, in return, maintains and eternalizes this uncertainty, giving it a fundamental nature since it protects against any rationalization, discussion or correction.

To sum up, the 'unique path' functions as a mechanism of social adaptation by correlating and integrating three levels of social reality and collective perceptions:

1. an authoritarian and paternalistic authority;
2. particularistic or 'scattered' masses, and
3. contemporary specialized institutions (of production, education, healthcare, elements of the market economy, etc.).

In other words, the institutional reality does not operate under the socio-cultural conditions described and analysed here if it is not (1) sanctioned by the authorities (in the form of *privilege*, favours, etc.) and (2) interpreted by the masses in terms of *'ours'*. Under such a system, available *institutional resources* (deliverables and benefits) can be exploited while avoiding functional *imperatives* (independence, responsibility, goal-orientedness, efficiency audits or improvement).

Conclusion

The mechanism of the 'unique path' mythologeme allows changes as long as they suit the *authorities* and are bearable for the *masses*. Hence the significance of the 'alibi' category introduced in this chapter: again, it is a common attitude to let the 'other' (whether it is new, Western or modern) exist but only as long as this takes place without us and without any unpleasant consequences for us. This may be viewed as an example of how the system creates gaps in social and cultural time. This means that the creation of such gaps is integrated in the structure and function of social institutions of reproduction – the school, the mass media and culture. This is exactly why history in the present socio-cultural environment is transformed into a repetition, ceremony or ritual and as another departure from its fundamentals (the 'loss' and 'grievance' for what has been lost) as well as yet another symbolic 'return' to order and stability, although again only for a brief period of time. In this way, the 'unique path' mythologeme becomes a serious obstacle to modernization.

Notes

1. The Levada Center, until 2004 called VCIOM, VCIOM-A.
2. Compare *Est mnenie! Itogi odnogo sotsiologicheskogo oprosa* [We Have an Opinion! Results of an Opinion Poll] (Moscow: Progress Publishers, 1990); and 'Sovetskii prostoi chelovek', *Cherty sotsialnogo portreta na rubezhe 1990-kh* ['A Common Soviet Person', *Social Profile Features at the Turn of the 1990s*] (Moscow: Mirovoi Okean, 1993).
3. For more information see L. Borusyak (2010), '"Staroe Dobroe Kino" i post-sovetskii opyt' ['Good Old Cinema' and Post-Soviet Experience], *Vestnik obshchestvennogo mneniya* [*The Russian Public Opinion Herald*], No. 1, pp. 90–101.
4. The idea and ideology of *Sonderweg* in Germany, as well as the emphasis on the uniqueness in Spain (*Hispanidad*), Turkey and other countries of delayed or belated modernization, are parts of a historical phase and do not constitute any fundamental mechanism of collective self-identification or symbolic reproduction of a 'lost' unity and the 'return' to it. The idea of multiple ways of modernization developed by a number of social and political scientists since the 1980s (see e.g. Eisenstadt S. N. (2009), *Multiple Modernities: Der Streit um die Gegenwart*. Berlin: Kadmos) makes senseless the ideologeme of a Russian 'unique path' with the content and functions given by Russian ideologues and analytically reconstructed in this article.
5. Compare the quote from Goethe's *Faust* 'In the beginning was the deed'.
6. Coser, L. A. (1974), *Greedy Institutions: Patterns of Undivided Commitment* (New York: Free Press).

6
Socio-Cultural Factors and Russian Modernization

Emil Pain

Introduction

On 12 November 2009 Russian President Dmitrii Medvedev announced in his address to the Russian Parliament that Russia would embark on a programme of modernization.[1] The public discussion that followed reflected the poor intellectual preparedness of the Russian elite to formulate an efficient modernization project. Various groups within the elite have different political agendas, although they often demonstrate an identical and nearly mystical attitude towards Russian culture as a destiny defining a Russian 'unique path' that differs fundamentally from the course of modernization in the West. In this chapter I discuss these ideas and raise questions about the nature of the socio-cultural conditions necessary for Russian modernization.

Socio-Cultural Factors and the Russian Debate

Russian political discourse interprets 'modernization' mainly as a national project designed to boost Russia's competitiveness in the world economy by innovation and advanced technologies. Hardly anyone challenges the innovative development goal; rather, the debate concerns the choice of ways to pursue that goal.

The currently most influential group in this discussion strongly promotes the traditional Russian 'top-down' method of modernization with major dependence on the political will of the authorities (or, as it is referred to nowadays, the 'vertical power structure') and command-and-control methods of regulation. A much smaller group of people, identifying themselves as liberals, propose a method based on the promotion of private initiative and free competition.

Although they seem to be two opposite approaches, they are practically identical in their narrow interpretation of modernization as a straightforward technological upgrade of the economy. Essentially, the debate simply concerns who is to be the major agency of this upgrade – the state apparatus or business. In my opinion this is a fictitious dilemma, since the fusion between bureaucracy and business in today's Russia makes it hard to discern where a bureaucrat ends and a businessman begins. It is often impossible to understand which private pockets – the bureaucrat's or the businessman's – are being lined with the funds allocated for public purposes, including the innovative development of the economy. Thus, both views share a strictly technocratic interpretation of modernization and pay minimal attention to socio-cultural conditions. This significantly hampers the understanding of the real mechanisms behind the establishment of an innovative development paradigm in Russia.

Socio-cultural changes have preceded technological change in human history. Europe's transition from agrarian and manufacture production to industrial production in the eighteenth and nineteenth centuries was preceded by changes that Max Weber called 'the disenchantment of the world'. A new rational consciousness gradually displaced the traditional mythological consciousness, and social relations regulated by law replaced informal traditional social relations. The turn of the twentieth and twenty-first centuries marked a new cycle of modernization – the transition from the industrial phase to a post-industrial phase and a 'knowledge economy' – bringing a change in social relations and social culture. The new economy requires popular initiative and creativity and cannot be dependent on forced labour mobilization. The fact that the Soviet totalitarian system was successful with its invented so-called *sharashkas* (research and development institutions with forced labour under the NKVD, the People's Commissariat for Internal Affairs) is no argument for mobilization-style methods of engaging the working population in an innovative economy. The phenomenon of creativity in sharashkas dates from the time of the Second World War, when defence of the fatherland outweighed enduring hardships such as forced labour in prisons and camps. In times of peace, the feeling of a lack of freedom is a factor that causes a massive brain drain from any repressive country.

It would not be correct to claim that the designers of Russian modernization projects are unaware of the impact of socio-cultural conditions. On the contrary, there is an active debate among the political elite regarding the link between culture and modernization, although it mainly concerns the myth of a predestined Russian mentality – of Russians lacking initiative and in need of a 'strong hand'. Such ideas view culture as a constant element, like a natural environment. For instance, a popular view is expressed as 'What can you do? Russian winters are fierce and the public consciousness is indestructibly paternalistic'. None of the parties to the debate considers that changing the socio-cultural environment is the ultimate goal of modernization.

The reasons why the authorities advocate such ideas are very clear. Maintaining the belief that fate is predestined and that nothing can be improved through public effort is for them a critical means of self-preservation.

Since the early 2000s, the Russian state-owned mass media have circulated the idea of a unique Russian civilization, determining a unique path of political and socio-cultural development. This idea was demonstrated in the 12-episode TV series called 'Culture is Destiny' that was aired in 2006, when the idea permeated official Russian politics. In a lecture held at the Russian Academy of Sciences in June 2007, Vladislav Surkov, First Deputy Head of the Administration of the President, said: 'Culture is destiny. God made us Russians, Russian citizens'.[2] Surkov told the Russian population that culture determines *eternal* features of the political system. In Russia's case it is centralized authority, in which the individual leader stands above the law. The Kremlin canonized the idea of a unique Russian civilization and a unique Russian path.

This dogma was accepted throughout the country without significant opposition. Many liberals who oppose the existing regime also essentially support the idea of Russia's uniqueness. The historian Yurii Afanasev published an article entitled 'We are not slaves? History is running on the spot: Russia's "unique path"',[3] which attracted a lot of public attention in late 2008. The article discusses the notion that Russian history since at least the seventeenth century still determines the servility of the Russian elite. Remarkably, Afanasev was one of the leaders of the 1990s democratic movement in Russia claiming that the victory of the liberals was inevitable. Today he interprets the idea of predestination differently and claims that there is no alternative to authoritarianism in Russia.

Why are the concepts of predestination and historical fatalism so popular in Russia today? One explanation is that these ideas are appropriate in times of stagnation, defined as a historical situation in which the ruling elite does not want to, and the opposition cannot or does not know how to, change life conditions. In the current period of Russian stagnation, both the authorities and the opposition operate according to the same myth about the predestined fate of the Russian state and the country's 'unique path'. Some liberal intellectuals reject the idea of a 'unique civilization' and the 'millennial greatness of Russia', but welcome the same myth in a different guise – as a civilization of 'millennial slavery'. In September 2010, at the 'What hinders Russian modernization?' press conference, the liberal economist Igor Yurgens, one of the architects of Medvedev's modernization programme, blamed the Russian public for failures in introducing the proclaimed modernization. According to Yurgens, the traditional consciousness and archaic cultural values of the Russian public are the obstacles to modernization, and the Russian people would not become 'mentally compatible with the average progressive European in understanding democracy'[4] until 2025.

We return to the discussion of this idea below, but the next section assesses how these ideas correspond to present Russian realities. The approach that views traditional culture as an obstacle to modernization used to be common in classical versions of modernization theory but then was heavily criticized. New versions of this theory, specifically 'neo-modernism', are based on principles that fundamentally differ from those supported by contemporary Russian modernizers.

Classic Modernization Theory under Revision

The concept of modernization as the progress of social change designed to ensure higher living standards was criticized in Russia in the 1970s and 1980s. At that time, the classical version of the theory, which had developed over almost a century and a half, was blamed for the empirical discrepancy between its theoretical postulates and the reality of third world countries undergoing modernization under pressure from external factors. In those years, modernization was commonly called 'enforced civilization and a tool of colonialism' since in some countries, primarily in Africa, the process of modernization was accompanied by the collapse of traditional institutions and lifestyles, and caused social disorganization. At the same time, it was premature to assess the results of industrial modernization. Positive results were not visible until the early 2000s, and only in those countries where the modernization process had been most complete and consistent. These countries managed to overcome, or significantly mitigate, the major problem plaguing the African continent – infant mortality.[5] They also developed relatively stable democratic regimes and 15 per cent growth in per capita income over the period 1995–2007. Most of Africa's autocratic countries, where the political elites had fought against the so-called export of modernization, showed negative trends in economic and social performance indicators[6] and were not able to deal with problems that had accumulated for centuries. In the 1970s, however, most Western intellectuals had demonized modernization in the third world as colonialism.

By the mid-1980s the scholarly debate had changed profoundly as new versions of modernization theory appeared that incorporated ideas from theories such as those of postmodernism. The term 'postmodern' was tacked on to the schemes, indicating a final stage of the modernization process with a specific relationship between material and moral values.

The build-up of a large bank of empirical data became an important stimulus for the development of modernization theory. As recently as the mid-twentieth century, all versions of this theory had rested only on historical arguments or on various historical accounts put forth by researchers. The 1980s modernization theory was for the first time supported by extensive sociological and cross-cultural research as the vast amount of data made it possible to draw conclusions about universal patterns of social development.[7] This research showed that there was a universal link between the change of technological structures (of the agrarian, industrial and new post-industrial society of the late 1980s) and a number of social processes, such as urbanization and changes in the social and demographic structure of the population. These studies freed modernization theory from the speculative arguments of philosophers and political theorists and strengthened it by stringent methodological procedures, using new sociometric and econometric methods to analyse social and cultural processes.

Under these conditions, a new version of modernization theory developed – neo-modernism – with innovations such as those described below.

1. Neo-modernism discarded all remnants of classical evolutionism and no longer emphasized any final goal or purpose of social development. Instead, it acknowledged the reversibility of historical changes and claimed that retrograde movement was no exception, but rather the rule. Many countries have experienced cyclic changes of reform and counter-reform, democratization of the political system, and then a reversion to authoritarian rule. In this regard, it is useful to note Samuel Huntington's concept of the three waves (or stages) of global democratization. According to Huntington, at each new stage a reverse wave eliminated a significant number of new democracies

from the democratic camp and pulled them back to traditional authoritarianism.[8] In my opinion, the concept of democratization waves and reverse waves can be applied to the analysis of Russian history, including the post-Soviet period.

2. According to the revised theory, modernization is a historically limited process for which only a specific collection of contemporary institutions and values is appropriate. Various scholars write about different sets of institutions and values. Jürgen Habermas believes that the universal features of modernity are characterized primarily by the development of civil rights and freedoms.[9] Alberto Martinelli emphasizes the drive for innovation in modern societies, and identifies the critical attributes of modernization as the 'increasing structural differentiation of societies and the formation of sovereign nation states'.[10]

3. A link between two types of modernization was established: one controlled and initiated by the elite ('project modernity'); and the other organic and based on spontaneous diffusion (dissemination, borrowing) of cultural norms and values. In addition, it was proven that the efficiency of controlled modernization is determined not only by the will of political elites, but also by the state of society. Moreover, at late stages of the modernization process, especially during the transition to a postmodern (post-industrial) society, the driving force is not so much the political elite as the initiative of the wider society. In other words, the 'top-down' type of modernization becomes historically replaced by modernization from below.

4. One of the basic hypotheses of the new modernization concept is the acknowledgement of diverse models of historical development. Consequently, there is also a diversity of modernization trajectories, depending on the initial conditions, historical experience, and cultural specifics of different countries.[11] This idea is most consistently reflected in S. N. Eisenstadt's concept of 'multiple modernities'.

How can the role of tradition in Russian society be understood from the perspective of new modernization theories?

A New Look at Russian Traditions

Classical modernization theory sees innovation as incompatible with tradition and assumes that innovation will displace traditions. Revised modernization theories, however, replaced these anti-tradition ideas with the *'modernizing potential' of traditions*. As Joseph Gusfield, one of the pioneers of the Neomodernism School, has remarked, 'traditional symbols and forms of leadership can be a vital part of the value system on which they are based'.[12] Another proponent of this school, the Russian scholar Piotr Sztompka, believes that it is necessary to 'identify "modernization traditions" and adopt them for further transformations'.[13]

Essentially, society can naturally accept innovative economic technologies only when innovations stem from traditions. To support this statement, I refer to Robert Putnam's classic study of Italian regions with different socio-cultural conditions as they were entering modernization. He showed that, in regions which successfully underwent modernization, civil society and democratic values usually had been strong as far back as the nineteenth century and were preserved in cultural traditions.[14]

Zygmunt Bauman put forward a similar but more categorical theory, alleging that society is doomed to destruction and complete collapse of its socio-normative system if new collective institutions fail to combine with traditional ones. A combination of new and old exists in many countries. Germany, for instance, has preserved traditional mechanisms of social regulation,[15] and traditional collective institutions (family, religion, neighbourhood associations, and craft guilds) have become the backbone and cultural mode for new types of institutions, such as those that engage youth, professionals or charities. About 60 per cent of the adult population in Germany, and almost 70 per cent in Scandinavian countries, participate in both new and traditional informal associations. Moreover, this is a question not only and not so much about natural reproduction of traditions as about the interest in a conscious cultivation of traditions on the part of politicians. In Germany, meeting public needs in the areas of culture, sports, tourism and communication through various associations costs a great deal less than it would cost an individual consumer. The potential influence of civil associations on the authorities or local government is far more effective than complaints by individuals.

Now, what do we have in Russia? There is a common belief that new institutions, primarily legal institutions, do not manage because they are not a part of traditional Russian culture and therefore do not fit into the Russian institutional matrix.[16] I do not agree with this point of view, hence my second statement: most urbanized Russian regions of Russia (which account for most of the country) suffer neither from a lack of tradition nor from any preserved traditional obstacles but from the destruction of the traditional institutional matrix.

What is cultural tradition? Tradition is the inter-generational handover of cultural norms, standard behavioural patterns, ideas and values that members of a certain society are supposed to endorse. Such a handover of accumulated experience over time is only possible if certain fundamental conditions for cultural transmission are preserved, primarily social institutions, which act as the carriers and keepers and above all as the controllers, ensuring compliance. Social control uses moral encouragement for observing traditions and moral sanctions against violation.

Certain nationalities in Russia, especially ethnic groups in the North Caucasus, have preserved such mechanisms. They often use their patriarchal traditions as a means of self-defence, as a sort of armour. There are many examples of how traditional societies used tradition to defend themselves against forced 'de-kulakization', collectivization, deportation and forced reinstatement of the 'constitutional order' in 1994–96, and how this defence saved thousands of human lives.

However, in most Russian regions with a predominantly ethnic Russian (or Slavic) population, mechanisms of social control were more or less completely demolished along with the institutions that maintained them. Village communities were forgotten as early as the mid-twentieth century. Religious communities, especially Orthodox parishes, were annihilated in the Soviet period and their role will probably never be restored, considering the fact that over 87 per cent of Orthodox believers do not consider themselves members of any particular parish and attend church services only sporadically. Until recently there were places where pensioners played dominoes while they kept an eye on their neighbours, and elderly women sat on benches at the entrance to an apartment block chatting about the morals of a particular family. This partially compensated for the lack of valid mechanisms of social control and operated on the principle of 'What will people say?' However, even that no longer exists.

With regard to family traditions the once close relationships of ethnic Russian families have been reduced to occasional contacts. In these circumstances, there is no doubt that the idea of Russian society as collectivistic, synodical and communal is a pure myth. On the contrary, today Russian society is one of the most atomized in the modern world. Based on the results of international studies (particularly the European Social Survey of 2004–05 and 2006–07), social scientists have concluded that Russians are leading in Europe in terms of atomization of social relations, and also have the lowest rates of values of collectivism.[17]

The same studies indicate that Russians are unwilling to participate in volunteer associations.[18] The country also has one of the lowest rates of mutual trust in Europe.

Social scientists and philosophers have long been discussing the specifics of traditional societies, such as those preserved in the North Caucasus, and the decentralized societies that are common throughout most of Russia. Francis Fukuyama in his study claims that traditional (he calls them 'familistic') societies are more socialized than ones in which traditions have been destroyed. Robert Putnam rejects this theory and refers to the example of Sicily, arguing that patriarchal societies are today antisocial and often produce mafia clans. I would argue that from the perspective of preserving group trust, group unity or joint survival, traditional patriarchal societies would appear to be better suited for a modern lifestyle in terms of everyday routine. However, the high level of trust within such societies is combined with an extremely high level of conflict between groups. This hampers national consolidation and preserves hard-line authoritarian political systems. In this respect, mainland Russia is far less prone to being overtaken by conflicts or hard-line authoritarianism, but it faces a set of other problems.

Today's Russian authorities build on the perception of Russian society as a traditional society. This does not hold true, however, because the major self-defence mechanism, which a majority of the public adopts in a situation when traditional group defence mechanisms have disappeared, is instead a simulation of obedience. There is a cynical saying from the Soviet days: 'You pretend you pay us, and we pretend to work'. This way of thinking has not only been preserved but actually developed further. Russia has become a country where everyone is simulating. This is why I believe it is wrong to subscribe to the idea shared by many social scientists that Russia has preserved authoritarian–paternalistic traditions. Russia is not a traditional but rather a new society of universal simulation. The federal authorities simulate democracy but pursue an authoritarian policy, which is losing most of the strong support that it previously enjoyed in popular culture. The regional authorities simulate the pursuit of authoritarian policy, while in fact they pursue a policy of anarchy, that is, they do what they want for their own benefit. The public pretends it approves all this and respects the authorities at all levels, whereas in fact they avoid any cooperation with the authorities and avoid any responsibility ('The master rules, so let him be responsible for everything'), evade taxes, and dodge the military draft. The Russian public also tries to avoid bureaucratic corruption, countering it with 'public fraud' ('Why should I pay the bureaucrat for a certificate if I can get one just around the corner for less money?'). This is not a tradition, but a defensive social reflex of the public. This behaviour not only lacks any signs of idolization of the authorities but also of respect; this is simulated obedience. The public neither resists the authorities nor obeys their will. Hence, small or large barricades or obstruction appear in all branches of the Russian 'power vertical'.

The probability that the norms of the rule of law will ever take root in Russia is very low, given the existing atomization of society and pervasive distrust. Besides, a modern innovative economy cannot develop without a legal institutional system – this is an axiom. So, what now? Is the door to Russian innovative modernization closed?

The 'Russian System' is not Traditional, but Inertial

This is yet another statement that I advocate. In my opinion, Russian inertia is based not so much on the pressure of past experience (cultural traditions) as on the lack of new experiences, above all self-organization, self-government and participation in the state administration. Russian citizens do not recognize the benefits of public solidarity and guarding public interests through collective action.

I believe that the difference between the pressure of traditional experience and the lack of new experience is a clear one, and I will illustrate this with an analogy. A person might not want to buy a new house because he is used to the old one, or because he does not have enough money to buy a new one. In the first instance, buying a new house means overcoming the stereotypes of consciousness, and in the second accumulating sufficient resources. This is exactly the choice Russia is facing after declaring that it will embark on national modernization. What should it focus on? Should it focus on overcoming existing stereotypes of consciousness or acquire new resources including new cultural skills? The potential for gaining new experiences and skills in a very short time is, in my opinion, supported by the 1990s experience, although those years are currently described mainly as a period of chaos and disorganization.

The then US ambassador to Moscow, George F. Kennan, wrote in 1951 about the sort of Russia it would be futile to look for. The first attribute he named was Russia's inability to build a market economy, and he supported his conclusion with the following reasoning: 'Russia has scarcely known private enterprise as we are familiar with it in this country'. In addition, trade and commerce were never regarded in Russia as an honourable business, as they were in the West.[19] Indeed, historically, trade was viewed in Russia more negatively than in Western Europe, America, Central Asia or the Caucasus, and this negativism was even more pronounced in the Soviet period. However, although Russia seemed to have lost all traces of private entrepreneurship during the years of Soviet rule, in 1991–94 it experienced an unprecedented boom in private entrepreneurship. In four years, the 'shuttle trade' sector alone involved 10 million individuals – former milkmaids, teachers, engineers and industrial workers.[20] The press was concerned that Russia had become a country of traders, while the intellectual community lamented that anything could be bought and sold.

It turned out that the struggle for survival and other extremely harsh conditions (in other words, 'strong external shocks') can in a short period of time change national cultural stereotypes that have been shaped by centuries of experience. I do not argue that Russia's experience is positive in terms of the accelerated expansion of entrepreneurs, but it is worth noting that this disproved the academic dogma that 'the level of education can be improved over a short period of time with appropriate investments, whereas the working culture is formed in the course of national historical development and traditions; that is why it can only change over a relatively extended period of time'.[21] However, professional orientations towards certain specific fields of work are regarded as the most inert elements of a working culture, although Russia managed to turn them around over a period of three to four years, that is, less time than it takes to get an academic degree (five or six years).

The European Social Survey (ESS), one of the most respected international benchmark surveys, in its 2004–05 and 2006–07 editions noted that 'modern Russia is close to most European countries'[22] in terms of its value structures, as measured on a scale showing both value preservation and readiness to change. Russia has the same rating as Belgium and the Netherlands, and the Russian public is rated as more prepared for change than that of some EU member states, such as Bulgaria and Poland. In most urbanized and industrialized Russian regions, the values of independence and readiness for risk-taking are leading social attributes for over half the number of respondents.[23]

Does this mean that socio-cultural conditions in Russia do not hinder innovative development? My answer to this question is 'No' and it would be a mistake to assume otherwise. First of all, the Russian initiative is anarchical. Russia has one of the lowest levels of respect for rules and norms in Europe, both formal (the law) and informal (religious, family, traditional ethnic, etc.). Second, Russia has the lowest level of mutual trust among the countries examined in the surveys. Qualities that in the Russian language express 'faith' are weakly developed, not just the word itself but also trust and confidence. In other words, this includes everything that relates to the likelihood of good things coming to people from God, from a partner or in the future.

One would assume that, with the current low level of trust in partners and low confidence in a prosperous future, such long-term capital projects as technology parks could never be developed by private enterprise. Under such conditions it would seem logical to rely on the government as the sole source capable of initiating, financing and executing the construction of large capital projects of innovative economic development. This is, in any case, how many major Russian economists view the potential for development. Thus, the economist Abel Aganbegyan notes that Russia does not have any sources of so-called long-term money in the private sector. There are almost no private pension funds, large insurance schemes, cooperative share funds, or ventures or any other funds functioning like the fund-raisers for long-term projects in the United States or Western Europe. Hence, he concludes, it is too early for Russia to relinquish the leading role of the state in the process of modernization, not least because the only potential source of innovative development is the Federal Stabilization Fund, which in any case is too large today.[24] The leading role of the federal government and the federal budget in innovative development has repeatedly been advocated by other prominent economists, such as Oleg Bogomolov and Ruslan Grinberg.

Leaving aside economic theories and returning to actual developments, we can note that the federal authorities failed to instil trust in them: it is not enough to simply redistribute cash from the stabilization fund to an industrialization fund. They also need to ensure that earmarked funds are not stolen and spent inappropriately. Obviously, even the highest-priority national projects, such as the Olympic Games, in addition to vast investments also require management by a personally trusted individual with special authority. It is hard to imagine that commissars can facilitate innovative projects in the Russian regions. The designer of the Topol intercontinental ballistic missile and the Bulava submarine-launched ballistic missile, Yurii Solomonov, said in March 2010 that 'vertical power' does not work even in the most disciplined, secret and, one would think, controlled industry – the defence industry. He believes that '"military police" management methods did not prevent the decay of the defence industry'.[25]

Another important point to note is that a reproduction of traditional Russian vertical, or 'top-down' modernization reproduces the same type of socio-cultural relations, especially alienation, legal nihilism and total distrust.

There is also a strong link between various manifestations of the vertical–hierarchical social organization and trust. Thus, concentration of power produces corruption, which in turn reduces trust in society. Nearly three quarters of Russian respondents are certain they will never be treated fairly by the bureaucrats. There is also a high rate of distrust in Hungary, although only 50 per cent of respondents reveal this sentiment in their answers. Only slightly more than a third of the respondents share the same view in Slovakia and the Czech Republic.[26]

Corruption undermines public trust not only in the authorities, with the exception of the top leadership, but also between individuals, not least because people have different access to corrupt contacts. Such connections are not transparent, and this alone breeds mutual suspicion. For instance, the following type of dialogue between two neighbours is common in Russia: 'I can't believe that neighbour X's son was admitted to university by fair selection; he had worse grades at school than my kids had. His parents probably pulled strings. However, I do not have such contacts, so now my children cannot study at university.' People have a similarly suspicious attitude towards other forms of social promotion or access to social benefits.

The research of Andrei Korobkov shows that corruption and practically unrestricted bureaucratic power are the major obstacles for 'even those Russian scientists living abroad who would like to return and help restore national science'.[27]

Thus, resurrection of the traditional Russian top-down form of modernization creates a vicious circle. The low level of both trust and respect for the law seems to necessitate stronger involvement by the state authorities in national modernization. In turn, such a concentration of power reduces the level of trust and erodes the legal consciousness of the public. How can this vicious circle be broken?

It is important to bear in mind that the rigid vertical administration structure is the cause rather than a consequence of the weak legal consciousness of the public and the low level of mutual trust in society. Consequently, it is virtually impossible to overcome alienation and distrust among people without ensuring a transparent environment and without encouraging initiative and independence. I also realize that positive social reforms cannot be carried out in the whole country simultaneously. For instance, the level of trust between individuals in the North Caucasus is very high, although they largely follow informal social norms. These groups and clans are extremely closed and have so far been highly resistant to universal legal norms, and they generally do not welcome any form of innovation. The situation is different in most other parts of Russia: here traditional norms are weak and society is atomized. At the same time, under the conditions of a low level of traditionality, a large group of individuals are ready to take risks and embrace innovations. According to the leading Russian social scientist, Nikolai Lapin, values do not constitute barriers for innovative economy development in urbanized Russian regions. Such barriers spring up when there is a gap between the interests of, on the one hand, major agents of innovation (architects of these ideas, investors, producers), and the present system of government in the country, which is run by interests far from any innovative development.[28]

Lapin's study produced some interesting findings. The Russian regions that show the best performance in terms of the actual evidence of an innovative economy (the creation of jobs and of innovative goods and services) are often characterized by a mediocre socio-cultural environment. The Perm Area, for example, is a region with average socio-cultural indicators but also the highest rates of achievement in the innovative economies of all surveyed Russian regions. How was this possible? The federal authorities did not invest any extra funds in the area, and the regional authorities had no resources for any independent development of an innovative character. However, the potential of local laws and experimental forms of administration was used to ensure that the local institutional environment was more propitious for innovative economic development than the average in Russia.

Thus, under the present institutional conditions, modernization in Russia will be patchy and will succeed only in those regions where the local authorities are capable of at least partially neutralizing the general national institutional unpreparedness for an innovative society and innovative economic development. Most of the country can be involved in this process only if the institutional, socio-political and cultural conditions change radically.

Changes in Political Institutions as a Prerequisite for Creating a New Cultural Climate

A new socio-cultural experience based on a rational mass consciousness and on legal relations can develop only in a certain political environment. You cannot learn to swim by reading a manual when you live in the desert, and you cannot master the practice of legal relations and legal ethics in a country that does not have an independent judiciary.

Therefore, establishing a free democratic institutional environment is a prerequisite for building a rational legal culture in society. This is why changes in Russian consciousness within a 25-year period (see the comment on Yurgens above) can be regarded as a pure utopia if they are not preceded by changes in political institutions. If this process is delayed, societal cultural changes will be delayed by the same number of years, or even longer given the inertia of public consciousness.

Culture is not only a variable that is entirely dependent on the political environment. It also affects the establishment of new political institutions. There were a few efforts in the 1990s to reform the political institutions in Russia but, unfortunately, most of them did not survive: the beginnings of a genuine federalism, local self-government, competitive elections and a free media are now things of the past. After the Orange Revolution, neighbouring Ukraine made even more radical changes in its political institutions. However, some eight or nine months after Viktor Yanukovich was elected president, in February 2010, most of the revolutionary gains were reversed without any significant social resistance.

The experiences of post-Soviet states confirm the conclusions put forth by many prominent political and social scientists (Charles Tilly, Robert Putnam, Ronald Inglehart and Christian Welzel among others) that democratic institutions will take root in society only if they are naturally integrated in people's cultural traditions and are based on such traditions. Only cultural traditions can legitimize new political institutions, but such traditions do not have to be centuries-old. Many countries have demonstrated that the establishment of a new political culture or a radical change in existing cultural stereotypes can occur over a historically relatively short period of time. A few post-Soviet countries managed a smooth transition from a Soviet to a modern liberal–democratic legal system. In addition to the Baltic states, with their Catholic or Protestant culture, this was also the case in Orthodox Moldova: in this extremely poor country, with high rates of emigration and vast numbers of other problems, the constitutional and legal environment allows both communists and anti-communists to legally alternate at the helm of the state within a constitutional and legal framework. What has Moldova in common with the Baltic states? These republics were the last to become a part of the USSR. Moldova (then Bessarabia) was incorporated in the USSR as late as 1940. As it turned out, Bessarabia managed to develop a political tradition of parliamentarism over the two decades or so that followed the breakup of the Russian Empire.

However, the psychological demilitarization of Germany and its rejection of the 'Sonderweg' (unique path) idea, not dissimilar to the present ideology in Russia, also took place over a couple of decades following the Second World War. It took the United States approximately the same length of time to eliminate much of the pervading racial prejudice after the civil rights movement first entered the scene. The span of 25–30 years represents the active lifetime of a single generation, and this often suffices for building a new cultural tradition.

Some might argue that this reasoning produces an inevitable, irrepressible conflict. Establishing a new culture requires political changes, but political innovations will not survive without a proper cultural tradition. So, what can be done?

In my opinion, there is no reason to raise expectations of such a serious conflict. In existing Russian conditions, as I have demonstrated, public culture does not obstruct the establishment of new political institutions, although they may nevertheless fail to take root in the public consciousness or be legitimized. Furthermore, a new political environment does not necessarily produce cultural changes: this requires a dedicated effort on the part of both the state and society. There should be a specific programme for nurturing a new culture, and it should be aimed primarily at creating rules of the game that encourage the interests of groups aligned with modernization and block the interests that oppose it. In addition, conditions for building new traditions should be created.

The post-Soviet states did not try to design any programme for the cultural development of democracy or the creation of a new culture. Such tasks were not even properly defined. In the 1990s some reformist politicians viewed culture as a simple consequence of political and economic change. Others mystified it and presented it as a kind of permanent property that had grown into the public body and acted as a fatal predeterminism.

It is useful here to note the original, ancient definition of culture as 'cultivation and nurturing'. Cicero called culture 'the cultivation of the soul'. In this respect the term 'invention of traditions', introduced in the scholarly discourse by Eric Hobsbawm in the 1980s, seems to be useful, but it has hardly been used at all in political practice.[29] An approach to culture that incorporates the designing of new traditions may help to eliminate inconsistencies in many modern processes and offer hope for positive social change in the foreseeable future.

Russia also needs a policy of cultivating traditions of modernization from the remains of traditional culture. The world has seen examples of policies based on designing a culture. For instance, the state of Israel resurrected the essentially forgotten language of Hebrew. Japan illustrates many of the features of such a policy. It is well known that socio-cultural factors played a significant role in creating the Japanese economic miracle. The Japanese maintain a tradition of loyalty to the company through the material and social encouragement of employees, including for instance the 'employment for life' system. All the same, this was a relatively new construct, which largely artificially incorporated ancient traditions of loyalty to the family, clan and community, and respect for elders. There was nothing like Japan's employment-for-life system during the economic crisis of 1929–33. On the contrary, that was a time of unprecedented job turnover in industry, whereas the countryside experienced a turbulent process of rural community disintegration and migration to the cities. The present employment for life system did not develop until the mid-twentieth century, and it is most common in small and medium-size business. In large companies, however, those employing over 5000 personnel, this form of employment extends to no more than a quarter of all employees, generally the skilled staff. This system is not used at all when business expands or radically modernizes. This explains why the famous top-manager Akio Morita, founder of the Sony Corporation, wrote, 'we could not rely on the traditional system of hiring new people to maintain healthy growth rates'.[30]

I am not suggesting that Russia should copy Japanese practice. I simply want to point to the paradigm of 'constructing traditions', which helps to legitimize innovations by attributing to them a traditional image. For instance, the elite could have supported the idea of restoring the Russian liberal tradition, which had a good track record in the late nineteenth and early twentieth centuries.[31] Only a few social historians remember this today, and it is practically unknown to the general public. Such a construction (or reconstruction) would be extremely useful for understanding liberalism and democracy as phenomena with Russian origins.

When constructing traditions of Russian modernization, it may be worthwhile to borrow from traditional Russian culture the values and ambitions of a 'great power'. This value system, like any other, can have both positive and negative effects. False ambitions could be used to justify passivity, and ambitions linked to phobias could be a source of aggression. However, this system could also serve as an incentive for development, not least because it is currently the basis for national consensus. All political groups in Russia agree that the country must not lag behind in the global economic competition and become a marginal participant. Both the government and various branches of the opposition agree that Russia should strive to be ranked among the leading states. The traditional saying 'Can't beat the Russians!' (*Znai nashikh!*) is an important incentive for innovative development.

Moreover, the preparedness of many Russians to accept innovations and to take risks needs to be reconstructed, primarily by ridding it of its anarchism and public disrespect for the law. In cultivating new values and transforming them into traditions, a special concern is the legitimization of the right to property, which has never been sacred in Russia. It is equally important to prepare society ethically to incorporate and legitimize the idea of a state ruled by law. The process of establishing the rule of law is usually a long process.

Conclusion

This analysis of Russia's socio-cultural conditions for modernization emphasizes that Russia cannot be characterized as an excessively traditional society – its traditions were destroyed by the years of totalitarianism. This specific feature should not be viewed exclusively as a constraint to modernization because it also contains a certain positive resource that could give Russia a competitive edge in introducing an innovative economy. My main conclusion is that the project of Russian modernization should be designed in rational, consistent steps. The first step should be to change the institutional environment, thereby paving the way for nurturing a culture and the development of traditions supportive of modernism. These new political, legal and social institutions will in turn ensure that political changes take root in society and withstand any opposition to them.

And yet, I believe that the critical obstacles to establishing a Russian democratic state ruled by law and to modernizing Russia are related not so much to traditional culture or the state of political institutions as to the psychology of hopelessness, which paralyses social activity. Imposing on the public consciousness an image of a unique Russian civilization as a predestined condition, as is currently done by the Russian leadership, exacerbates feelings of hopelessness. This is why political groups that support the task of modernizing Russia must reject the present dominating psychology, which suppresses the belief that Russian society can improve life by its own efforts.

Notes

1. Presidential Address to the Federal Assembly of the Russian Federation (2009) Moscow, 12 November, Grand Kremlin Palace, http://www.kremlin.ru/transcripts/5979.
2. V. Surkov (2007), *Russkaya politicheskaya kultura. Vzglyad iz utopii* (Russian Political Culture. Outlook from Utopia), (Moscow: Presidium of Russian Academy of Sciences) 8 June, http://surkov.info/publ/4-1-0-55.
3. Yu. Afanasev (2008), 'My – ne raby? Istoricheskii beg na meste: "osobyi put" Rossii' [Aren't We Slaves? Historical Running on the Spot: The Russian 'Special Path'], *Novaya gazeta*, 5 December.
4. M. Sergeev and S. Kulikov (2010), 'The public is to blame for modernization failures. This is also why Dmitry Medvedev should remain in power, according to Igor Yurgens, the head of the Russian Institute of Contemporary Development (INSOR)', *Nezavisimaya gazeta*, 29 September, http://www.ng.ru/economics/2010–09–16/1_modernize.html.
5. Benin, Botswana, Namibia, Niger, Lesotho, Mauritius, Mali, Madagascar, the Seychelles, Senegal and a few other countries (*c.* 25% of the African states) managed to accomplish, on average, an 18% reduction in infant mortality over the period 1995–2007. J. Siegle, Morton H. Halperin and Michael M Weinstein (2005), *The Democracy Advantage: How Democracies Promote Prosperity and Peace* (New York: Routledge).
6. Ibid.
7. The World Values Survey (WVS) fund has been conducting annual research since 1981, covering 52–88 countries in various years. At about the same time GlobalNR and Gallup International started annual sociological and cross-cultural research programmes covering over 60 countries. Russian scholars from the Sociology Institute of the Russian Academy of Sciences participated in the 'European Sociological Study' (ESS) in 2005–07, covering 27 countries.
8. S. Huntington (2003), *The Third Wave: Democratization in the late XX Century* (In Russian) (Moscow: ROSSPEN).
9. J. Habermas (1985), *Der Philosophishe Diskurs der Modern* [The Philosophical Discourse on Modernity] (Frankfurt: Suhrkamp).
10. A. Martinelli (2006), *Global Modernization: Rethinking the Project of Modernity* (St Petersburg: St Petersburg State University Publishers), p. 23.
11. See e.g. S. N. Eisenstadt (1999), *New Modernization Paradigm: The Comparative Study of Civilizations*, An anthology edited by B. S. Erasov (In Russian) (Moscow: Aspekt Press).
12. J. R. Gusfield (1967), 'Tradition and Modernity: Misplaced Polarities in the Study of Social Change', *American Journal of Sociology*, Vol. 72, Issue 4, January.
13. P. Sztompka (1996), *Sotsiologiya sotsialnykh izmenenii* [The Sociology of Social Change], translation from English, edited by V. A.Yadov (Moscow: Aspekt Press), p. 183.
14. R. Putnam (1993), *Making Democracy Work: Civic Traditions in Modern Italy* (Princeton, NJ: Princeton University Press).
15. Former Russian nationals who moved to Germany had a hard time adjusting not to new laws (which are actually similar to Russian laws but better

enforced) but to the informal control, such as neighbours constantly reminding them what they should or should not do at home or in the street.

16. S. Kirdina (2004), 'Institutsionalnaya struktura sovremennoi Rossii: evolyutsionnaya modernizatsiya' [Institutional Structure of Modern Russia: Evolutionary Modernization], *Voprosy Economiki*, No. 10, pp. 89–98; and S. Kirdina, *Institutsionalnye matrisy i razvitie Rossii* (Institutional Matrices and Development in Russia) (Novosibirsk: Russian Academy of Sciences).

17. M. Magun and E. Rudnev (2008), 'Zhiznennye tsennosti rossiiskogo naseleniya: skhodstva i otlichiya v sravnenii s drugimi evropeiskimi stranami' [Values of the Russian Public: Similarities and Differences as Compared with Other European Countries], *Vestnik obshchestvennogo mneniya*, No. 1, p. 44.

18. E.g. neighbours living on the same floor of an apartment complex can still agree on something, whereas it is harder for neighbours living in the same section of the apartment block to agree about anything, and tenants in the whole building would agree on something only in extreme need.

19. G. F. Kennan (2001), 'Amerika i russkoe budushchee' [America and the Russian Future], *Novaya i noveishaya istoriya*, No. 3. The article appeared in *Foreign Affairs*, Spring 1990, but was first published in 1951: see http://www.foreignaffairs.com/articles/45446/george-f-kennan/america-and-the-russian-future-1951.

20. 'Shuttle traders' are individuals who move commodities across borders in personal luggage. 'History of Shuttle Trade Entrepreneurship in Russia' (2007), 18 April, http://www.bishelp.ru/vne_format/detail.php?ID=30103.

21. O. I. Shkaratan and V. V. Karacharovsky (2002), 'Russkaya trudovaya i upravlencheskaya kultura. Opyt issledovaniya v kontekste perspektiv ekonomicheskogo razvitiya' [Russian Labour and Management Culture. A Study in the Context of Economic Development Perspectives], http://p1.hse.ru/journals/wrldross/vol02_1/shkar_kar.pdf.

22. Magun and Rudnev (note 17), p. 44.

23. N. I. Lapin (2010), 'Tsennosti "sokhranenie-otkrytost izmeneniyam" i setevye innovatsionnye instituty' [Values of 'preservation – availability for change' and web innovative institutions, Lecture at the symposium in memory of Samuel Huntington 'Culture, cultural change and economic development' (Moscow: State University Higher School of Economics), 24–26 March.

24. A. Aganbegyan (2009), 'Ne vykapyvaite kartoshku ranshe vremeni' [Do not dig out the potatoes before it's due], *Stolitsa NSK. Informatsionno-analiticheskii zhurnal* (Novosibirsk), No. 2, September, p. 18.

25. '"Yadernaya vertikal ne rabotaet!" – priznal genkonstruktor "Bulavy"' [Nuclear vertical does not work!, admitted the General Designer of the Bulava missile], Russian Information Agency, 'Novyi Region', http://www.nr2.ru/policy/275338.html.

26. See D. Lovell (2002), 'Doverie i politika v postkommunistichesom obshchestve' [Trust and Politics in Post-Communist Society], *Pro et Contra*, Vol. 7, No. 3, Summer, http://www.carnegie.ru/ru/pubs/procontra/67145.htm.

27. I. Dubinskaya (2009), 'Diagnoz rossiiskoi nauke' [Diagnosis for Russian Science: Brain Drain], http://www1.voanews.com/russian/news/Analysis-and-perspectives/Russian-Science-Open-Letter-Part-Two-2009–10–06–63710747.html.

28. Lapin (note 23).

29. E. Hobsbawm and T. Ranger (1983) (eds), *The Invention of Tradition* (Cambridge and New York: Cambridge University Press), pp. 1–2.

30. Yu. Morozov (1991), 'Sotsio-kulturnye osobennosti yaponskogo puti modernizatsii', Ver. 1 [Socio-cultural specific of Japanese modernization, Ver. 1], http://www.sociodinamika.com/puti_rossii/05.html]. See also Yu. Malenova (2007), 'Chto takoe klassicheskii yaponskii menedzhment? [What is Classic Japanese Management?] http://shkolazhizni.ru/archive/0/n-6808.

31. *Rossiiskii liberalizm: Idei i lyudi* (2007), [Russian Liberalism: Ideas and People] (Moscow: Novoe Izdatelstvo), p. 904; and A. A. Kara-Murza (2009), *Intellektualnye portrety: Ocherki o russkikh myslitelyakh xIx–xx vv. Vypusk 2* [Intellectual portraits: Essays on Russian Thinkers of xIx–xx centuries. Issue 2] (Moscow: Izdatelstvo IFRAN), p. 160.

Part III

Piecemeal Reform under Putin and Medvedev

7
The Policymaking Process in Putin's Prime Ministership

Stephen Fortescue

Introduction

In deciding – in the first half of 2008 – to undertake a study of the contemporary Russian policymaking process, it had been my intention to examine that process in 'normal' times. In particular I was interested in whether changes made when Vladimir Putin became prime minister in May 2008 would lead to improvements in policymaking. However, the global financial crisis intervened soon afterwards and I was left no choice but to recognize that the nature of the project was, for the moment, going to change. That was unfortunate even if only because one could reasonably suggest that policymaking is easier in crisis circumstances, since there is a greater sense of unity among policy actors and reduced need to deal with lower priority distractions.

Although much of the period covered by the study so far has been in crisis conditions, there was a brief period between Putin becoming prime minister in May 2008 and the 'official' recognition in September that year that the crisis had hit Russia during which Russian policymakers considered themselves to be operating in normal times. Furthermore, since the later months of 2009 the sense that the worst is over was sufficient for the authorities to speak of the need to think in terms of post-crisis policymaking. We therefore have enough experience of policymaking since Putin became prime minister in both crisis and 'normal' circumstances to be able to undertake an evaluation of the effectiveness of Putin's approach to policymaking.

Note that I am talking about the process of making policy, not the content. I am not concerned with whether policy is good or bad. Nor am I concerned with implementation. I do not have a precise definition of what is a good or a bad policy process, but very roughly a good one is one that gets to the decision stage reasonably quickly and after appropriate consultation. By appropriate consultation I mean enough to ensure that a policy issue is subject to examination from a full range of interested parties, but not to such a degree as to drag the process out interminably and in a way that the ultimate policy is stripped of meaningful content through long negotiation.

How Policy is Made

A general outline of how policy process is made is required before deeper analysis of the Putin case can be undertaken. What follows is a quick outline of the policy process, applicable to any political system but presented in such a way as to assist in the analysis of contemporary Russia.[1] I suggest that what shapes a modern policy process is what I call the logic of specialization. This is not because I believe that the phenomena to be described are determined, but because they do have a logic of their own and develop along a predictable route unless specific countermeasures are taken. Given that the logic is driven by good functional reasons, interfering with it requires care and judgement.

In complex societies there is specialization of knowledge and, more importantly for us, specialization of functional organization. Different organizations, in our case primarily but not necessarily exclusively government bureaucratic agencies, have specialized functions. An expectation arises, probably on the part of both the agencies themselves and the political leadership, that the former be engaged in policy processes related to issues involving their specialized function. Because an issue is likely to be related to more than one specialized function and therefore organization, their involvement in the policy process entails multilateral consultation. Such consultation requires a specific structure and procedures. The required structure is a collective decision-making body, in the case of a political system a cabinet made up of representatives of the key specialized organizations. Procedures include not just decision-making rules within the cabinet, but also for the pre-meeting circulation and sign-off of documentation. As important as such procedures are if cabinet meetings are not to become chaotic and marathon talkathons, they have the potential to delay the policy process to the point of paralysis or to produce outcomes so full of compromise as to greatly reduce their value.

This negative outcome can be avoided if it so happens that the interests of the policy participants are sufficiently aligned for them to be able to arrive at a policy outcome of their own accord. This could well have been what happened in the tax administration case mentioned above. But if interests are not well aligned – and often they will not be – political leadership is needed to encourage or force the resolution of policy deadlocks. But for a whole variety of reasons political leaders are sometimes unwilling or unable to push for resolution. They might be unwilling to take sides if they are engaged in the classic 'divide and rule' tactic in a factionalized political environment – they cannot afford to favour one side over the other. They might be too committed to a particular policy participant who does not want resolution, usually because the status quo suits its interests. The leader might be too weak, in terms of personal characteristics such as decisiveness, energy and health or politically in terms of constitutional arrangements or the balance of political forces.

In democratic systems pressure is placed on governments to act decisively by the electorate, often through the representations of the opposition. An indecisive government, harried by an opposition, is likely to be replaced before the consequences of its indecision become too severe. Non-democratic countries do not have that mechanism and so rely to a considerable degree on the personal commitment of the political leadership to drive through policy change. In tyrannical regimes, leaderships can do so without let or hindrance, although they are unlikely to enjoy policy success if they take no notice of specialized organizations in the policy process. Non-democratic regimes that are less than tyrannical are likely to lack both the motivation (particularly when, as is often the case, they are using the divide-and-rule tactic) and means (being short on both coercive power and legitimate authority) to do so.

Policymaking during the Putin Presidency

Putin's presidency was not democratic, and it specifically lacked the democratic institution of an opposition that is particularly useful in punishing indecisive governments. I would not, however, classify Putin's regime as tyrannical. It is therefore not surprising that there were signs during his presidency of a policy process in which the logic of specialization was out of control.

Indeed, what spurred me to examine the contemporary Russian policy process was a realization that during Putin's presidency the process presented a very mixed picture. Some policy issues were dealt with very efficiently and some not so efficiently. Two case studies that I had examined in some detail provided very different evaluations. The reform of tax administration procedures, a very sensitive issue post-Yukos, produced vigorous debate and bureaucratic manoeuvring, but a relatively quick outcome was reached with which all participants were more or less happy.[2] By way of contrast the rewriting of the Law on Subsurface Resources became a policy marathon lasting many years, which produced outcomes that are still contested.[3]

I saw enough in the second of these two cases, as well as more superficial knowledge of other policy issues (military reform, administrative reform, corruption, strategic development of the energy sector, industry policy) to suggest that there might be serious flaws in the policy process, although with enough examples of successful cases (tax reform, agricultural land) to require some discriminating explanation.[4]

As just suggested, I see the rewriting of the Law on Subsurface Resources as an example of a poor policy process, one in which the logic of specialization got out of control. Early in the debate over the legislation we saw a classic sign-off standoff, when the then competing Ministries of Natural Resources and Economic Development and Trade refused to bring a compromise draft of a new law to cabinet, and as long as they were unwilling to do so Prime Minister Kasyanov refused to allow the matter to be discussed.[5] Similar obstructionist tactics were used in the following years as the various agencies involved fought to protect and advance their interests.[6] More detail on some other so-called soglasovanie marathons is provided below. (*Soglasovanie* is the Russian word for the bureaucratic process of 'sign-off'.)

Putin's intervention in these cases did not necessarily lead to a resolution of the matter. They did when his own personal power was involved. Matters such as the appointment of governors or changes in electoral procedures were finalized with considerable dispatch. That suggests that in cases where he did not achieve a resolution it was because he was not strongly motivated to do so. There could well have been a personality factor involved, or even a personal ambiguity as to which policy approach was better. One senses in Putin a hankering for traditionally harsh Russian centralized control cohabiting with a recognition derived from his Soviet life experience that ultimately it is an ineffective approach. Presumably his commitment to the standard 'divide and rule' tactic also had a lot to do with it. He could not afford too clearly to take sides in important policy debates, as can be seen in the characteristic ambiguity or support of both sides in many of his public interventions.[7]

While there were political and perhaps personality reasons why Putin often failed to exercise the political leadership needed to break policy deadlocks, there were structural obstacles as well. Russia has generally been seen as a highly centralized, super-presidential system, where the president has close to absolute power.[8] This is, in fact, not the case, and not only because Russia is a very large, unruly place that is hard to rule from the centre. Constitutionally the power of the president to engage in policymaking is above all the power to rule by decree. It is a power that Yeltsin used extensively to push through radical policy change. However, Putin made very little use of his decree power through his two terms. In the economic area in particular, he essentially ceased issuing decrees.[9] Why might that have been?

To do so would, of course, have required him clearly to take sides in a policy debate, something which, as suggested above, he was often reluctant to do. But there were other reasons as well. He did not want to be seen as doing things the way that Yeltsin did, and he would have noted anyway that Yeltsin struggled to have his decrees accepted as legitimate normative documents by implementing bureaucrats. There is also the constitutional issue that the president's decrees have normative force only if they are not contradicted by parliamentary legislation. For Yeltsin there was no existing legislation in the most controversial policy areas. However, by the time Putin came to power much of the policy space was occupied by existing legislation, meaning that most controversial policy change required the amendment or annulment of existing legislation. Such change cannot constitutionally be achieved by presidential decree.[10]

That means that most policy change during the Putin presidency was achieved through legislation presented to parliament by the government. (In Russian parlance the government [*pravitelstvo*] is a separate political institution from the presidency.)[11] And because formally speaking Russia is a semi-presidential system, the government is headed not by the president but by a prime minister.[12] The prime minister is both constitutionally weak, without the power to hire and fire ministers, and until Putin's appointment was also politically weak, as both presidents Yeltsin and Putin appointed nonentities and got rid of them quickly if they showed any signs of gaining in power and status. This meant that the prime minister was unable to force through policy decisions. Most of the '*soglasovanie* marathons' took place within the government apparatus and its ministries. The president was too remote from the government apparatus to intervene directly, and when he did it would almost inevitably look as if he was undermining the prime minister, making the long-term problem worse.

Putin as Prime Minister

Putin was aware of the problem and when forced by the constitution to vacate the presidency decided to switch to the prime ministership, in order to be closer to the day-to-day processes of policymaking. He also introduced structural and procedural changes to the way in which policy was made. In fact, it could be argued that he tinkered with the policy process in such a way as to allow for greater dispatch in policymaking without having to commit himself too decisively.

He attempted to streamline cabinet decision-making by setting up an inner cabinet, the presidium.[13] He also rehabilitated the long-established practice that he had abolished as part of his presidency's administrative reform of appointing a number of first deputy and deputy prime ministers whose main task was to resolve policy differences between agencies. The institution had been abolished because multiple deputy prime ministers had come to be seen as part of the *vedomstvennost* problem, that is, of strong vertical hierarchies – usually based on a sector of the economy – claiming the loyalty of all officials in that sector, including those with ostensibly a top-down directive role. To quote Huskey, writing of the Yeltsin period, 'the deputy prime ministers often exhibit less loyalty to the premier than to the ministries they oversee'.[14] Their restoration by Putin was a reversal to traditional practice that was not unexpected. It had been said in 2006 that Prime Minister Fradkov was so frustrated at his inability to get warring ministers to agree that he was seeking to have multiple deputies restored.[15]

However, there was an important difference in the new deputy prime minister arrangements. Rather than each deputy having responsibility for a single broad area of policy responsibility and a set list of reporting ministries, each now had a list of specific policy issues (admittedly generally within a single broad area) for which he was responsible.[16] Deputy prime ministers were empowered to give directives (*porucheniya*) to whichever ministries were involved in a listed policy issue, including ministries outside the deputy's broad 'sectoral' area. For example, Deputy Prime Minister Igor Sechin sent directives to the Ministries of Defence, Industry and Trade, and Economic Development, as well as the Federal Property Agency (Rosimushchestvo), that the controversial transfer of Ministry of Defence assets to the state holding company Oboronprom be completed without delay.[17] On other issues these ministries would receive directives from other deputy prime ministers. There is clearly flexibility – and no doubt at times internal conflict – over which deputy gets carriage of which issue. In the Oboronprom case, Sechin was the responsible deputy prime minister despite the fact that the defence industry is explicitly excluded from his official list of responsibilities.[18] Zubkov was in charge of the highly controversial Law on Trade, presumably because of his agricultural responsibilities but despite foreign and domestic trade being listed as the responsibility of Shuvalov on the government's website. This matrix-type approach was clearly designed to break down the tight-knit sectoral hierarchies that were so typical of the Soviet period and which were not slow to reassert themselves in the post-Soviet period.[19]

The deputy prime ministers used as a major forum for their activities the so-called *soveshchanie*. *Soveshchanie* is a common Russian bureaucratic word, which has become exceptionally popular in recent times. Although applicable to various types of gathering, it generally has a sense of a one-off meeting without formal, normative status, and therefore without the power to issue formal directives or normative acts. It is therefore to be distinguished from various commissions and councils that have normative acts setting out their areas of activity and competencies. *Soveshchaniya*, in the form of small, very informal meetings of the 'lock them up until they come to agreement' type, were used in the later years of the Putin presidency to resolve policy deadlocks. For example, they were used to bringing resolution to the negotiations on foreign access to strategic assets and the related reform of the Law on Subsurface Resources.[20] (See also a description of the budget planning process in 2006, during which meetings of the formal Commission on Budget Planning were postponed because participants were unable to agree on which set of data to use, with ultimately the real work being done in *soveshchaniya* chaired by Sobyanin, then head of the presidential administration, and Medvedev, then a first deputy prime minister.[21])

Another attack on the logic of specialization came after the reality of the crisis in Russia had been acknowledged, but it appears not to have been driven by the crisis. The government's formal consultation and sign-off procedures were amended in late 2008 to allow those drafting normative acts to proceed to the registration of those acts as legally valid and enforceable if other parties involved in the sign-off process had not responded within a month of their having been circulated.[22] The change was made explicitly to counter the deliberate misuse of sign-off procedures to obstruct the policy process. There was some difference of opinion as to the application of these procedural rules. In one newspaper, *Vedomosti*, it was suggested that they applied only to the decrees (*rasporyazheniya* and *prikazy*) of ministries and equivalent agencies; in another, *Kommersant*, it was said that they also applied to draft legislation, the area of greatest difficulty for the policy process.[23] Whatever the case, the changes strongly suggested that Putin expected a more flexible approach in the preparation of legislation.

As suggested in the introduction to this chapter, there was only a brief period of normal times after Putin introduced these changes in which their efficacy could be tested. The signs were not good. Despite some early positive statements, including regarding Putin's decisiveness,[24] the classic 'soglasovanie marathons' continued. One example was gas pipeline access to producers other than Gazprom. Not surprisingly, Gazprom was opposed to such a change and without even being a government agency was able to delay the proposal throughout this period (with the crisis providing the opportunity for resolution to be delayed indefinitely).[25]

Efforts were made to subject *soveshchaniya*, one of the major instruments of the new approach, to the routinized processes of consultation and sign-off. For example, at the end of September 2008 a Monday meeting of the presidium of the cabinet scheduled to approve the 2020 strategic plan was cancelled at the last moment and convened as a *soveshchanie* chaired by Putin because the requisite sign-offs had not been obtained at a *soveshchanie* chaired by Shuvalov the previous Friday.[26] The normative documents required to legalize the transfer of the state's shares in a large number of companies that were to make up the state-owned holding company Rostekhnologiya dragged on procedurally for months, despite the apparent – but as usual somewhat ambiguous – determination of two presidents, Putin and Medvedev, to bring it to a conclusion.[27] As part of the process a *soveshchanie* to be chaired by Putin was called off the day it was to be held because not all invitees had submitted their positions on a matter that had been intensely debated in some form for two years.[28] At a *soveshchanie* on gas pipeline access Gazprom had its objections to the outcome recorded in the minutes, to ensure that those objections would be appended to the formal documentation presented to cabinet.[29]

Although six months is perhaps not a sufficient period on which to base a judgement of the success or otherwise of Putin's new approach to policymaking, the signs were not good. The new procedures were not enough to overcome bureaucratic interests and reticent political leadership. How did the new approach cope with the crisis?

The Crisis

Crisis management policymaking saw the full mobilization of the new structures and procedures. The deputy prime ministers were very heavily involved in consultations, negotiations and decision-making. *Soveshchaniya* were used both for consultation and the hard business of decision-making, essentially replacing formal decision-making bodies. As noted by one commentator in October 2008, the most recent anti-crisis decisions of the government were taken at *soveshchaniya* chaired by Dmitrii Medvedev, not by Vladimir Putin. The formal headquarters, the presidium of the government, yet again had its meeting cancelled because its members were too busy, and the date of its next meeting was unknown.[30]

In this context we will ignore the reference to the tandem; as far as meetings of the presidium, and the cabinet itself, are concerned, they did return to something like a regular schedule, but the evidence is that they played a largely formal role in approving decisions that had already been made at *soveshchaniya*. One commentator described a meeting of the presidium in February 2009 as essentially a PR exercise to demonstrate to the population that their individual lives would not be affected by the crisis – 'the meeting of the government became a routine psychotherapy session'.[31] Some minor changes could be made, but they were unlikely to be dramatic.[32]

Once the reality of the crisis had hit a series of *soveshchaniya* devoted to key affected sectors – banking, the automobile industry, defence industry, construction – produced immediate fire-fighting measures,[33] including share market intervention, a programme of loans from the state-owned Vneshekonombank to companies facing immediate debt repayments or margin calls on loans from foreign banks, state injections into bank capital, and a list of priority 'system-forming' firms. *Soveshchaniya* preceded the formal approval of the amended 2009 budget and the two anti-crisis plans;[34] they were also used to deal with very specific issues, such as how to get emergency assistance to the car manufacturer AvtoVAZ.[35]

Soveshchaniya operated according to a rough hierarchy. At sectoral level representatives of the business community and other interested parties were invited to attend. At this level they were usually although not always chaired by a deputy prime minister. That was followed by a *soveshchanie* of deputy prime ministers chaired by either Putin or Medvedev. The attendance at these *soveshchaniya*, at which the final decisions were made, was limited to the deputy prime ministers and perhaps a small number of lower level officials and a few people from outside government structures.[36]

As the crisis continued, the approach was maintained. The second attempt by the government to get credits to enterprises through the banking system represents a good example. An initial attempt made in late 2008 was deemed to have been a failure. The first we heard of a new approach was at a special *soveshchanie* on the matter chaired by Medvedev on 14 May 2009. Reports of that meeting revealed that Medvedev had held a *soveshchanie* two days earlier with members of the banking community, who had declared that they were happy with the new approach. Kudrin presented relevant amendments to the Budget law at the 14 May meeting. A Ministry of Economics source revealed to reporters that, although the ministry had not seen the amendments before the meeting, they were acceptable to his organization.[37] In more 'normal' policymaking that would be unheard of – that a key agency would not have seen the proposals in advance and that it would accept them if it had not. The next week the documentation was approved at a meeting of the presidium of the cabinet,[38] and by 29 June the amendments had gone through parliament and the enabling decrees were issued.[39]

Soveshchaniya managed to retain their relatively informal nature, without being subjected to complex and potentially obstructionist consultation and sign-off procedures. It is interesting in this regard to consider the fate of the Commission for Maintaining the Resilience of the Russian Economy (popularly known as KURS). Early in the crisis the Russian Union of Industrialists and Entrepreneurs (RSPP), an important big business lobbying organization, had expressed its dissatisfaction with the widespread use of *soveshchaniya* in crisis management, presumably because they did not guarantee business representation, and asked for the establishment of a formal anti-crisis council reporting to the president, in the expectation that such a council would have business representatives among its membership.[40] KURS, which appeared soon afterwards and was expected to be the real headquarters of crisis management policymaking, had a statute and formal operating procedures.[41] But it did not, perhaps for that very reason, become a major policymaking body. Its role was largely limited to policy implementation – above all dealing with claims for funds from 'system-forming' enterprises,[42] and even then it seemed on occasion to struggle. In mid-March 2009 the commission was trying to decide how to get emergency funding to AvtoVAZ. In the end it took a *soveshchanie* chaired by Sechin to decide the matter, and then what was probably a PR *soveshchanie* at the plant held by Putin to announce it.[43] One commentator writes of KURS: 'At its meetings one could die of boredom – no major decisions, just the "dumb selection" of anti-crisis bids coming in from every corner of our huge country'.[44]

The same story is evident at the sectoral level. Two formal bodies were set up specifically to deal with the crisis in the metals sector: the Coordination Council for Industry Policy in the Metals Sector, set up in October 2008 by the Ministry of Industry and Trade; and the governmental Commission for the Development of the Metals Sector, created in February 2009 and headed by Igor Sechin. There is no record of the former meeting before November 2009, when it was convened during the International Trade Fair 'Metal-expo'.[45] Despite its statute requiring meetings at least quarterly, it was noted by Sechin at a meeting of the latter in February 2010 that, although a majority of its members had participated in various *soveshchaniya* on the sector, the commission itself had not formally met until that date.[46]

The ability to keep things flexible was not because there was no vigorous policy debate. The arguments, essentially between the fiscal conservatives, personified by Kudrin, and the 'spenders', a broad coalition of just about everyone else, were fierce. The policy process did not have the easy task of coping with a situation in which there was a lot of consensus before it even started. Nevertheless, while there are certainly arguments about the appropriateness of particular decisions, there is little to criticize in the decision-making process itself. It was broadly consultative, but able to produce rapid and focused outcomes.

Post-Crisis

The policy process that served Russia reasonably well in crisis circumstances was not set up for that purpose. It was designed for 'normal' times. No one can be sure that normal times have returned. But Russian economic performance appears to have bottomed out, and certainly by the second half of 2009 the authorities were stressing the need for a shift from the 'hands on' management of the crisis to more strategic post-crisis policy issues.[47] In the brief period before the onset of the crisis, the signs were not good that it would work well in such times. How is Putin's approach to policymaking coping in the post-crisis period, as such big issues as the growth (now known as modernization) versus stability debate, taxation, pensions, administrative reform and corruption return to the policy agenda? The period is too brief to allow much more than some speculation based on a limited amount of evidence.

As described above, Putin undertook reform of the policy process in three areas: the reintroduction of deputy prime ministers, the use of *soveshchaniya* and changes to *soglasovanie* procedures. How have they fared since the crisis?

The multiple deputy prime minister system was abolished early in the Putin presidency because of its contribution to *vedomstvennost*. It was reintroduced because the prime minister was not able to handle the cabinet, but with a matrix element to reduce its *vedomstvennost* potential. That appears to have worked reasonably well in crisis circumstances, but one wonders whether the pressure of sectoral loyalties – particularly when they are reinforced by ideological and factional values – will increase in normal circumstances. The jurisdictional overlap can be considerable, particularly when it is also taken into account that deputy prime ministers often have other positions as well. The case cited above, of Sechin giving directives to a whole range of ministries over the privatization of assets destined for Oboronprom, was complicated by the fact that before doing so Sechin, in his other capacity as chair of the board of directors of Oboronprom, complained in a formal letter to Medvedev about the Ministry of Defence's obstructionism. Despite the fact that Medvedev did no more than note receipt of the letter, Sechin went ahead and sent his directives.[48] One imagines that in more settled circumstances such behaviour will draw a response from ministries that do not see themselves as 'naturally' subordinate to the directive-issuing deputy prime minister, as well as from their 'natural' deputy prime ministers. Having said that, one notes, however, the comments of Gaman-Goluvtina and her co-authors that the appointment of Dmitrii Kozak as deputy prime minister with responsibilities going beyond the boundaries of the Ministry of Regional Development has helped deal with major coordination problems in regional policy.[49]

Regarding *soveshchaniya*, we have seen that in the brief period of normalcy before the crisis hit there was pressure to have them subjected to the routinized procedures of consultation and sign-off. That pressure has been resisted in crisis circumstances. How do things stand now?

There are signs of them becoming more routinized, including being postponed because *soglasovanie* cannot be achieved in advance, for example, the 2010 budget *soveshchaniya*.[50] One might indeed expect them to fade away as formal decision-making bodies and the more established procedures of consultation and sign-off between institutional agencies return as the norm.[51] In the defence industry sector the inter-agency commission on assistance to the defence-industry complex, headed by a deputy Minister of Finance, has remained as an important body, including in dealing with the never-ending demands of Rostekhnologiya's Sergei Chemezov.[52] In the oil and gas sector, relatively unaffected by the crisis, the Commission for the Fuel and Energy Sector also remains an important operational body, albeit one with serious *soglasovanie* problems.[53]

However, *soveshchaniya* certainly have not disappeared. Although there is no need for daily emergency meetings to deal with financial emergencies, they are still used to advance the policy process outside formal bodies. Tough, daily meetings were used to lay the groundwork for drawing up budget policy for 2011–13. [54] They were also used in classic, out-of-hours, logjam-busting style to iron out the final details of the marathon Law on Trade legislation,[55] even if implementation became a matter of inter-agency battles through formal bodies.[56]

Little has been heard of the changed *soglasovanie* procedures since they were introduced in late December 2008, but what evidence there is suggests that they have only half-worked. The changes themselves left considerable room for playing bureaucratic games: a consulted agency can still send a negative opinion within the month allotted and thereby set in train a long negotiation process, and a consulted agency that does not respond within a month can appeal even after the document has been registered. Those, and other appeals, go to a deputy prime minister. It appears that the result has been a great increase in the number of draft policy documents arriving at the government administration with lack of agreement formally noted and so requiring deputy prime ministerial *soveshchaniya* to arrive at a final resolution.

It was on the grounds that this development was not conducive to speedy policymaking that in November 2009 Putin again changed the consultation rules to exempt completely the government administration's Commission on Administrative Reform from *soglasovanie* requirements.[57] One also sees in practice examples of some softening of the most rigorous demands of *soglasovanie*, with documents that have not been signed off being partially sent forward to decision-making bodies. For example, First Deputy Prime Minister Viktor Zubkov allowed parts of a draft government degree on the methodology of implementation of the ever-controversial Law on Trade to go to the working group in charge of implementation even though the draft had not been signed off. A government official was quoted in *Kommersant* as saying: 'The draft decree prepared by FAS [Federal Anti-Monopoly Service] was not presented to the government apparatus in signed-off form. Therefore only individual aspects of this issue will be examined. And directives will be issued that further work be done on the methodology according to established procedures, with sign-off being obtained from the ministries of economics, finance, industry and trade, the Russian statistical office.'[58]

It is very clear that *soglasovanie* has not been abandoned, but some leeway is being allowed. Another example concerns another big policy issue, state funding of innovation. A draft plan submitted to the government apparatus for presentation to Putin's commission on high-tech and innovation was returned to the Ministry of Economics for further work, after objections had been lodged during *soglasovanie* by the Ministry of Finance and other agencies. However, Sobyanin directed that work begin on the implementation of those components of the plan that were not controversial.[59]

In the Law on Trade case it was noted that if the disagreements could not be resolved Zubkov would determine 'additional sign-off measures, but now on the basis of a table of disagreements'. A 'table of disagreements' is also referred to in the case of amendments to the Law on Bankruptcy, for which the Ministry of Economics had been unable to obtain sign-off from the Ministry of Finance.[60] Presumably, a table of disagreements is drawn up when preliminary procedures have been exhausted and resolution will be required at a higher level, as noted at the beginning of this section.

Perhaps in response to some weakening of *soglasovanie* procedures the major agencies have moved in other ways to strengthen their automatic right to be involved in the policy process. At the end of 2009, at the same cabinet meeting at which Putin directed that the Commission on Administrative Reform be freed from *soglasovanie* procedures, the Ministries of Finance and Justice gained the right to issue a 'finding' (*zaklyuchenie*) on any proposal coming from any government agency.[61] Later the Ministry of Economy pushed for and obtained the same right, although seemingly related to policy documents related to business.[62] One would have expected these agencies already to have had such a right under normal *soglasovanie* procedures. The fact that they have pushed for it in this specific form suggests that normal *soglasovanie* procedures have indeed been weakened.

There are recent examples of policymaking in which Putin's approach continues to be used, and apparently to good effect in the sense that a controversial issue is – after a reasonable amount of debate and argument – rammed through. An example is the new project-based approach to drawing up the budget championed by the Ministry of Finance. Kudrin first raised the issue (at least in a way that reached the public eye) at a meeting with Putin in January 2010.[63] Putin referred to it, very carefully and diplomatically but as if it were a done deal, at a *soveshchanie* on federal programme funding in early March.[64] Kudrin intended to take it to cabinet on 18 March, but the objections of the Ministry of Economics, recorded in the form of a table of disagreements, were such that the matter was not put on the agenda.[65] Kudrin then went to Medvedev, who at a meeting between the two on 24 March expressed support for the idea.[66] That was followed by another *soveshchanie* chaired by Putin, described as having gone late into the night, at which he approved the new approach and directed the Ministry of Economics to prepare the implementing documentation.[67] The matter was taken to a government apparatus-sponsored inter-branch working group chaired by Sobyanin and Kudrin.[68] It was decided there that the Ministry of Finance's budget programme, which included the new approach, should be accepted 'as a whole' (*v osnovnom*) and that objections should be taken into account only 'to the extent possible' (*po vozmozhnostyam*), that is, they should not be allowed to stop the process.[69] Putin then announced on 14 May at a joint board meeting of the Ministries of Finance and Economics (this was a showcase meeting with a very large attendance) that the matter would go to cabinet soon.[70] At a cabinet meeting on 20 May Kudrin's programme was approved. Some of the details were still not signed off, but Kudrin suggested that he would use his position as deputy prime minister to issue directives to resolve those issues speedily.[71] So while some details remained to be tidied up, the issue seems to have been resolved in a fraught couple of months, with the policy process being driven along despite persistent *soglasovanie* problems.

Medvedev and the Policy Process

Putin appeared to be satisfied with the policy process at the moment. He was able to be relatively non-committal on controversial issues and yet progress was made. Medvedev was less satisfied, and made his own effort to push things along. He famously vented his frustrations at the failure of government agencies to implement his directives. Presidential directives (*porucheniya*), despite their uncertain legal status, are an important instrument in the hands of a president determined to use them.[72] It was said that Medvedev's directives were more specific – demanding the preparation of specified draft legislation and normative acts – than Putin's, who used them more for getting matters on the agenda. There also was a very large and increasing number of them – 1354 in 2008 and 1753 in 2009.[73] To the extent that Medvedev's directives demanded the preparation of documentation on matters that have not been subjected to full discussion – and *soglasovanie* – within the government, they represented a real attack on the capacity of agencies to control the bureaucratic process.

Agencies were certainly less than enthusiastic about implementing them, as it was generally claimed that the main reason for failure to meet directive deadlines is sign-off delays.[74] In August 2009 Medvedev

put the head of the Control Administration of the presidential apparatus, Konstantin Chuichenko, in charge of controlling the fulfilment
of his directives in the area of employment policy.[75] By 2010 he was
pushing hard for Chuichenko to more rigorously control the fulfilment
of all his directives, reaching a climax in June in a videoconference
showing off the full panoply of his bossiness and technological prow-
ess. Chuichenko, who sounded far from enthusiastic, was charged with
ensuring that full disciplinary measures, up to dismissal, were taken
against recalcitrant bureaucrats.[76] It was a matter for discussion whether
these were the actions of a frustrated figurehead president or the serious
use of a previously little-noted presidential weapon to force through
policy change and even to achieve elite turnover.[77] Putin responded
by applying the lowest level of administrative penalty against deputy
ministers in six ministries, most of whom let it be known in one way or
another that they were being held (lightly) responsible for something
over which they had no control.[78]

Conclusion

The evidence is that the policy process coped with the crisis quite well.
Decisions were made quickly, but not without consultation. The structures that performed well – *soveshchaniya* and deputy prime ministers,
as well as a relaxation of *soglasovanie* procedures – were introduced into
the policy process by Putin before the crisis hit. They were continued
to be used as the urgency of the crisis diminished, and with some good
effect. Although the impatient Medvedev was not satisfied with the system, the relatively relaxed Putin was able to push things along without having to commit himself too strongly and publicly to one side or
another. It was, however, still difficult to say whether, as the big policy
issues returned to the top of the agenda, the pressures of the logic of
specialization – of which there were plenty of signs – would come to
dominate and then challenge Putin either to allow the policy process to
stagnate or to adopt a more vigorous leadership style.

Notes

1. The following section is a summary of Stephen Fortescue's, 'Institutionalization
   and Personalism in the Policy-making Process of the Soviet Union and Post-
   Soviet Russia', in Stephen Fortescue (ed.) (2010), *Russian Politics from Lenin to
   Putin* (Basingstoke: Palgrave), chapter 2.

2. Stephen Fortescue (2006), 'Business–State Negotiations and the Reform of Tax Procedures in Post-Yukos Russia', *Law in Context*, Vol. 24, No. 2, pp. 36–59; Aleksandr Shokhin (2006), 'Ot dobra dobra ne ishchut' [You Don't Seek Good from Good], *Vedomosti*, 17 August.
3. Stephen Fortescue (2009), 'The Russian Law on Subsurface Resources: A Policy Marathon', *Post-Soviet Affairs*, Vol. 25, No. 2, pp. 160–84.
4. For a policy balance sheet of the Putin presidency, see Ol'ga Proskurnina, 'Ot pervogo litsa – ko vtoromu' [From the First Person – to the Second], *Vedomosti*, 12 May 2008.
5. Fortescue (2009) (note 3), p. 163.
6. Petr Netreba (2009), 'Belomu Domu udvoili obem bumazhnoi raboty' [The White House Doubled the Paperwork], *Kommersant*, 19 January.
7. For an example see his statement made during a fierce struggle between the centre and regions over regional access to the resource licensing process: 'The ownership, use and assignment of natural resources must be to the benefit of the whole Russian people, every citizen of our country. And at the same time the interests of the population living in the territory where national wealth is exploited by one company or another must be recognized.' V. V. Putin (2005), 'Vstupitelnoe slovo na soveshchanii s chlenami Soveta palaty Soveta Federatsii' [Introduction at the Meeting of Members of the Federation Council], 7 December, www.kremlin.ru/text/appears/2005/12/98572.shtml. For another good example of his preference for compromise, see his contribution – as prime minister – to the growth versus stability debate: 'The budget has to be used as a factor for development – that's obvious. But it's just as obvious that the budget must be balanced. Up until now you [the ministries of finance and economics] have been able to find a healthy, clear, pragmatic compromise, and I hope that you will continue to do so.' Vadim Visloguzov (2010), 'Ministerstva torguyut tsenami na neft'' [Ministries are Trading with Prices on Oil], *Kommersant*, 17 May.
8. Steven M. Fish, 'The Executive Deception: Superpresidentialism and the Degradation of Russian Politics', in Valerie Sperling (ed.) (2000), *Building the Russian State: Institutional Crisis and the Quest for Democratic Governance* (Boulder: Westview), chapter 8.
9. Moshe Haspel, Thomas F. Remington and Steven S. Smith (2006), 'Lawmaking and Decree Making in the Russian Federation: Time, Space, and Rules in Russian National Policymaking', *Post-Soviet Affairs*, Vol. 22, No. 3, July–September, pp. 264–7.
10. Scott Parrish, 'Presidential decree authority in Russia, 1991–95', in John M. Carey and Matthew Soberg Shugart (eds) (1998), *Executive Decree Authority* (Cambridge: Cambridge University Press), chapter 3; Thomas F. Remington (2000), 'The Evolution of Executive–Legislative Relations in Russia Since 1993', *Slavic Review*, Vol. 59, No. 3, p. 506; Haspel, Remington and Smith (note 164), pp. 252–3.
11. The president also has the power of legislative initiative, that is, he can send draft legislation directly to parliament, bypassing the government, but Putin rarely used that power. The president was the least common source of parliamentary bills on economic policy between 1996 and 2004. Paul

Chaisty (2006), *Legislative Politics and Economic Power in Russia* (Basingstoke: Palgrave), p. 73.

12. Eugene Huskey (1996), 'The Making of Economic Policy in Russia: Changing Relations between Presidency and Government', *Review of Central and East European Law*, Vol. 22, No. 4, pp. 365–87; Oleh Protsyk (2006), 'Intra-executive Competition between President and Prime Minister: Patterns of Institutional Conflict and Cooperation under Semi-presidentialism', *Political Studies*, Vol. 54, pp. 219–44.

13. Petr Netreba (2008), 'Gosudarstvennye raskhody v Belom dome obsudili v kremlevskom stile' [State Expenses Discussed in the White House in the Kremlin Style], *Kommersant*, 3 June.

14. Eugene Huskey (1996), 'The Making of Economic Policy in Russia: Changing Relations Between Presidency and Government', *Review of Central and East European Law*, Vol. 22, No. 4, p. 369.

15. Valerii Vyzhutovich (2006), 'Nastroika bez igry' [A Configuration without Game], *Politcom.ru*, 21 June.

16. For the distribution of responsibilities, see the government website at http://www.government.ru/content/rfgovernment/rfgovernmentvicechairman/d4da4820–24dd-42d8–9b06-d90b3e0c2fe8.htm.

17. Elena Kiseleva (2009), 'Igor Sechin topit voennykh' [Igor Sechin Heads the Military], *Kommersant*, 20 November.

18. See http://www.government.ru/gov/activity/#person8.

19. Huskey (note 14), p. 370.

20. Nadezhda Ivanitskaya (2008), Svetlana Ivanova and Yuliya Belous, 'Medvedev prislushalsya' [Medvedev Listened], *Vedomosti*, 18 March.

21. Petr Netreba (2006), 'Minfin ne uspevaet za byudzhetnymi zaprosami' [Ministry of Finance Has No Time for Budget Requests], *Kommersant*, 23 May.

22. 'O vnesenii izmenenii v Pravila podgotovki normativnykh pravovykh aktov federalnykh organov ispolnitelnoi vlasti i ikh gosudarstvennoi registrat-sii' [On the introduction of changes in the rules of preparing normative legal documents of federal executive bodies and of their state registration. Regulation by the Government of the Russian Federation], *Postanovlenie Pravitelstva Rossiiskoi Federatsii*, 29 December 2008, No. 1048.

23. Evgeniya Pismennaya and Mariya Tsvetkova (2009), 'Lichno otvetyat [To Personally Respond], *Vedomosti*, 13 January; Dmitrii Butrin and Petr Netreba (2009), 'Vsya vlast vitse-premeram' [All Power to the Deputy Prime Ministers], *Kommersant*, 13 January.

24. Tatyana Stanovaya (2008), 'Putin vozglavil partiyu rosta' [Putin Heads the Party of Growth], Politcom.ru, 2 June; Evgeniya Pismennaya (2008), '"My podgotovimsya k ryvku za 4 goda" – Igor Shuvalov, pervyi zamestitel predse-datelya pravitelstva Rossii' [We Prepare for a Breakthrough in Four Years – Igor Shuvalov, First Deputy Chairman of the Russian Government], *Vedomosti*, 5 September; Petr Netreba and Elena Kiseleva (2008), 'Ministry ne veryat v svoi polnomochiya' [Ministers Do Not Trust their Credentials], *Kommersant*, 2 June.

25. Dmitrii Butrin (2009), 'Pravila igry' [The Rules of the Game], *Kommersant*, 19 January; 'Vektor', *Vedomosti*, 23 March 2009.

26. Petr Netreba (2008), 'Ekonomisty Belogo Doma perevedeny v turborezhim' [The Economists of the White House Have Moved to a Turbo-Regime], *Kommersant*, 30 September.
27. Tatyana Stanovaya (2008), 'Chemezov vs pravitelstvo' [Chemezov vs the Government], Politcom.ru, 16 June.
28. Evgeniya Pismennaya and Anna Nikolaeva (2008), 'Pauza zatyanulas' [The Break was Protracted], *Vedomosti*, 16 June.
29. 'Deneg ne pokazhet' [Money not on Display], *Vedomosti*, 5 August 2008.
30. Dmitrii Butrin and Petr Netreba (2008), 'Krizis dushat osnovatelnostyu' [They Choke the Crisis with Basics], *Kommersant*, 21 October.
31. Tatyana Stanovaya (2009), 'Molochko antikrizisnoe, putinskoe' [Anti-Crisis Milk of Putin], Politcom.ru, 10 February.
32. For examples of minor changes being made to the amended 2009 'crisis' budget and the second anti-crisis plan, see Nadezhda Ivanitskaya, Natalya Kostenko and Mariya Shpigel (2009), 'Melkii torg' [Small Bargaining], *Vedomosti*, 24 March; Petr Netreba and Dmitrii Butrin (2009), 'Pravitelstvo vyneslo antikrizisnyi plan' [The Government Issued an Anti-Crisis Plan], *Kommersant*, 20 March.
33. Dmitrii Butrin and Petr Netreba (2008), 'Krizis zavalivayut dengami' [A Crisis Flooded with Money], *Kommersant*, 17 October.
34. Dmitrii Butrin (2008), 'Vse raskhody zapisany' [All Expenses are Written Down], *Kommersant*, 10 November.
35. Dmitrii Belikov (2009), 'AvtoVAZ ishchet dorogu k gosstredstvam' [AvtoVAZ Looks for the Road to State Money], *Kommersant*, 30 March.
36. Nadezhda Ivanitskaya (2009), 'Dengi – k letu' [Money – Towards the Summer], *Vedomosti*, 19 March.
37. Evgeniya Pismennaya and Vasilii Kudinov (2009), '30 dnei do garantii' [30 Days until Warranty], *Vedomosti*, 15 May.
38. 'Predsedatel Pravitelstva Rossiiskoi Federatsii V.V. Putin provel zasedanie Prezidiuma Pravitelstva RF', 25 April 2009 [The Chairman of the Russian Government V.V. Putin Chaired a Meeting of the Presidium of the Russian Government], http://premier.gov.ru/events/news/4227/.
39. As reported by Putin at a meeting on the budget, 29 June 2009, http://premier.gov.ru/2009/6/29/.
40. When the council was eventually set up, in the form of KURS, there was no business representation. RSPP's spokesperson nevertheless declared the association to be satisfied, noting the business representation on the expert groups that would report to KURS. 'As a rule, the practical work always gets done at the level of the experts'. Butrin and Netreba (note 30).
41. For its statute and membership, see http://www.government.ru/content/coordinatingauthority/b2c0e3b6–447d-42b1-ad2b-782b044995d6.htm.
42. Evgeniya Pismennaya and Nadezhda Ivanitskaya (2009), 'KURS Shuvalova' [Shuvalov's KURS], *Vedomosti*, 14 January; Dmitrii Belikov, Petr Netreba and Dmitrii Smirnov (2009), 'V Belyi dom pustyat GAZ' [The White House Starts Up GAZ], *Kommersant*, 30 January.
43. Dmitrii Belikov and Petr Netreba (2009), 'AvtoVAZ poekhal po osoboi doroge' [AvtoVAZ Went a Special Way], *Kommersant*, 18 March; Belikov (note 35).

44. Evgeniya Pismennaya (2009), 'Chelovek nedeli: Aleksei Kudrin' [The Person of the Week: Alexei Kudrin], *Vedomosti*, 2 March.
45. 'Soveshchanie koordinatsionnogo Soveta metallurgicheskoi promyshlennosti pri Minpromtorge Rossii' [Meeting of the Coordinating Council of the Mettalurgical Industry at the Russian Minpromtorg], 6 November 2009, http://www.minprom.gov.ru/activity/metal/news/92.
46. 'Zamestitel Predsedatelya Pravitelstva Rossiiskoi Federatsii I. I. Sechin provel zasedanie Pravitelstvennoi komissii po voprosam razvitiya metallurgicheskogo kompleksa', 17 February 2010 [The Deputy Chairman of the Russian Government I. I. Sechin Chaired a Meeting of the Government Commission on Problems of Developing the Metallurgical Industry], http://government.ru/docs/9433.
47. 'Stenograficheskii otchet o soveshchanii po ekonomicheskim voprosam', 9 September 2009 [Minutes from a Meeting on Economic Issues], http://www.kremlin.ru/transcripts/5409; 'Rabochaya vstrecha s zamestitelem predsedatelem pravitelstva – ministrom finansov Aleksandrom Kudrinym', 6 April 2010 [Working Meeting with the Deputy Chairman of the Government – Minister of Finance Alexander Kudrin, http://www.kremlin.ru/transcripts/7367.
48. Kiseleva (note 17).
49. O. V. Gaman-Goluvtina et al. (2009), 'Effektivnost gosudarstvennogo upravleniya v Rossiiskoi Federatsii v 2008 godu' [The Efficiency of State Management in Russia in 2008], *Ezhegodnyi doklad InOP "Otsenka sostoyaniya i perspektiv politicheskoi sistemy Rossii"* (Institut obshchestvennogo proektirovaniya) [Yearly Report of the InOP "Evaluation of the Situation and the Perspectives for the Russian Political System". Institute of Social Planning], p. 74, http://www.inop.ru/page529/page484/.
50. Dmitrii Butrin, Petr Netreba, Irina Granik and Oleg Sapozhkov (2010), 'Ne vsegda poruchaetsya' [Not Always Entrusted], *Kommersant*, 17 March.
51. For a list of such bodies, see http://www.government.ru/content/coordinatingauthority/.
52. Evgeniya Pismennaya (2009), 'Chemezovu pomogut' [Chemezov Gets Help], *Vedomosti*, 5 March.
53. Dmitrii Kazmin and Alena Chechel (2009), 'Reforma zatyanulas' [The Reform is Delayed], *Vedomosti*, 22 January.
54. Dmitrii Butrin and Petr Netreba (2010), 'Byudzhetnoe poslanie k rabochemu stolu' [A Budget Message to the Work-Table], *Kommersant*, 30 June.
55. Dmitrii Butrin (2009), 'Pravila igry' [The Rules of the Game], *Kommersant*, 14 December.
56. Petr Netreba and Kristina Busko (2010), 'Zakonu o torgovle dobavyat metodichnosti' [Orderliness is Added to the Law on Trade], *Kommersant*, 25 March.
57. 'Rabochii den' [The Work Day], 24 November 2009, http://premier.gov.ru/events/news/8336/; Dmitrii Butrin (2009), 'Vsya vlast yuristam i finansistam' [All Power to the Lawyers and Financers], *Kommersant*, 25 November; Tatyana Stanovaya (2009), 'Pravitelstvo i reformy' [The Government and Reforms], Politcom.ru, 30 November.
58. Netreba and Busko (note 211).

59. Evgeniya Pismennaya (2010), 'Innovatsii po vyzovu' [Innovation on Demand], *Vedomosti*, 29 March.
60. Oleg Sapozhkov and Petr Netreba (2010), 'Zakon o bankrotstve upersya v konflikt interesa' [The Law on Bankruptcy Ran into a Conflict of Interest], *Kommersant*, 27 April.
61. 'Materialy k zasedaniyu Pravitelstva Rossiiskoi Federatsii 24 noyabrya 2009 g.', 24 November 2009 [Material for the Meeting of the Russian Government, 24 November 2009], http://government.ru/docs/8330/; Butrin (note 57); Stanovaya (note 57).
62. Maksim Tovkailo (2010), 'Novyi kontroler' [The New Controller], *Vedomosti*, 24 March.
63. 'Rabochii den' [The Work Day], 16 January 2010, http://premier.gov.ru/events/news/9007/.
64. 'Rabochii den' [The Work Day], 9 March 2010, http://premier.gov.ru/events/news/9672/.
65. Maksim Tovkailo (2010), 'Byudzhet trebuet kultury' [Budget Demand on Culture], *Vedomosti*, 9 April.
66. 'Rabochaya vstrecha s zamestitelem predsedatelem pravitelstva – ministrom finansov Aleksandrom Kudrinym', 6 April 2010 (note 202).
67. Tovkailo (note 65).
68. Evgeniya Pismennaya and Maksim Tovkailo (2010), 'Kudrin otrezhet' [Kudrin Cuts], *Vedomosti*, 14 April.
69. Petr Netreba (2010), 'Tsel opravdyvaet sredstva byudzheta' [The Purpose Justifies the Budget Means], *Kommersant*, 19 April.
70. 'Rabochii den' [The Work Day], 14 May 2010, http://premier.gov.ru/events/news/10586/.
71. Petr Netreba (2010), 'Polet fantazii pridavali kalkulyatorom' [A Calculator was Added to the Flight of Fantasy], *Kommersant*, 21 May.
72. Iaroslav Startsev (2000), 'Les instructions du President de la Russie: Analyse d'un instrument d'action discretionnaire', *Revue d'etudes comparatives Est-Ouest*, Vol. 31, No. 2, pp. 137–55.
73. Butrin, Netreba, Petr and Sapozhkov (note 205).
74. Ibid.
75. Tatyana Stanovaya (2009), 'Pravitelstvo pod kontrol' [Government under Control], Politcom.ru, 6 August.
76. 'Soveshchanie po voprosu ispolneniya poruchenii Prezidenta' [Meeting on the Problem of Implementing Presidential Instructions], 21 June 2010, http://news.kremlin.ru/news/8126.
77. Olga Mefodeva (2010), 'Medvedev razbushevalsya' [Medvedev Flew into a Rage], Politcom.ru, 22 June.
78. Mariya Tvetkova, Maksim Tovkailo and Alena Chechel (2010), 'Vzyskanie za myagkost' [Punishment for Softness], *Vedomosti*, 8 July.

8
Business Representation in the State Duma

Paul Chaisty

Introduction

In a very general sense social scientists use the concept of modernization to describe the ways in which less developed societies achieve the standards reached by more developed societies at a particular point in time. This meaning is shared by scholars and politicians as distinct as the late American political scientist Samuel Huntington and Russia's chief ideologist Vladislav Surkov.[1] However, it is a controversial concept that has been criticized for its linear understanding of modern development; and even those scholars who apply the concept hold different views on the forms that modernization can take. Modernization has many dimensions – economic, political, social and cultural – and the causal relationship between them remains a point of dispute.

In keeping with the theme of this book, this chapter focuses on the political dimension of modernization in Russia. More specifically, it is concerned with the area of parliamentary representation. Contemporary Western political science generally associates modernity with liberal democracy, and democratic processes in modern industrial societies have tended to produce legislative politicians with particular social and professional characteristics.[2] This chapter explores the extent to which Russia's parliamentarians converge on or diverge from this pattern of development.

Focusing on the elected lower house of the Federal Assembly, the State Duma, the chapter pays particular attention to the over-representation of business interests. It describes the predominance of business backgrounds in the career profiles of deputies, and it explores how the capacity of deputies to lobby their interests has changed over time. Finally, the chapter considers the implications and consequences of business representation for both political and economic modernization in Russia.

The Representation of Business Interests in Legislative Politics

The Russian Parliament has a poor reputation as a political institution. Although the Federal Assembly played a prominent role during the first decade of the 1993 Constitution, it has been less influential in more recent times.[3] Comparative legislative analysis also shows that the assembly fares poorly in cross-national measurements of parliamentary power. In the most recent global survey of national parliaments, Steven Fish and Matthew Kroenig rank the Federal Assembly among the weakest – below the parliaments of Georgia, Ukraine and Kyrgyzstan in the non-Baltic former Soviet Union, and at the same point in the scale as countries like Azerbaijan, Haiti, Liberia, Iran and Yemen.[4] Even the Russian political elite are willing to admit the limitations of the formal legislative process. Russian President Dmitrii Medvedev's 2008 election pledge to tackle what he called Russia's 'legal nihilism' posed serious questions about the capacity of the parliament to create the legislative foundations for a modern society.

Nonetheless, membership of the assembly is still considered worthwhile by members of Russia's political and economic establishment. For Russia's business elite in particular, seats in the assembly have been much sought after since the introduction of the new parliament in 1993. This is illustrated by Figure 8.1, which summarizes the percentage of newcomers to the parliament's lower house, the State Duma, who were elected from a business background between 1993 and 2010.[5] Contrary to the trend of weakening legislative power, it shows that business candidates make up a growing proportion of politicians elected to the lower house. In the Fifth Duma (2007–11), the number of deputies elected from a business background reached almost 40 per cent, which was double the number of deputies with a corresponding background that had been elected to the First Duma (1993–95).

Indeed, figures such as these probably underestimate the full extent of business linkages in the Russian Parliament. The data illustrated in Figure 8.1 are based on the official biographies of Duma deputies, and it is unlikely that all deputies were willing to reveal the full extent of their wealth in official publications.[6] Nor does this information capture the business interests that Duma deputies acquire during their time in office. Despite legal limits on their business activities, deputies have

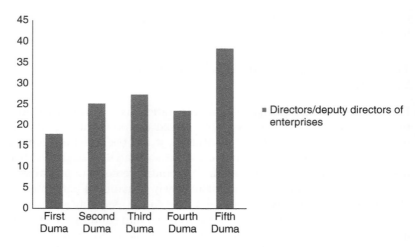

Figure 8.1   Percentage of Duma newcomers with a business background, First to Fifth Dumas (1993–2011)

many opportunities to cultivate business contacts. According to research on the Fifth Duma conducted by the Russian branch of Transparency International, even the officially declared wealth of Duma deputies increased significantly over the first two years of the parliamentary term.[7]

With the introduction of electoral reforms that have strengthened the proportional component of the Russian electoral system since 1993, political parties have become the main conduit for business interests in the lower house. The electoral lists of most political parties contain candidates with business backgrounds, many of whom have no previous experience of working for the parties they are competing to represent. In fact there are examples of individuals standing as candidates for different parties in different elections – even parties as ideologically opposed as the Union of Right Forces and the Communist Party.[8] Moreover, it is not unheard of for parties that have achieved representation in parliament to find seats for businesspeople during a Duma term. In the most extreme case, Vladimir Zhirinovskii's Liberal Democratic Party of Russia created a seat for a business sponsor in the Fifth Duma by expelling a sitting party member from the lower house.[9]

Yet, business representation is not simply a feature of party rule. Seats in the non-partisan upper house, the Federation Council, are also coveted by individuals with well-known business empires. The opportunities available to such individuals increased in 2002 when the method for forming the upper house was changed. The power of regional assemblies and chief executives to appoint 'senators' under the new rules enabled well-established figures from business to acquire seats across the country. They included individuals like Sergei Pugachev, a banking tycoon who became one of the richest men in Russia in the early 2000s, and Valentin Zavadnikov, a former deputy chair of Russia's largest electricity utility, RAO UES.

Therefore, business backgrounds are predominant in the career paths of Russian parliamentarians. Table 8.1 shows the percentage of Duma newcomers elected from different occupational backgrounds during the first five Dumas. Despite some fluctuation between different parliamentary terms, these data provide interesting differences from the typical profile of parliamentary elites in modern industrialized democracies.

Professions that tend to dominate in European parliamentary democracies – law, education, journalism – do not feature so prominently in Russia. In contrast to many democracies, there are few Duma deputies with a background in law in the lower house, and educational professions are in decline – this is the main reason for the sharp drop in the number of deputies included in the Education, Science and Health category in Table 8.1. These data also highlight the low share of representatives from the public sector. Health professionals, for example, make up a very small proportion of elected Duma deputies. Additionally, while the number of party and regional representatives is significant in the occupational backgrounds of Duma members, a career pattern that is also increasingly important in European democracies,[10] many deputies who have had political experience at the regional level have had careers in business, too. Indeed, when compared with countries with traditionally high levels of business representation, like the United Kingdom and the United States, the dominance of business in the Russian Duma is still notable. In the United Kingdom, the number of MPs with backgrounds in business varies according to the partisan composition of the parliament, and even during periods of Conservative Party rule, when business representation tends to be greatest, there remains equally high numbers of MPs with backgrounds in politics, law and public affairs.[11] In the United States, business has historically followed law as the most likely career path of the members of Congress, and in recent times it has been superseded by public service.[12]

Of the business sectors that feature in the career profiles of deputies, four areas predominate: manufacturing, agriculture, finance and energy (see Table 8.2). These data mirror the key sectors of the Russian

Table 8.1 Percentage of Duma newcomers from different occupational backgrounds, First to Fifth Dumas

	First Duma	Second Duma	Third Duma	Fourth Duma	Fifth Duma
Business Leadership	18	25	27	23	38
Regional Government	18	16	21	21	26
Political Parties, Business & Civil Society Organizations	12	14	13	15	11
Education, Science & Health	18	12	13	9	5
Federal Government	8	7	3	11	6
Military, Police & Security Services	4	8	6	7	4
Media, Arts & Sport	7	4	5	4	8
Business Workforce*	8	9	8	5	1
Law	3	1	1	2	0.4
Other	3	2	2	1	0

Notes: If newcomers held careers simultaneously in public office and other occupations prior to their election (e.g. an individual who remained active in business while holding a position in regional government) the original career is counted, not the position in public office.

*'Business Workforce' refers to newcomers who held manual or middle-level managerial positions in corporations and enterprises before their election to parliament. This category is distinguished from 'Business Leadership', which covers the directors and deputy directors of corporations and enterprises.

economy, and include those areas of the economy where big business is most concentrated. On average, almost 70 per cent of deputies with a background in business were either directors or deputy directors of companies with interests in one of these sectors.

The standard deviations shown in Table 8.2 highlight the variation in levels of representation over time, however. The high standard deviation for agriculture is the result of a significant decline in the number of deputies with backgrounds in agribusiness. Along with other traditional areas of the economy, notably the military-industrial sector, the size of the agricultural lobby has diminished in successive post-Soviet parliaments. In part this reflects the decline in the representation of leftist parties, especially the Communist and Agrarian parties, which had close connections to these sectors, but it is also a consequence of the greater concentration of Russian big business representation

Table 8.2 The mean percentage of Duma newcomers from different sectors of the economy, First to Fifth Dumas

Economic sector	Mean	Standard Deviation
Manufacturing	26.9	7.18401
Agriculture, forestry and fishing	17.3	11.09842
Financial and insurance activities	14.9	7.892401
Mining/Energy	13.52	8.328085
Construction	7.38	1.833576
Wholesale and retail trade	5.9	3.660601
Transportation and storage	2.64	1.050238
Other	11.34	7.540424

Notes: The coding of industrial sectors followed the United Nation's International Standard Industrial Classification. See http://unstats.un.org/unsd/cr/registry/regcst.asp?Cl=27&Lg=1.

The category 'Mining/Energy' is formed from the UN classification for the 'Mining and quarrying' and 'Electricity, gas, steam and air conditioning supply' sectors. It therefore covers both upstream and downstream productivity in the fuel sector, which is often difficult to demarcate for many energy companies in Russia.

from the energy and finance sectors. The number of deputies from finance and energy backgrounds increased significantly in the Third Duma (2000–03), when the assembly's power was at its peak. This Duma included individuals like Sergei Lobov, the general director of the Slavneft-Kostromanefteprodukt oil company, as well as the banking tycoon Suleiman Kerimov. In more recent times, the Yukos affair[13] and the decline in the parliament's political influence in the Fourth and Fifth Dumas have contributed to a slight fall in the proportion of newcomers from big business, especially finance. In the Fifth Duma, this shortfall was filled by deputies from medium-size businesses associated with sectors such as retail, food and construction. The newcomers elected to this parliament also tended to have more diverse business portfolios.

The importance of business concerns in the legislative activity of the parliament is further underlined by the types of legislation that have been at the centre of lobbying campaigns in the lower house. The data summarized in Table 8.2 suggest that economic legislation is at the centre of most lobbying campaigns in the assembly.[14] Much of this activity has been concerned with the budget and fiscal policy, and with general framework legislation that affects all areas of the economy. A significant proportion of this legislation also clustered around those economic sectors that have featured predominantly in the career profiles of deputies.

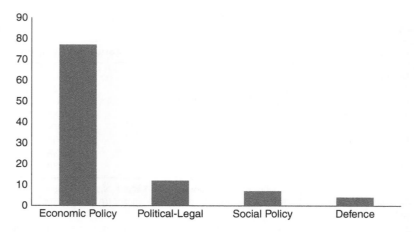

Figure 8.2   The percentage of lobbying campaigns by policy area, First to Fourth Dumas

Three sectors feature most consistently in lobbying campaigns in the lower house: agriculture and related manufacturing in the alcohol and tobacco industries; finance, which includes legislation that regulates the banking and insurance sectors; and energy – legislation affecting the oil, gas and electricity industries. These policy areas were well represented in the parliament by deputies who had close personal ties to each sector. They included, on energy issues, Valerii Yazev, the head of the Russian Gas Society and founder of Yava Invest, a company that is reportedly linked with the gas giant Gazprom; on agriculture issues, Gennadii Kulik, a former agriculture minister and deputy prime minister responsible for agricultural issues, and head of the Association of Grain Producers and Exporters; and on finance and insurance issues, Vladislav Reznik, who served on the boards of two banks, three insurance companies and seventeen businesses, and in the late 1990s was chairman of the Russian State Insurance Company.[15]

Thus, business interests have maintained a strong presence in the State Duma since its inception in 1993. The number of deputies with business ties has increased over time, and they have typically come from the most powerful sectors of the Russian economy. Yet the capacity of business interests to influence the lawmaking process also changed over the first five Dumas. The opportunities available to initiate, modify and veto legislation as it passed through the legislature declined with the growth in the legislative power of the executive branch. As a consequence, the rationale for business involvement in parliamentary politics has changed over time, too.

Patterns of Business Influence in the Duma

The emergence of parliaments with genuine legislative influence during the perestroika period provided a parliamentary focus for influence-seeking economic actors. Mikhail Gorbachev's legislative reforms of the late 1980s gave the communist economic *nomenklatura* new lobbying opportunities within the political system. Managers and directors of state corporations and collective farms formed deputy groups in the newly formed All Union Congress of People's Deputies. These groups were influential in shaping some of the key economic legislation of the time, most notably the 1991 Law on Privatization. One such group, the Scientific–Industrial deputy group, formed the basis of Russia's main post-Soviet business organizations, the Russian Union of Industrialists and Entrepreneurs.

In the early post-Soviet period, the Russian Supreme Soviet (1990–93) was also a magnet for established economic interests and emerging business forces. The combination of the parliament's substantial constitutional and financial powers and weak party political control made Supreme Soviet deputies particularly attractive to powerful lobbies. Traditional economic interests in agriculture and heavy industry were represented by deputy groups like the Agrarian Union and the Industrial Union, and Russia's nascent financial and banking sector was attracted to the substantial budgetary funds controlled by the assembly. Interestingly, even the speaker of the parliament, Ruslan Khasbulatov, formed his own expert group on finance and banking, which included many key names from Russia's emerging banking community: Vladimir Vinogradov (then chair of Inkombank), Mikhail Khodorkovskii (then chair of Menatep bank) and Vladimir Gusinskii (then chair of Most-Bank).[16]

Since 1993, the Federal Assembly, and the State Duma in particular, has continued to be an arena for interest lobbying. Although the 1993 Russian Constitution conferred substantial legislative powers on the president and the government, the parliament retained a number of important legislative and budgetary powers. However, the nature of business involvement has changed over time. In the early Dumas – the First (1994–95), Second (1996–99) and Third (2000–03) – the relative weakness of executive control over the legislative process provided opportunities for economic lobbies to influence lawmaking. In the first two parliaments, the agrarian lobby was a major beneficiary of the parliament's leftist orientation and influence over the budgetary process. In the Third Duma, which coincided with Vladimir Putin's first term, there was a notable increase in the involvement of big business. For example, the number of inter-party associations created to lobby on behalf of specific economic interests increased exponentially in this parliament. According to one estimate there were more than 30 inter-party groups by the end of the spring session of 2001. This number included the group 'Russian Energy', which was led by former Prime Minister Viktor Chernomyrdin. The Third Duma was also defined by the lobbying activities of individual energy companies, in particular the Yukos oil company. Indeed, Yukos's lobbying against government tax legislation is often cited as a factor that contributed to the arrest of Mikhail Khodorkovskii towards the end of this parliament.

In the Fourth (2004–07) and Fifth Dumas (2008–11), the executive's greater control over the parliament's activities reduced the latitude that business interests had enjoyed in earlier assemblies. During the Fourth Duma, which was dominated by the question of who would succeed Vladimir Putin as Russian president in 2008, parliamentary discipline was tightened, and lobbying was contained mainly within the executive branch. Occasional conflicts between the president and the government did spill over into the assembly during President Medvedev's tenure, however. Legislation regulating retail trade in the Fifth Duma, for example, provoked intense lobbying by producer (notably agricultural) and retail groups and, in the absence of a clear position within the executive, the parliament played a part in resolving this conflict.[17] Yet when the executive branch took a united position on legislation, the capacity of business representatives to exert influence was limited. This was illustrated by equally controversial legislation on the regulation of the pharmaceutical industry in the Fifth Duma, which drew sharp criticism from the pharmaceutical lobby in the parliament.[18] Despite the legislation attracting a large number of amendments, the Health Ministry was able to steer the bill through parliament without significant changes being made.

This pattern of business influence in the assembly reflects the overall decline in the parliament's legislative power. The political dominance of the executive branch has removed much of the parliament's legislative autonomy, which in turn has affected the internal mechanisms for decision-making in the lower house. Control over the legislative agenda has been centralized in the hands of the pro-executive United Russia Party. Legislative committees and other formal venues and processes such as passage of the annual budget, which in previous parliaments had provided a key focus of lobby activity, have become less central to the parliament's work (although not entirely inconsequential).

In the early Dumas, the relative weakness of executive control gave economic interests multiple opportunities to exert influence over the lawmaking process. In order to build the majorities that were required to enact legislation, the key agenda-setting actors in the assembly – party, parliamentary and committee leaders – were the prime focus of lobby activity.

The partisan organization of the State Duma made parties the main target for businesses that sought to influence the legislative process. Through their financial support of party election campaigns and membership of parliamentary party groups, business interests were well placed to shape party strategy on legislative issues. A number of parliamentary groups had particularly strong associations with business groups. In the First Duma, for example, the pro-presidential parliamentary group Stability received the backing of a number of powerful financial and industrial concerns, including Menatep, Alfa, LogoVaz and Gazprom,[19] and in the Second Duma the parliamentary groups Russia's Regions and Our Home is Russia were closely associated with companies in the energy sector.

The greater power and influence of the parliament at this time meant that business interests could make significant headway with the support of party leaders. Drawing comparisons between the Fifth Duma and earlier Dumas, the influential United Russia legislator, Viktor Pleskachevskii, revealed: 'Ten or twelve years ago it was enough [for business lobbies] to agree with one faction, to finance some of its activities, and it would, without any hesitation, stand on their side. Now if you wish to pass legislation it is necessary to get the agreement of three subjects – the Duma, government and president. This is more difficult.'[20]

Membership of political parties also enabled well-resourced candidates to acquire key legislative positions in the assembly. Senior positions in the parliamentary leadership and in legislative committees were highly valued. This was most evident in the Third Duma, which, unlike the ideologically divided Second Duma and the executive-controlled Fourth Duma, was the one most dominated by big business interests. The appointment of Vladimir Dubov to head the Duma's sub-committee on taxation is a good case in point. A former company executive and shareholder in the Yukos oil company, Dubov was widely recognized as the main force behind legislation at the Third Duma to reduce the tax burden on oil companies.

It is not surprising therefore that rankings of the most influential Duma 'lobbyists' for the early parliaments included deputies who held top positions in either the parliamentary leadership, committees or parliamentary factions and groups.[21] This pattern continued into later Dumas. The political resources, contacts and legislative expertise that legislative leaders enjoy have remained correlated with legislative influence. In studies of lobbying at the Fourth and Fifth Dumas, the Centre for the Study of Business–State Relations (*Tsentr po izucheniyu problem vzaimodeistiya biznesa i vlasti*) lists many party and committee leaders in their rankings of top lobbyists.[22] However, the main difference with earlier Dumas is that all the deputies identified in these studies were members of just one party, United Russia. These findings reflected the very different system of decision-making in the later Dumas, which gave business interests fewer points of access into the legislative process.

The election of a two-thirds majority for the United Russia Party in December 2003 produced a majoritarian organization in the State Duma.[23] One consequence of this was that the de facto centre of legislative decision-making in the lower house moved from formal agenda-setting organs like the Council of the Duma and legislative committees to bodies internal to the United Russia parliamentary party. They included the presidium of the parliamentary party, which drew up and confirmed the legislative agenda of the Duma in close consultation with officials from the government and the presidential administration, and ad hoc bodies formed by the parliamentary faction from the heads of the relevant profile committees and executive agencies to coordinate and resolve conflicts over legislation before bills were discussed in committees and on the floor. According to one estimate, just a tenth of the number of deputies at the Fifth Duma was involved in the real process of decision-making.[24]

This development went a long way towards making the legislative process more efficient, but it also rendered the formal stages of the decision-making process increasingly ceremonial. Committee hearings, for example, became less important in shaping the detail of legislation, as indicated by the reported decline of government representation at committee meetings.[25] Plenary discussions also ceased to perform an influential role in lawmaking. Even the government's official representative in the Duma, Andrei Loginov, was prepared to admit that: 'Objectively speaking, once one of the factions received a constitutional majority, the plenary sessions of the State Duma, took a procedural form. The First, and especially the Second and Third convocations were a time of lively assemblies. Then, much depended on the credibility of the arguments put forward in the chamber. This is rare today. As a rule the faction United Russia and all the other factions enter the chamber with prepared positions on this or that question. Discussion has become more formal.'[26]

The relative decline in the importance of the formal lawmaking process was most evident in the formation of the annual budget. In the earlier Dumas, the annual budget was the main focus of lobby activity. Seats in the Budget Committee were the most coveted by deputies; in the words of one former Communist deputy, Vladimir Semago, the committee was the parliament's 'most professional economic lobbyist',[27] and night-long sessions to resolve conflicts between deputies and government officials became an annual feature of the Duma's work.[28] In later Dumas, this practice was effectively undone by a series of measures aimed at usurping executive control over the budgetary process. In the Third Duma, the government used informal consultations with their coalition partners in the parliament (so-called zero readings) to reconcile key differences before the formal process commenced; in the Fourth Duma, a three-year budget cycle was introduced to mitigate the lobbying of deputies within the majority party, United Russia;[29] and, in the Fifth Duma, the time allocated to the formal consideration of the budget was reduced.[30] As a consequence, the budgetary process became swifter, more exclusive and opaque. Those deputies involved in real budget making tended to be senior figures within the United Russia faction – just one-fifth of Duma deputies exercised any real influence over the formation of the budget, according to one study[31] – and the impact that deputies had on real expenditure was significantly reduced.

Therefore, the increase in business representation in the parliament has not resulted in greater business influence over the internal activities of the assembly. The emergence of a powerful executive during the presidency of Vladimir Putin constrained the parliament's legislative autonomy and limited the opportunities available to legislators to shape the decision-making process. This development increased the capacity of the Kremlin to curb particularistic behaviour in the lower house. Potentially, it raised the ability of Russia's political leadership to bring about much-needed policies of economic modernization. However, the predominance of business interests in the lower house was also symptomatic of deeper obstacles that faced government modernization programmes aimed at delivering sustainable economic development.

Obstacles to Political and Economic Modernization

The over-representation of business interests within the Russian Parliament contrasts with the general trend that has been observed for modern industrial societies. Notwithstanding the variation in parliamentary recruitment patterns within and between Western Europe and North America, the underlying tendency is for modern democracy to produce career politicians with distinctive paths of recruitment. In modern democracies, politics is a career increasingly restricted to individuals with backgrounds in public service, with the 'gradual exclusion from the ranks of MPs... of those who have only a background in productive or distributive economic activities (like entrepreneurs, managers, workers, and agriculturalists)'.[32]

This development is understood in terms of the complexities generated by modern political systems. The opening up of political systems to different social groups, institutions and processes, it is argued, requires politicians who are more than simply similar in social profile: 'For representation to be effective, a more qualified personnel seems necessary', Cotta and Best hypothesize.[33] Central to this understanding of representation is the notion that legislators are capable of responding to the wishes of their electorates. Hence the development of representation is linked to broader democratizing processes.[34]

In Russia, the weakness of democratic representation has prevented the emergence of a responsive legislative branch. The high number of business newcomers is one feature of this problem. 'Representation' in this context is little more than a descriptive concept to encapsulate the election of businesspeople. It is not meant to imply the capacity of legislators to respond to broader electoral demands. Even the particularistic legislative influence that was associated with economic interests in the earlier parliaments became less evident with the tightening of executive control.

With the decline in the parliament's political and legislative influence, the explanations typically put forward to account for the high levels of businesspeople have focused on the personal protection that individuals gain from acquiring seats in parliament. They include, first and foremost, immunity from prosecution. In Russia's turbulent world of business, this consideration is not insignificant. Since 1994, only three Duma deputies have had their immunity revoked by the assembly for fraudulent business activity, while many more have successfully evaded prosecution with parliamentary backing. According to one estimate, 27 Duma deputies were at the centre of criminal scandals in the Fifth Duma alone (2007–11).[35]

Membership of the assembly also provides businesspeople with a means of protection in Russia's bureaucratized market system. By achieving the rank of Duma deputy or Federation Council senator, legislators become government officials. This status commands the capacity to avoid or minimize the side-payments and intrusive scrutiny that face ordinary business actors. As noted by one of Russia's most experienced former Duma deputies, Aleksei Mitrofanov, the status of deputies is a potent deterrent to predatory law enforcement agencies; faced with the threat of investigation, he explains, business deputies can always retort 'I'm in the team, I'm a member of the parliament, goodbye...'.[36]

For a society that has historically viewed officialdom with suspicion, such explanations for business representation in the Russian Parliament do little to bolster the legitimacy of representative institutions. The perception of legislators as self-serving is a contributory factor in accounting for low public confidence in the parliament. This was highlighted by the public ridicule of legislators for low attendance in Duma debates during the Fifth Duma. Even insiders sought to explain high rates of absenteeism in terms of the distractions that parliamentarians faced from outside business activities. Accounting for President Medvedev's measures to increase attendance, for example, one Duma insider explained that it was aimed at businesspeople who 'having received a mandate and who had solved their problems on Okhotnyi ryad[37] ceased to attend, saying "Leave me alone". And now that they have received the answer "It's necessary to attend" they reply "How can I possibly attend, I have a business to run".'[38]

Yet there is also a political rationale for the maintenance of this status quo. Many businesspeople who win seats in the assembly are part of the coalition that underpins the authority of Russia's political leadership. Over a quarter of United Russia's newcomers who were elected from business backgrounds in the Fifth Duma had previously held positions in regional government, mainly in regional parliaments. These individuals represented an important constituency that formed the basis of United Russia's majority in the lower house and contributed to Russia's democratic reversal.[39] Consequently, a career in public service in Russia is not indicative of the democratizing processes that have shaped parliamentary recruitment in European democracies. Indeed, as Table 8.1 shows, the recruitment of parliamentarians with a background in federal or regional government increased as the democratic nature of the regime decreased in later Dumas.

The task of constructing authoritarian coalitions is generally thought to create negative externalities for economic development. Rent seeking is one such key feature in many authoritarian regimes.[40] The exclusive nature of winning coalitions under authoritarianism, it is contended, enables their members to acquire private goods at the expense of policies that are for the public good.[41] As Bueno de Mesquita et al. argue, what constitutes good politics in an authoritarian regime (i.e. survival in office) often means bad policy: 'leaders working under institutional arrangements correlated with authoritarianism are wise to establish special privileges for their backers ... Doling out special privileges often is vital to their political survival. Autocrats can be forgiven bad policy, but they are not likely to survive the elimination of patronage or the corrupt benefits of cronyism. For autocrats, what appears to be bad policy often is good politics'.[42]

The obstacles to political modernization in Russia might therefore be expected to have had a negative effect on modernization in the economic sphere. This analysis is prominent in much of the writing on Russian politics.[43] The argument that democratic reversal has bolstered bureaucratic opposition to policies intended at promoting economic innovation is supported by a growing body of research. Studies that have stressed the increasingly conservative nature of the legislative agenda during Putin's second term,[44] and indicators like the World Bank's 'Ease of Doing Business' index, which shows a deterioration over time in the supportiveness of Russia's business environment,[45] fit with this overall analysis.

This backsliding has principally been the result of opposition to economic reform from within the executive itself. The parliament's ability to veto economic policy has been limited since the early 2000s. Yet the composition of the parliament still provides a useful insight into those economic elites who have benefited from Russia's partial economic transition from communism and who seek to maintain this status quo.

The findings of this chapter suggest that deputies from traditional and large economic sectors predominate among business actors in Russian parliamentary circles, albeit with some variation over time. This is broadly consistent with the general nature of late Soviet and early post-Soviet economic policies, which prioritized the distribution of existing property over economic development. For the Russian political scientist Oksana Gaman-Golutvina, this path of economic transition has had the effect of the 'de-modernization and re-traditionalization' of political rule.[46] In her analysis, power and property became merged in Russia leading to a 'quasi-feudalization' of the state.[47] The corollary for representative politics has been the absence of new enterprises and small business interests that could provide the support for policies aimed at sustainable economic development. With the exception of the First

Duma, deputies from small business backgrounds have been under-represented in the assembly. Such crowding out of small business is frequently identified as a major obstacle to the economic modernization of Russia and, given the state's reliance on the revenue from big business, will be difficult to overcome.[48]

Conclusion

The challenges of economic and political modernization are closely related. The task of creating a dynamic and innovative economy requires decision-makers who are capable of taking decisions that can facilitate those economic forces that drive change. In Russia, the phenomenon of business over-representation in legislative politics is symptomatic of a general problem that constrains economic modernization at all levels of government. The merger of power and property undermines the political authority that is needed to bring about such a fundamental transformation of Russian society. No matter how powerful the legislature has been in post-communist Russia, the belief that legislators are ultimately self-serving (whether accurate or not) has shaped the popular perception of representative institutions.

The weakness of political institutions is a major obstacle for leaders who are intent on modernizing any society, whether democratic or authoritarian. In modern democracies, the notion of professional politicians is meant to describe decision-makers who have the ability to bring about change; politics in other words gains a degree of autonomy, which ultimately derives from popular authority. Without the need to acquire this authority, leaders lose the capacity and/or incentive to make policies that are conducive to economic development, as the post-Stalin Soviet Union illustrated. In present-day Russia, more compliant political institutions have been interpreted as a sign of political success. However, they have also been acquired at the expense of more inclusive representative institutions that might stand a better chance of gaining the authority that is needed to engender change within society. This feature of post-Soviet political development diminishes the political resources that are available to any Russian government that attempts to modernize.

Notes

1. See S. P. Huntington (1968), *Political Order in Changing Societies* (New Haven and London: Yale University Press); M. Leontev (2010), 'Eksklyuziv: mezhdu

strok. Intervyu Vladislava Surkova' [Exclusive: Between the Lines. Interview with Vladislav Surkov], *Odnako,* 7 December, http://www.odnakoj.ru/exclusive/interline/vladislav_syrkov_mxdolzhnx_gotovitqsya_k_bydyshcej_vojnedot_nasamom_dele_kbydyshcemy_miry/.

2. See H. Best and M. Cotta (eds) (2000), *Parliamentary Representatives in Europe 1848–2000* (Oxford: Oxford University Press).

3. See T. F. Remington (2007), 'The Russian Federal Assembly, 1994–2004', *Journal of Legislative Studies,* Vol. 13, No. 1, pp. 121–41; P. Chaisty (2011), 'The Federal Assembly and the Power Vertical', in G. Gill and J. Young (eds), *Handbook of Russian Politics and Society* (London: Routledge).

4. S. M. Fish and M. Kroenig (2009), *The Handbook of National Legislatures: A Global Survey* (Cambridge: Cambridge University Press), pp. 756–7.

5. These data include deputies who were the directors and deputy directors of business and economic enterprises before their election to parliament.

6. MPs' biographies were used to code all newcomers. A. H. Arinin and A. S. Kosopkin (eds) (2006), *Gosudarstvennaya Duma Rossiiskoi Federatsii: Tom 2, 1993–2006* [The State Duma of the Russian Federation: Volume 2, 1993–2006] (Moscow: Rossiiskaya politicheskaya entsiklopediya); E. Belov et al. (2008), 'Vsya Duma' [The Whole Duma], *Kommersant Vlast,* No. 2, http://www.kommersant.ru/doc.aspx?DocsID=843330.

7. A. Litoi and L. Tagaeva (2010), 'Dokhodnyi ryad' [The Income Row], *Novaya gazeta,* No. 61, 9 June.

8. Yurii Korgunyuk describes the example in the Fifth Duma of the Communist MP Aleksei Bagaryakov, who had stood as a candidate for the centre–right Union of Right Forces party in the elections to the previous parliament. Bagaryakov, who initially failed to get elected in 2007, became a Duma deputy only after the Communist Party created a vacancy for him. Y. Korgunyuk (2010), 'Party Funding in the Russian Federation: A Tool of Bureaucratic Control', in Anthony Butler (ed.), *Paying for Politics: Party Funding and Political Change in South Africa and the Global South* (Auckland Park: Jacana Media).

9. T. Shkel (2008), 'Parlament po-slavyanski' [Parliament in a Slavic Way], *Rossiiskaya gazeta,* No. 25, 7 February.

10. Best and Cotta (note 2).

11. P. Hackett and P. Hunter (2010), *Who Governs Britain? A Profile of MPs in the New Parliament* (London: Smith Institute), http://www.smith-institute.org.uk/publications.html?category_id=3.

12. J. E. Manning (2010), *Membership of the 111th Congress: A Profile,* Congressional Research Service Report for Congress, http://opencrs.com/document/R40086/.

13. In the summer and autumn of 2003 the owners of Russia's largest oil corporation, Yukos, were arrested. Among them was Mikhail Khodorkovskii, who at the time was Russia's leading business tycoon. This event was interpreted by business as a sign of the state reasserting its control over the economy.

14. These data were compiled from a sweep of the main books, expert reports and newspaper articles on parliamentary lobbying published since 1994. They include V. M. Gerasimov, A. A. Derkach, A. S. Kosopkin and T. I. Nefedova (1999), *Psikhologiya parlamentarizma* [Psychology of Parliamentarianism]

(Moscow: Status-Kvo 97); P. A. Tolstykh (2006), *Praktika lobbizma v Gosudarstvennoi Dume Federalnogo Sobraniya Rossiiskoi Federatsii* [Lobbying in the State Duma of the Russian Federation] (Moscow: Kanon); S. Lolaeva and G. Cherkasov (2007), *Povsednevnaya zhizn deputatov gosudarstvennoi dumy* [Everyday Life of the Deputies of the State Duma] (Moscow: Molodaya gvardiya); P. A. Tolstykh (2007), *GR Praktikum po lobbizmu v Rossii* [GR Practical Work on Lobbying in Russia] (Moscow: Alpina Biznes Buks); P. A. Tolstykh (ed.) (2007), *Luchshie lobbisty Gosudarstvennoi Dumy FS RF IV sozyva: 2003–2007* [The Best Lobbyists of the 4th State Duma: 2003–2007] (Moscow: Tsentr po izucheniiu problem vzaimodeistviia biznesa i vlasti) [Centre for the Study of Interaction Problems between Business and the Authorities]; *'Tenevaya Duma': interesy dumskikh lobbistov* (2001) [The Shadow Duma: Interests of Duma Lobbyists] (Moscow: Tsentr politicheskoi informatsii). This sweep of the literature produced a dataset of 100 laws for the first four Dumas.

15. At the time of writing, the Fifth Duma had not completed its term; hence comparable analysis was not available for that parliament. Yet it is interesting to note that one of the main lobbying campaigns at the Fifth Duma involved the Law 'On Trade'. This legislation was at the centre of a struggle between the food producer and retail sectors – two areas of the economy that achieved much higher levels of representation in the Fifth Duma.

16. P. Chaisty (2006), *Legislative Politics and Economic Power in Russia* (Basingstoke: Palgrave Macmillan), p. 149.

17. See T. Stanovaya (2009), *Zakon o torgovle: politika i lobbizm* [The Law on Trade: Policy and Lobbying] http://www.politcom.ru/9334.html; I. Kalinina (2010), 'Petlya bumeranga' [The Loop of the Boomerang], *Biznes-zhurnal*, No. 3, 20 March, http://offline.business-magazine.ru/2010/169/330352/page/1/.

18. See D. Nikolaeva (2010), 'Lekarstvam propishut popravki' [They Prescribe Amendments to Medicine], *Kommersant*, No. 20, 5 February; D. Nikolaeva (2010), 'Lekarstva upakovany pod kontrol tsen' [Medicine is Packed under Price Control], *Kommersant*, No. 43, 15 March.

19. Y. Fedorov (1995), 'Economic Interests and Lobbies in the Formulation of Russian Foreign Policy', *Post-Soviet Business Forum Briefing*, No. 5 (London: Royal Institute of International Affairs), p. 2.

20. E. Glybina, V. Dyatlikovich and A. Tsygankov (2010), 'Kak rabotaet russkaya demokratiya' [How Russian Democracy Works], *Russkii reporter*, No. 35, 9 September.

21. Chaisty (note 16), p. 141.

22. Tolstykh (2006) (note 247); P. A. Tolstykh (ed.) (2010), *Luchshie lobbisty Gosudarstvennoi Dumy FS RF V sozyva: 2007–2010* [The Best Lobbyists of the 5th State Duma: 2007–2010] (Moscow: Tsentr po izucheniyu problem vzaimodeistviya biznesa i vlasti) [Centre for the Study of Mutual Problems between Business and the Authorities].

23. P. Chaisty (2005), 'Majority Control and Executive Dominance: Parliament–President Relations in Putin's Russia', in Alex Pravda (ed.), *Leading Russia: Putin in Perspective* (Oxford: Oxford University Press).

24. Tolstykh (2010) (note 14).

25. V. Khamraev (2007), 'Zakonodatelnaya vlast "otlichilas" ispolnitelnostyu' [The Legislature was 'Singled Out' by the Executive Power], *Kommersant*, No. 213, 20 November.

26. M. Barshchevsky (2009), 'Dokumenty s temnym proshlym' [Documents with a Dark Past], *Rossiiskaya gazeta: yuridicheskaya nedelya*, No. 5009, 1 October.
27. B. Stolyarov (2000), 'Lobbit po-russki – 2' [Lobbying in Russian – 2], *Novaya gazeta*, No. 30, 17 July.
28. See V. Belchenko (2010), 'Ona byudzhetu otdana' [The Budget Is Presented], *Ogonek*, No. 6, 15 February; L. Tagaev (2010), 'Nizhnyaya palata N. 5' [The Lower Chamber no. 5], *Novaya gazeta*, No. 44, 26 April.
29. Khamraev (note 25).
30. E. Zubchenko (2010), 'Uskorenie byudzheta' [Speeding-Up the Budget], *Novye izvestiya*, No. 102, 15 June.
31. Tolstykh (2010) (note 14).
32. Cotta and Best (note 2) p. 14.
33. Ibid., p. 18.
34. H. Pitkin (1967), *The Concept of Representation* (Berkeley: University of California Press).
35. I. Petrov (2010), 'Deputatam postavili na vid' [Under Deputies' Scrutiny], *RBK Daily*, 23 September.
36. Glybina, Dyatlikovich and Tsygankov (note 20).
37. Okhotnyi ryad (Hunters' Row) is the historic name for the street in central Moscow where the State Duma is located.
38. Glybina, Dyatlikovich and Tsygankov (note 20).
39. See O. J. Reuter and T. Remington (2009), 'Dominant Party Regimes and the Commitment Problem: The Case of United Russia', *Comparative Political Studies*, Vol. 42, No. 4, pp. 501–26.
40. R. Wintrobe (1998), *The Political Economy of Dictatorship* (New York: Cambridge University Press).
41. B. Bueno de Mesquita, A. Smith, R. M. Siverson, and J. D. Morrow (2003), *The Logic of Political Survival* (Cambridge, MA and London: MIT Press), p. 8.
42. Ibid., p. 19.
43. E.g. see M. McFaul and K. Stoner-Weiss (2008), 'The Myth of the Authoritarian Model', *Foreign Affairs*, Vol. 87, No. 1 (January/February), pp. 68–84.
44. T. F. Remington (2008), 'Patronage and the Party of Power: President–Parliament Relations Under Vladimir Putin', *Europe–Asia Studies*, Vol. 60, No. 6, pp. 959–87.
45. World Bank (2010), *Doing Business 2011: Making a Difference for Entrepreneurs* (Washington, DC: World Bank).
46. O. Gaman-Golutvina (2007), 'Political Elites in the Commonwealth of Independent States: Recruitment and Rotation Tendencies', *Comparative Sociology*, Vol. 6, No. 1–2, p. 136.
47. O. Gaman-Golutvina (2008), 'Changes in Elite Patterns', *Europe–Asia Studies*, Vol. 60, No. 6, p. 1034.
48. S. Gehlbach (2008), *Representation through Taxation: Revenue, Politics, and Development in Postcommunist States* (Cambridge: Cambridge University Press).

9
De-bureaucratizing the Small Business Sector

Eugene Huskey

Introduction

Much of the Western analysis of Russian economic policy in recent years has focused on the heavy hand of the Russian state in large-scale firms that operate in strategic sectors of the economy.[1] However, alongside the renewed Russian state interest in the commanding heights of the economy, there have been notable efforts by the government to de-bureaucratize the environment for small business formation and development. Launched in 2001 with the adoption of the Law on the Registration of Juridical Persons, this initiative has gone through several iterations and is now one of the most high-profile policy concerns of the Putin–Medvedev tandem.[2]

In order to show how bureaucratic agents have resisted change and how the political leadership has responded to this resistance, this chapter examines the development of laws and policies designed to minimize transaction costs in the small business sector. The numerous reforms introduced since 2001 were intended to reduce the opportunities for state officials to use registration, licensing, state contracts, and inspections to extract rents from small business owners.[3] The focus of this chapter is on policy and practice relating to inspections, specifically on the reforms introduced since Medvedev's accession to the presidency in 2008.

Legislative Reform on the Deregulation of Small Business

In a speech to the State Council on 26 March 2008, shortly after he took office as president, Dmitrii Medvedev launched the latest round in the deregulation of Russian small business. After noting that 'small business…is the foundation for the expansion of a middle class', Medvedev reaffirmed the ambitious target contained in the 'Putin Plan for 2020' of a small and mid-sized business sector that should account for 60–70 per cent of employment.[4] In a speech to the government in July 2008, Putin continued this theme by noting that during the preceding three years the number of small businesses in Russia had grown from 840,000 to 1.14 million,[5] yet that still represented less than 12 per cent of total employment and less than 17 per cent of the country's GDP. These figures contrasted unfavourably with those from Eastern and Western Europe.[6]

Russia's political leadership recognized that there were many causes of the lag in the development of the small business sector, but they focused on deregulation as the appropriate state response to the problem. In Putin's words, 'the businessman, as before, confronts various forms of barriers and difficulties. We have to use the most decisive means to clear away these bureaucratic hurdles [*zavaly*]'.[7] In perhaps the most powerful critique of the state bureaucracy as the enemy of the small business owner, President Medvedev warned on a visit to Gagarin, Smolensk *oblast*, in early August 2008 that 'our law enforcement agencies and other state authorities must stop terrorizing [*koshmarit*] business!'[8] Coming immediately after Medvedev had signed a decree attacking state corruption, this visit was a carefully orchestrated media event, in which the Russian president bantered for the cameras with local business owners. When he asked them who 'was biting them the most', who was 'drinking [their] blood', the immediate response from locals was Rospotrebnadzor, the agency responsible for inspections in the field of retail trade. Medvedev then turned to two leading law enforcement officials who accompanied him on the trip – Yurii Chaika, the Procurator-General, and Rashid Nurgaliev, head of the Ministry of Internal Affairs (MVD) – who were busy taking notes. The Russian president observed that in Russia signals are important, and he had just given them a signal to take action on this issue.[9] Medvedev was speaking to the leaders of two law enforcement agencies that had been among the most persistent opponents of earlier measures to deregulate Russian business.[10]

New Policy on Registration, Licensing and Inspections

The latest round of policy initiatives on the deregulation of business has led to new legislation on three different fronts: registration, licensing and certification, and inspections. Although it is tempting to view these changes as cosmetic, or virtual, reforms launched by political leaders who merely feign indignation at the predatory practices of their 'agents' in the Russian state, there are elements in the new policies that seem to go beyond the usual half-measures. This is especially evident in the philosophical foundations of certain changes to the registration and licensing regimes. The traditional Russian approach to business regulation has been to assume the dishonesty of the merchant and to legislate accordingly. The result, as Thomas Owen noted with respect to the state regulation of business in the tsarist era, was 'rigid laws tempered by arbitrary exceptions for favored petitioners'.[11] On certain matters, however, recent legislation has been based on a level of trust in the petitioner that is altogether unusual for Russia, an approach that has been championed by the primary institutional source of liberalizing policy during the past decade, the Ministry of Economic Development.[12]

For example, a government directive issued in July 2009 allows small businesses engaged in 36 different kinds of activity to inform the relevant state agency of their intent to conduct business rather than forcing them to seek permission from state officials ahead of time.[13] This policy not only removes a bureaucratic toll-keeper but also begins to shift the conceptual ground that governs relations between the state and the business community. Instead of a presumption of culpability, the new policy introduces a presumption of decency [*dobrosovestnost*], which has the potential to reduce the heavy hand of the state in Russian business. This approach, called the notification method, or *uvedomitelnyi poryadok* in Russian, is also being applied to the certification of products. This promises to reduce the share of products requiring state certification from 85 per cent at present to 15 per cent. Moreover, in 2011 it will be possible to provide the information to the relevant state agencies online.[14]

There are of course caveats to what appears to be a revolution in this area of business regulation. First, as suggested above, some licensing and certification will not be subject to the 'notification method', specifically those goods and services that pose a potential threat to health or security. Second, there are numerous state agencies that are refusing to adhere to the notification method and continue to require that businesses receive documentation from the state (*spravki*) before offering goods and services to the public.[15] One study showed that, whereas 69 per cent of officials in the Federal Tax Service and 65 per cent of local government officials approved of this reform, only 29 per cent of personnel in the fire inspectorate favoured the change.[16] To ensure that the law is implemented as written, the country's leadership will need to demonstrate the requisite political will, whether through direct signals to state agencies or by holding governors or regional procurators accountable for punishing agencies that fail to respect the laws on the notification method.

Since Medvedev's accession to the presidency, the political leadership has devoted special attention to state inspections as an impediment to the development of small business. According to Prime Minister Putin, state agencies were conducting 20 million inspections of businesses each year, which cost the state 160 billion roubles, not including the cost to business. Each of those inspections was an opportunity for the receipt of bribes by state officials. In some cases, inspectors accepted money directly from business owners to cover up an actual violation of rules, instead of reporting the offence and requiring the business to pay a fine to the state; in other instances, inspectors extorted money from business owners by finding violations when none was there or by threatening to perform monitoring activities that were either expensive or intrusive. Medvedev himself reported that the system of state inspections imposed an unofficial tax on businesses that equalled approximately 10 per cent of revenues, which is an especially heavy burden on small businesses that operate with very narrow margins.[17]

As part of his larger campaign against corruption, in May 2008 President Medvedev issued a decree that outlined an initiative to improve the business climate in Russia, in part by reducing the scope for self-dealing by state inspectors who review the activities of small and mid-size businesses. This wide-ranging decree, entitled 'On Immediate Measures for Reducing the Administrative Barriers to the Conduct of Business', ordered the preparation within two months of legislation that would introduce various safeguards against the abuse of power by state agencies charged with the oversight of businesses. It also called for simplifying and reducing the cost for connection to the electric grid by small and mid-sized businesses, expanding access of businesses to long-term leases of government buildings, and forming a council for the support of small and mid-sized businesses in each federal district, with business representatives to be included on the councils.[18]

Based on the principles outlined in the May decree, in December 2008 the Russian Parliament passed one of the most important pieces of legislation on state–business relations in the post-communist era.[19] It was, in effect, a revision and expansion of a predecessor law that helped to launch the initial round of reforms of small business at the beginning of Putin's presidency.[20] The new law contained several provisions designed to limit the exposure of small and mid-sized businesses to state inspections. First, it expanded from two to three years the length of time between planned inspections of businesses. Second, it allowed unplanned inspections only in cases where violations of state regulations threatened the life or health of consumers, and even in these instances the state agency had to receive advance permission from the regional procuracy for the unplanned inspection. Third, the law reduced the total inspection time per year to 20 days for small companies, 50 hours for most proprietorships, and 15 hours for what are termed microenterprises, such as small shops and kiosks. There are also a number of other regulations that limit the freedom of manoeuvre of state inspectors, such as the need to obtain signed approval for an inspection from the head or deputy head of the inspecting agency and to inform the firm of the specific subjects of the inspection in advance.

The law of December 2008, most of whose provisions went into effect on 1 July 2009, also injected the Procuracy into the system of planned inspections by requiring that state agencies provide, by 1 September each year, a list of planned inspections for the following calendar year. By 1 October, the Procuracy is to compile and publish a consolidated schedule of planned inspections. By introducing the Procuracy as a gatekeeper in the process of planned inspections, the political leadership appeared to have three goals in mind: to ensure advanced notification of inspections, whether on-site or 'documentary'; to combine inspections where appropriate in order to lessen the administrative burden on small and mid-sized businesses; and to ensure that the three-year gap between planned inspections is respected by state officials.

Finally, the law of December 2008 restricted the MVD's involvement in businesses to criminal investigations of business activity. Previously, the police had frequently used what were called 'extra-procedural' methods to impose sanctions on businesses for purely administrative violations, a practice that heightened the vulnerability of businesses to bribe-taking. As a directive from the Procurator-General noted in March 2008, 'the MVD had not taken adequate measures for decriminalization of the business sphere'.[21] Many studies of the attitudes of business owners towards the state illustrate that the police have been viewed as among the most heavy-handed representatives of the state in Russian business.[22]

Implementing the New Legislation on State Inspections

Because the new legislation on state inspections came into effect as recently as the summer of 2009, it is not possible to draw firm conclusions about its impact on relations between business and the state in

Russia. The initial evidence, however, suggests that the efforts of the political leadership to lighten the regulatory burden on small and mid-sized business are being at least partially realized. Assessing the first six months of experience under the new legislation, Prime Minister Putin remarked in a meeting with Elvira Nabiullina, Minister of Economic Development, that the Procuracy has thus far rejected 48 per cent of requests from state agencies for unplanned inspections. 'Not bad results [*eto samo po sebe neplokho*]', according to the prime minister.[23]

Not surprisingly, the burden of inspections on small and mid-sized businesses continues to vary widely across the country. In Moscow, home to a quarter of all Russian small and mid-sized businesses, former Mayor Yurii Luzhkov suspended all planned inspections for the second half of 2009 and the city Procuracy turned down 75 per cent of all requests for unplanned inspections during the summer of that year.[24] According to one source, Moscow led all areas of the country in 2009 in the share of unjustified requests for unplanned inspections, which is in accordance with the city's longstanding reputation for inspections and other administrative barriers that are unusually disruptive to business activity.[25]

A report from the Procuracy in the Urals Federal District noted that procurators had received 3500 requests for unplanned inspections in the last seven months of 2009, of which 1400, or 40 per cent, were turned down. The Procuracy in this federal district even rejected half of the planned inspections for the 2010 calendar year, either because the subject enterprises had already been inspected within three years or because they had been operating for less than a year. In other words, the various inspectorates in the vast Urals Federal District were requesting approval for unplanned inspections that clearly violated basic provisions of the law of December 2008.[26]

This latest round of de-bureaucratization of the business environment has not, of course, created a neo-liberal regulatory regime in Russia. First, the recent legislative and policy changes have not restricted inspections conducted by a whole range of state agencies, including those concerned with taxation, anti-monopoly policy, foreign investment, and payments to the Social Fund.[27] Second, and predictably for any bureaucracy, inspection agencies are exploiting loopholes in the law to reclaim their access to small and mid-sized businesses. For example, after being turned down by the Procuracy in their attempt to conduct an unplanned on-site inspection of firms, two agencies organized off-site 'documentary' inspections instead.[28] Third, many state officials are simply circumventing the Procuracy and conducting unplanned and unsanctioned inspections. It is difficult to obtain accurate information on the scale of this phenomenon, but it appears to be widespread. Finally, based on reports from the Procuracy, MVD officials continue to exceed their authority by conducting administrative inspections under the guise of criminal investigations.[29]

Yet despite the limits of reform legislation and the robust resistance of many state agencies to the introduction of a more business-friendly regulatory regime, there is evidence that among the many concerns of small and mid-sized businesses, state inspections are imposing lower transaction costs than in the past. The Government Commission on Small Business Development, headed by Igor Shuvalov, reported in early 2010 that if one excludes the inspections conducted by tax and law enforcement agencies, the number of state inspections of small and mid-sized businesses declined from 20 million in 2006 to 1.2 million as of the second half of 2009.[30] The results of a multi-year, World Bank-supported survey indicate that the intensity of state inspections in the small business sector has declined from 3.3 for each business in a six-month period in 2002 to 1.3 per business in a six-month period in 2009. The same study reported that, whereas almost 30 per cent of small and mid-sized firms in Moscow experienced pressure to give bribes during state inspections, that figure had fallen to about 13 per cent by late 2009.[31]

Conclusion

At a meeting in March 2010 that was organized by the small-business association OPORA (the All-Russian NGO of Small and Medium-sized Businesses), Prime Minister Putin insisted that the ban on baseless state inspections 'is not some kind of *kampaneishchina*, not a temporary anti-crisis measure, but the essence of state policy'.[32] Given Russia's long history of half-measures and virtual reforms in economics, law, and public administration, a considerable measure of scepticism is in order regarding the outcome of the latest effort to de-bureaucratize the Russian economy. In some respects, the mobilization of the procuracy in the fight against corruption is very much in keeping with traditional Russian responses to the pathologies of a statist regime. When in doubt, create yet another checking mechanism or strengthen those already in existence, and then watch while those institutions are infected by the disease they are asked to cure. One of the vice-presidents of OPORA complained in April 2010 that the Procuracy was already losing the battle with other state agencies intent on maintaining their freedom of manoeuvre with regard to business owners. In the words of this individual, 'it seems that the "Procuracy barrier" set out in the law has stopped working'.[33]

However, there are two elements of this latest round of reforms that may represent a break with the past. The first, and more problematic, is the application of the 'theory of one *krysha*'. As Konstantin Sonin has observed, when the 'process of the collection of bribes is fully decentralized, and the sanitation inspector, and fire inspector and all the other inspectors don't coordinate their activity – the burden on firms will be greater than in the case when bureaucrats follow the orders of a single '*krysha*'.[34] Thus, with the Procuracy serving as a single *krysha* – by dramatically reducing the number of bureaucratic agents who answer to the principal – Russian businesses should be able to operate in a less intrusive administrative environment, as long as the Procuracy enjoys the support of the political principal and is able and willing to constrain the agents who operate beneath it.

It is likely, of course, that the Procuracy will become an essential pillar in a new 'corruption vertical'.[35] It has the authority to conduct unplanned inspections itself and to serve as the gatekeeper for inspections of most other state agencies, which considerably increases its ability to extract bribes from business owners. In this regard, the value of its currency rose considerably in early 2010 when the Procuracy was granted the right to vet applications for inspections of big businesses as well as small. However, as suggested above, even a more corrupt Procuracy would probably lower the overall transaction costs for Russian business by consolidating rent collection in a smaller number of hands. This consolidation should also make it easier for the political leadership to manage the state bureaucracy and its relations with business.

Finally, the emphasis of recent policy on the 'notification method' also considerably reduces the scope for bribe taking. This reform clears away administrative barriers by allowing, in many cases, a simple submission of documentation to replace the formal receipt of state approval for the certification of products and the commencement of business activity. Thus, since 2001, the trajectory of de-bureaucratization of business in Russia has proceeded from a complex regulatory regime with multiple gatekeepers to a simplified set of regulations with fewer gatekeepers, some of whom run interference for petitioners with other state agencies, to, in some cases, a form of self-reporting and self-regulation that rests on the presumption of decency rather than culpability of Russian business owners. The task ahead is to carefully assess the impact of this policy trajectory on everyday relations between business and the state.

In this sphere at least, policies adopted in the past decade appear to serve as a countervailing current to the hardening of political relations between state and society.

Notes

1. See e.g. P. Hanson and E. Teague (2005), 'Big Business and the State in Russia', *Europe–Asia Studies*, Vol. 57, No. 5, pp. 657–80; and P. Domjan and M. Stone (2010), 'A Comparative Study of Resource Nationalism in Russia and Kazakhstan, 2004–2008', *Europe–Asia Studies*, Vol. 62, No. 1, pp. 35–62.
2. Kontseptsiya administrativnoi reformy v RF v 2006–2008 godakh, Rasporyashenie Pravitelstva RF Ot 25 oktyabrya 2005g. N1789-g [The Concept of Administrative Reform] (2005). In October 2005 Russia adopted a Concept on Administrative Reform for the period from 2006 to 2008 that promised, on paper at least, to redefine relations between business and the state. Building on Putin's remarks to the country in his State of the Union message that year, the Concept document noted that, '[i]n essence, the realm of state administration has turned into a constraining factor for socio-economic development of the country and the raising of its international competitiveness'.
3. As Nonna Barkhatova observed with regard to the barriers to entry for small business in the 1990s, 'To set up a trading point (kiosk or small shop) required 40 state departments and licenses costing 40,000 rubles'. N. Barkhatova (2000), 'Russian Small Business, Authorities, and the State', *Europe–Asia Studies*, Vol. 52, No. 4, pp. 657–76; see also E. Huskey (2007), 'Lowering the Barriers to Entry for Russian Small Business', in K. Hendley (ed.), *Remaking the Role of Law: Commercial Law in Russia and the CIS* (Juris Publishing).
4. Vstupitelnoe slovo na zasedanii prezidiuma Gosudarstvennogo soveta 'O preodolenii administrativnykh barerov v razvitii malogo biznesa i merakh nalogovoi politiki, napravlennykh na stimulirovanie ego rosta, 27 marta 2008, Tobolsk [Introduction at the Meeting of the Presidium of the state council "On Overcoming Obstacles in the Development of Small Business, and Measures of Tax Policy to Stimulate the Growth of this Business, 27 March 2008], www.kremlin.ru/text/appears/2008/03/200925.shtml.
5. M. Kalmatskii (2008), 'K bareram' [To the Barriers], *Novye Izvestiya*, 15 July no. 123, p. 3.
6. 'Vstupitelnoe slovo' [Introduction] (note 4); A. Zhuplev (2009) 'Small Business in Russia: Trends and Outlook', *Baltic Rim Economies*, Expert Article 416.
7. Kalmatskii, 'K bareram' (note 5).
8. A. Latyshev (2008), 'Khvatit koshmarit biznes!' [Stop Horrifying Business], *Izvestiya*, www.izvestia.ru/russia/article3119031/.
9. Latyshev ibid.
10. T. Mukhamatulin (2009), 'Khot koshmarit nakonets perestanut' [If Only They Stopped Horrifying Business], *Vzgliad*.
11. T. Owen (1991), *The Corporation under Russian Law, 1800–1917: A Study in Tsarist Economic Policy* (Cambridge: Cambridge University Press), p. 210.

12. E. Zibrova (2010), '"Malysham" uproshchayut zhizn' [Life of Small Business is to Become More Simple], *RBK Daily*, 29 January.
13. Ob uvedomitelnom poryadke nachala osushchestvleniya otdelnykh vidov predprinimatelskoi deyatelnosti, Postanovlenie Pravitel'stva RF ot 16.07.2009 N 584 [On the Notifying Procedure at the Beginning of Different Kinds of Business Activity].
14. Maksim Tovkailo (2008), 'Obogashchaites na zdorove' [Get Enriched on Health], *Gazeta*, no. 128, 11 July 2008, p. 9.
15. Zibrova (note 12).
16. *Monitoring administrativnykh barerov razvitiya malogo predprinimatelstva: rezultaty 7-mi raundov, 2001–2009* [Monitoring Administrative Barriers for the Development of Small Business] (Rossiiskaia shkola: CIFER, 2009); Anatoly Zhuplev (2009), 'Small Business in Russia – Trends and Outlook', Baltic Rim Economies, Expert Article 416, 30 October.
17. 'Vstupitelnoe slovo', 'Introduction' (note 4).
18. This presidential decree followed on the heels of a directive by the Procurator-General that ordered procurators to do more to protect business from unnecessary inspections, in part by coordinating inspections of state agencies to prevent duplication. 'O neotlozhnykh merakh po likvidatsii administrativnykh ogranichenii pri osushchestvlenii predprinimatelskoi deyatelnosti, Ukaz Prezidenta RF ot 15 maia 2008 g, N 797 [On Urgent Measures to Liquidate Administrative Restrictions on Business Activities. Presidential Decree, 15 May 2008]; Ob organizatsii prokurorskogo nadzora za soblyudeniem prav subektov predprinimatelskoi deyatelnosti (s izmeneniyami na 30 aprelya 2009 goda),' Prikaz Generalnoi Prokuratury RF ot 31 marta 2008 g, N 53 [On the Organization of Surveillance by the Prosecutor Monitoring the Rights of the Subjects of Business. Order by the Prosecutor-General, 31 March 2008].
19. O zashchite prav yuridicheskikh lits i individualnykh predprinimatelei pri osushchestvlnenii gosudarstvennogo kontrolya (nadzora) i munitsipalnogo kontrolya, Federalnyi zakon N 294-F3 ot 26 dekabrya 2008 g. [Defending the Rights of Judicial Persons and Individual Businessmen in Connection with State Control (investigation) and Municipal Inspection, Federal Law of 26 December 2008].
20. O zashchite prav yuridicheskikh lits i individualnykh predprinimatelei pri provedenii gosudarstvennogo kontrolya (nadzora), Federalnyi zakon ot 8 avgusta 2001, N134-F3 [Defending the Rights of Judicial Persons and Individual Businessmen in Connection with State Control (investigation) and Municipal Inspection, Federal Law of 8 August 2001].
21. Ob organizatsii prokurorskogo nadzora za soblyudeniem prav subektov predprinimatelskoi deyatelnosti (s izmeneniyami na 30 aprelya 2009 goda), Prikaz Generalnoi Prokuratury RF ot 31 marta 2008 g, N 53 [On the Organization of Surveillance by the Prosecutor Monitoring the Rights of the Subjects of Business. Order by the Prosecutor-General, 31 March 2008].
22. See e.g. *Monitoring administrativnykh barerov razvitiya malogo predprinimatelstva: rezultaty 7-mi raundov, 2001–2009* (note 16).
23. D. Butrin and A. Shapovalov (2010), 'Vertikal goskontrolya zamknut na Prokuraturu' [The Vertical of State Control is Reserved for the Procurator], *Kommersant*, No. 15, 29 January, p. 2.

24. Evgeniya Zubchenko (2010), 'Oni prosto zverstvuyut' [They Just Commit Atrocities], *Novye izvestia*, 20 May; Anatoly Zhuplev (2009), 'Small Business in Russia –Trends and Outlook', *Baltic Rim Economies*, Expert Article 416, 30 October.

25. Kseniya Batanova (2010), 'Genprokuratura upolovinila proverki biznes' [The Procurator- General Cut by Half the Investigation of Business], *Gazeta*, 20 January.

26. 'Itogi nadzornoi deyatelnosti organov Prokuraturoi Uralskogo federalnogo okruga po zashchite prav yuridicheskikh lits i individualnykh predprini-matelei pri osushchestvlenii gosudarstvennogo kontrolya (nadzora) i munit-sipalnogo kontrolya', 18 June 2010 [Conclusions of the Investigative Activity of the Procurator of the Ural Federal District Concerning the Defence of the Rights of Judicial Persons and Individual Businessmen During State and Municipal Control (Investigation)], www.genprok-urfo.ru/library/?cid=6.

27. There are consistent reports from business owners that in the wake of the economic downturn and the concomitant pressures on state revenues, tax inspectors have become especially aggressive in their dealings with busi-nesses, although in these cases the payments are far more likely to go into the coffers of the state rather than the pockets of the bureaucrats. The tax office is perceived as one of the least corrupt of the state institutions.

28. 'O rabote organov prokuratury oblasti po zashchite subektov predprinima-telskoi deyatelnosti, Prokuratura Kalingradskoi oblasti' [On the Work of the Regional Procurator on Defending Subjects of Business Activity], www. prokuratura39.ucoz.ru/news/2010–01–27–304.

29. Ilya Zinenko (2010), 'Chinovniki nashli sposoby koshmarit biznes v ramkakh zakona' [Officials Found Ways to Horrify Business Within the Framework of the Law], *Gazeta*, 22 April.

30. '24 fevralya sostoyalos zasedanie Pravitelstvennoi komissii po razvitii malogo i srednego predprinimatelstva' [On 24 February a Meeting of the Government Commission on the Development of Small and Medium-Sized Business Took Place] Obshchestvennyi sovet po razvitiyu malogo biznesa [The Public Council on the Development of Small Business], 26 February 2010, www.osspb.ru/osnews/5673/.

31. *Monitoring administrativnykh barerov razvitiya malogo predprinimatelstva: rezultaty 7-mi raundov, 2001–2009* [Monitoring Administrative Barriers to the Development of Small Business: Results of the 7th Round, 2001–2009] (Rossiiskaya shkola, CIFER: 2009).

32. A. Kolesnikov (2010), 'Malyi biznes zashchitili ot maloi vlasti' [Small Business Was Defended from Local Authorities], *Kommersant*, 24 March.

33. I. Zinenko (2010), 'Chinovniki nashli sposoby koshmarit biznes v ramkakh zakona', *Gazeta*, 22 April.

34. K. Sonin (2007), 'Pravila igry: uspeshnaya reforma' [The Rules of the Game: A Successful Reform], *Vedomosti*, 18 June; and A. Shleifer and R. Vishny (1993), 'Corruption', *Quarterly Journal of Economics*, Vol. 108, No. 3, pp. 599–617.

35. D. Butrin and A. Shapovalov (2010), 'Vertikal goskontrolya zamknut na Prokuraturu' [The Vertical of State Control is Reserved for the Procurator], *Kommersant*, No. 15, 29 January, p. 2.

10
United Russia's Political Recruitment in the Russian Regions and 'the Strengthening of the Power Vertical': The Case of Novgorod Region

Clementine Fauconnier

Introduction

This chapter presents a regional case study that analyses the role of the 'party of power', United Russia, in the policy of centralization pursued by Vladimir Putin since he became president in 2000. How does the party's increasing influence on political recruitment at the regional and local levels contribute to the reinforcing of central authority over regional elites, especially the governors? I focus on the candidate selection process in the Novgorod region – which is situated in the northwestern federal district of Russia, between Moscow and St Petersburg – and more specifically on the developments of 2007–08, when a significant part of the former regional political elite was replaced. The study of United Russia's political recruitment in the Russian regions will also shed light on the party's role and autonomy in the contemporary Russian political system.

After a decade characterized by state weakness and the development of contract federalism[1] between Boris Yeltsin and the leaders of the most powerful regions, one of the most challenging issues for Vladimir Putin was the establishment of new relations between Russia's federal centre and the regions. In his first State of the Union Address, in July 2000, the newly elected president affirmed the necessity to 'admit that federative relations in Russia have not been fully built and developed [and that] regional autonomy is often interpreted as a sort of permission to disorganize the State'.[2] He then announced his wish to 'increase presidential vertical structures in the regions, ... [and] enhance the effectiveness of state power'.[3] This programme of federal reforms, conducted under the slogan of 'strengthening the power vertical', considerably reinforced central authority over regional political elites,[4] especially after the elimination of gubernatorial elections that came into force in 2005.

At the same time, the adoption since 2001 of new legislation on political parties and elections[5] also contributed to changing the nature of political competition – or non-competition – especially in the regions.[6] The many constraints imposed by the law on political parties led to the disappearance of regional political formations and the marginalization of many others, while the shift from a mixed electoral system to a fully proportional one with a 7 per cent barrier to elect the deputies to the lower house of the Parliament – the State Duma – *imposed a party affiliation on all candidates*. If the proclaimed goal of these reforms from the outset was to strengthen political parties[7] in a party-system until then described as 'fragmented' and 'weakly institutionalized',[8] they above all benefited one political formation: the United Russia Party.

Created in December 2001 to support the President, United Russia differs from the 'parties of power' – 'electoral blocs organized by state actors to participate in parliamentary elections'[9] – that existed under Yeltsin by virtue of its complex organization, its dimensions – officially 2 million members in 2008 – and its electoral successes. Not only has United Russia had an absolute majority of the seats in the State Duma since 2003 (including 238 of the 450 seats that were filled in December 2011), but the party also occupies a dominant position in most regions (see Tables 10.1, 10.2 and 10.3). In this context, United Russia plays an

Table 10.1 United Russia's share of national and regional representation in the executive and legislative branches, 2004–08[a]

	2004		November 2008	
	United Russia	**Total**	**United Russia**	**Total**[b]
State Duma deputies	304	450	315	450
Senators	45	178	117	166
Governors	36	89	74	83

Notes: [a]Tables 10.1, 10.2 and 10.3: official data from the party's website: http://edinros. er.ru/er/rubr.shtml?110112.
[b]With the programme launched in 2003 to merge some of the federal subjects, the number of federal entities decreased from 89 to 83 in March 2008.

Table 10.2   United Russia in regional assemblies, 2004–08

	2004 (of 89)	November 2008 (of 83)
Number of regional assemblies where more than two-thirds of the deputies are members of United Russia	14	43
Number of regional assemblies where more than half and fewer than two-thirds of the deputies are members of United Russia	25	36
Number of regional assemblies where fewer than half of the deputies are members of United Russia	50	4

Table 10.3   United Russia in local executive and legislative organs (including regional administrative centres, percentages)

	2004	November 2008
Executive branch	22.6	63.4
Legislative branch	13.8	40.5

increasing role in the recruitment of elected officials: in the executive and the legislative branches, at the national, regional and local levels.

Obviously, the new party of power benefited from reforms that were aimed directly at encouraging national-level political parties. Its domination has been an important means of achieving the consolidation of central executive power, control of the legislative branch and marginalization of the opposition. But the ability of the party's central structure to control regional branches, keep them independent of regional administrations and allow them autonomy in the selection of their candidates remains in question. To what extent did the fact that the majority of regional and local elected officials progressively became United Russia members contribute to establishing new – more hierarchical – relations between the federal centre and them? One way of answering this question is to analyse the party's candidate recruitment: who is selected and how? Did the former regional elite manage to retain power after joining the party and, if so, under which conditions? Or to what extent did United Russia's domination result in the replacement of former political office holders by new people? The analysis of the degree of centralization in the candidate selection process will help us to understand more precisely how and to what extent the domination of the party of power gave the central authorities more influence in the selection of elected officials and then contributed to the establishment of new centre–regional relations and to the process of power centralization that had been launched in 2000.

As well as this, an empirical analysis of United Russia's candidate selection process will allow us to consider the place occupied by the party of power. For Darrell Slider, United Russia is not 'a truly independent political party with the structures and mechanisms needed to become more fully functional and capable of enforcing its own internal discipline', which he considers as part of the Kremlin's strategy.[10] Nevertheless the definition by Vladislav Surkov[11] in February 2006 of United Russia as the principal mechanism for the continuity of the regime and the objective he set to provide the party's domination for the next 15 years[12] has renewed debates about the nature of the Russian political system. Bearing in mind the distinction made by Barbara Geddes between personalist and single-party regimes, the possibility for United Russia to 'dominate access to political office and control over policy' with, at least sometimes, the possibility to exercise 'some power over the leader'[13] and not only be a 'support party', that is, a tool for the ruling elite, remains an open issue.[14]

As shown in the case of Novgorod region, the implementation of federal reforms and the adoption of the laws on political parties strongly reinforced the position of the party of power and inversely weakened the governors, who became more and more dependent on the centre. In this context, as Andrew Konitzer[15] writes: 'Given the nature of "partification" in Russia's regions, political leaders were thus faced with two options – take on a national party label or face marginalization and opposition from within their region. With the increasing popularity of both Putin and United Russia, the choice was usually clear'. The evolution of Novgorod Governor Prusak's situation from 2002 to 2007 will demonstrate how both Putin's reforms and the rise of United Russia progressively reduced the governors' margin of manoeuvre. In Novgorod region, the first years after the creation of the party's regional branch were characterized by the continuity of political elites, who mainly remained under the control of the governor, even if they gradually joined the party. But the few months between August 2007 and March 2008 – which at the national level corresponded to the period between the beginning of the legislative campaign up to the election of Dmitrii Medvedev to the presidency – many changes occurred with (1) the resignation of the governor, (2) the designation of new deputies to the State Duma under new electoral rules, and (3) the organization of elections in the regional administrative centre, Velikii Novgorod. If the regional political system instituted by the governor in the 1990s has been widely documented,[16] the 2007–08 turn in the political trajectory of the region is especially interesting. Not only does it reduce the centralization of the party structure but it also allows us to analyse the role United Russia played in the replacement of regional political elite.

A New Governor and the End of the Regional Branch's 'Privatization'

Appointed head of the Novgorod regional administration by Boris Yeltsin in 1991, Mikhail Prusak[17] was re-elected governor in 1995 and in 1999 with 92 per cent of the vote. As Olga Kryshtanovskaya has written, Prusak belonged to the group of seven 'strong governors' who at the end of the 1990s were re-elected with more than 90 per cent of the vote.[18] In addition, Prusak, like many governors at the end of the 1990s, was able to control legislative recruitment in the region. According to Kryshtanovskaya, among the 26 regional deputies elected in October 1997, 24 were supported by him.[19] After 16 years in office, the governor's unexpected resignation on 3 August 2007, a few months before the legislative and presidential elections, constitutes a major development in the history of the region. Before analysing how this event reflects the transformation of relations between the centre and regional elites – especially the *heads of regional administrations* – it is necessary to briefly analyse the role Prusak played in the region's political trajectory and the way he coped with the rise of United Russia.

The Novgorod Oblast During The 1990s: A Regional Political System Dominated by the Governor

After the USSR collapsed, Novgorod region – poor in natural resources and with an industry that had specialized in petrochemicals, forestry and electronics – found itself in a tough situation.[20] From the start of the 1990s, Prusak set up an original strategy of political, economic and social development. In particular the liberal market-oriented reforms he implemented and the attractive business climate he created were quite successful. As Nicolai Petro writes,[21] 'While Russia's GDP declined by 2.7% annually from 1995 to 1998, the same period saw an annual growth of 3.8% for the Novgorod region. In 1999 industrial production grew 13.8%, compared to 8% for Russia, while unemployment rates fell by one-third'. The choice to encourage foreign direct investment provided more financial independence, unlike the position in other regions that continued to rely on the resources allocated by the federal centre. According to Nicolai Petro, the share of federal funding in the regional budget decreased from 50 per cent in 1994 to 26 per cent in 1998 and 8 per cent in 2000.[22] That is how the originality and accomplishments of Prusak's policies attracted the attention of many Russian and international experts who considered the economic and political development of the region as a 'model'.[23]

Many studies dedicated to centre–regional relations during the Yeltsin era emphasized the autonomy by default that regional leaders enjoyed, in a context of central state weakness. They also showed how the different ways in which they coped with economic and political difficulties contributed to the emergence of various kinds of regional political regimes. Vladimir Gelman[24] proposes a four-case typology to describe them: 'elite settlement', 'struggle over the rules', 'war of all against all' and 'winner takes all'. Because of the enormous degree of influence that Prusak had concentrated in his hands and the absence of political opposition, Gelman classified the Novgorod region in a fourth category that he defined as follows: when 'an actor can achieve total dominance over other actors and maximize its control over resources'.

But unlike many other governors, Prusak did not join the electoral coalition Fatherland-All Russia headed by Yurii Luzhkov (ex-Mayor of Moscow) and Mintimer Shaimiev (then President of Tatarstan) which, on the eve of the 1999 legislative elections, entered into competition with Unity,[25] which had been created by Yeltsin's entourage.[26] Despite the criticisms he made of some aspects of the federal government, the Novgorod governor was always loyal to Moscow and to President Boris Yeltsin.[27] In February 2000, while Putin was interim president but not yet formally elected, Prusak published with Evgenii Savchenko and Oleg Bogomolov –governors of Belgorod and Kurgan regions, respectively – a letter in which he stated that Russian federalism should be reformed and submitted a list of propositions, among which was the appointment of governors by the president.[28]

After Putin's election in March 2000, a merger process between Unity and Fatherland-All Russia was launched that was completed at United Russia's First Congress, on 1 December 2001. On this occasion, Vladimir Putin affirmed that Russia needed national parties, especially a strong party of power, deeply institutionalized in the regions[29] and able to win the majority. How did Prusak respond to the gradual rise of a major nationwide structure such as United Russia? What kind of strategy did this strong and independent governor adopt while the new President was launching his programme of reforms?

The Strategy of the Governor Facing the Rise of the United Russia Party

Eager to show his loyalty to the president but at the same time retain some degree of autonomy, Prusak's strategy consisted first of all of taking the direction of a satellite party,[30] the Democratic Party of Russia, loyal to the Kremlin and with the clear objective of undermining support for the liberal Union of Right Forces.[31] Because of his obvious lack of involvement,[32] Prusak was excluded from the Democratic Party of Russia in February 2003, but he still did not join United Russia. He even turned down an invitation to attend the second Party Congress, saying: 'Let us not delude ourselves: becoming a member of United Russia would not open new perspectives to the region. Besides we already have good relations with all the ministers'.[33] Two months later, he secured the replacement of the United Russia's Regional Political Council Secretary, Evgenii Zelenov – who had been elected to the State Duma by the Novgorod single-mandate district in 1999 – by one of his confidants, Anatolii Boitsev, who was also the regional assembly speaker.

The fact that Prusak affirmed that he did not need to attend the Party Congress because he already had good relationships with national leaders and had a capacity to negotiate the replacement of United Russia's Regional Political Council Secretary is described by Andrew Konitzer[34] as a sign of the 'partial privatization' of some regional United Russia Party structures. This was, said Konitzer, 'indicative of ... the dependence of United Russia organizations on particularly strong governors' such as Prusak, who was reelected head of the regional administration for the third time in September 2003 with 78 per cent of the vote and the support of the party of power even if he was still not a member.[35]

Last but not least, it was the candidate supported by Prusak – Aleksander Filippov – who was elected to the State Duma as an independent in December 2003 against United Russia's candidate and former Regional Political Council Secretary Evgenii Zelenov.[36] From the beginning, Zelenov had positioned himself as in opposition to the regional administration and the governor. When the new Velikii Novgorod mayor, Nikolai Grazhdankin, was elected in December 2002 with 40 per cent of the vote, Zelenov declared that 'the results of the elections show the real situation and relations of Novgorodians towards events: for the first time in ten years, there were really opposition candidates and for the first time in ten years during the campaign, discontent towards regional administration was precisely and clearly formulated. ... 40 per cent voted for the policy of Prusak, who supported this candidate. But 47 per cent voted for other candidates who pronounced against this policy. These results show that the regional administration must think again about its method and work'.[37] The ability of the governor to retain his control of political recruitment, with to some extent the agreement of United Russia leaders even though it was in conflict with their regional party representatives, reflects the situation of the party of power during its first year of existence and its dependence on governors for whom 'gubernatorial support [was] more important than dozens of devoted party members'.[38]

This situation ended in 2005 when the new system of gubernatorial appointment became effective. The decision announced by Putin after the Beslan hostage-taking tragedy of September 2004 to replace the direct election of governors by a system in which regional legislatures (where United Russia was increasingly dominant) approve candidates proposed by the president was a major turning point in Russian federalism. Deprived of the right to be elected, the governors' fate became exclusively dependent on their relations with the federal centre. It also strongly reinforced United Russia's regional branches, since many had joined to show their loyalty to the president.[39] According to the president of the *Institute of Contemporary Politics*, Vladimir Lysenko, from 2004 to March 2005 the number of regional heads of administration who were members of United Russia increased from 30 to 50. Prusak himself finally joined United Russia in June 2005, but was nevertheless able to negotiate his membership and assume the direction of the party's regional branch.

In October 2006 Prusak agreed to head the United Russia Party's list in elections to the regional assembly, which was the first occasion for the party of power to have an electoral victory in the region. United Russia won 16 of the 25 seats in the regional assembly. Apart from the support of Prusak himself, this success was also facilitated by electoral reforms that made it compulsory for half the regional deputies to be elected through a party-list system, whereas until then most regional elections had been held under a majoritarian system. As Aleksander Kynev has put it,[40] 'electoral reforms in the Russian regions were just as integral an element in the construction of the vertical of power as the reforms that preceded them'. They not only benefited the party of power but also allowed it to absorb the heads of regional administrations into the party. After the new mode of gubernatorial appointment, most of them agreed to head United Russia lists in the parliamentary elections as well. With this new role as 'party locomotives', they accepted direct responsibility for United Russia's results and also put their leadership and administrative resources at its service.

While many governors used the opportunity to request a vote of confidence before the end of their mandate,[41] Prusak repeated several times, on the last occasion in July 2007,[42] that he would not ask for one. But on 3 August 2007 he announced his resignation and four days later the regional assembly unanimously accepted the candidacy of Sergei Mitin, who had been deputy minister of agriculture and a native of Nizhnii Novgorod, on the proposal of the President's plenipotentiary representative in the North-Western Federal District, Ilya Klebanov. A few days later Mitin announced that he would head the regional list in the December 2007 Duma election – as Prusak had been preparing to do – while the Regional Assembly Deputy Speaker, Sergei Fabrichnyi, became secretary of the regional political council at the end of August.

Summing up this part of the discussion, the resignation of Prusak can be seen as a second step in United Russia's regional institutionalization after a period of 'privatization' in which the regional head of administration had been able to retain some autonomy towards Moscow and exercise some control over regional party structures. Besides, while in 2005–06 most governors were maintained in their function – as Darrell Slider notes, 'of the first forty-eight governors appointed, thirty-three were reappointments'[43] – Prusak was not the only one who was replaced at the beginning of 2007 on the eve of the legislative elections;[44] another, for instance, was the governor of Sakhalin region, Ivan Malakhov.

The Selection of New Deputies: The Primaries and the Constitution of a 'Cadre Reserve'

If we assume that the case of the Novgorod regional executive's resignation was a turning point in United Russia's candidate selection, to what extent does the selection of federal legislative candidates confirm the idea of a transformation in political recruitment? During Putin's second term (2004–08), the constitution of 'cadre reserves' became a central topic in the leader's discourses,[45] including United Russia's leaders. On the eve of the December 2007 legislative elections, and with the party of power increasingly dominant in regional parliaments, several procedures were instituted for candidate selection, including 'primaries' and a particular attempt to recruit young candidates.

State Duma Candidate Selection: The Decision to Run 'Primaries' in the Regions

Since 1993, half of the 450 seats in the Duma had been filled by proportional representation and another half had been elected through single-mandate districts. Putin announced in his speech to the government in September 2004 that the 2007 elections would be conducted on an exclusively party-list and proportional basis, with the eligibility threshold raised from 5 to 7 per cent. In addition, the 'against all' option was removed. Last but not least, only political parties would be allowed to compete, knowing that the laws on political parties had already strongly limited their ability to register. Apart from the so-called federal troika – the top three candidates who headed the electoral lists[46] – all the candidates had to be split into regional groups. That is how, in order to submit candidate lists to its party congress in October 2007, United Russia regional leaders had the task of organizing primaries in their regions.

The first reference to the term 'primaries' dates from 2006 during the preparation of the October 2006 regional elections. On this occasion, the party organized a special project named *Politzavod* (Political Factory), dedicated to the selection of young candidates, since the United Russia Supreme Council had decided in April 2006 that the entire party electoral list had to include a 20 per cent quota of young people. The day of the Politzavod contest finale, Ivan Demidov, the ideological and political coordinator of the 'Young Guard',[47] explained: 'We are experiencing an historical moment because, in fact, for the first time we have organized primaries ... "Primaries" is an English word that we could translate as preliminary elections of candidates amongst the members of one party"'.[48]

If the primaries were at the beginning used only for the selection of young candidates, the party afterwards decided to apply this selection procedure to all the candidates on the 2007 electoral list. In April 2007, the Centre of Social and Conservative Policy (CSCP) – a discussion club related to United Russia – published on its website a meeting report entitled 'Cadre Reserve: Approaches and Methods'.[49] After a detailed review of all the kinds of primary elections that are organized in the world – in the United States, in Italy, in Bulgaria – the authors of the document examined the 'positive' and 'negative' effects of such a procedure. For Russia's own legislative elections, they finally recommended 'semi-closed and media-covered primaries that would allow a prolonged campaign, attract media attention, consolidate the electorate and catch floating voters'.[50]

The De Facto Centralized Selection Procedure

In the Novgorod region, the final selection of candidates confirmed the dissociation between the regional primaries and the real choice of future Duma deputies. On 23 and 24 August 2007, at the close of meetings between electors, sympathizers, members and potential candidates, the regional leaders of the party established a ten-name list of winners from the primaries and then submitted it to the party's central authorities. But, at the same time, they underlined 'the ideological signification of this vote, which aims at uniting people around the ideas defended by the party... [and at] finding candidates able to create a Cadre Reserve and then hold functions in the organs of power'.[51]

On 1 October 2007 the Party Congress published the definitive Novgorod candidates list and added the two names of those who, in fact, would become Duma deputies: Galina Izotova and Vladimir Golovnev, since they were put respectively in second and third place on the list (see Table 10.4). Neither had any ties with the region and both were elected for the first time. At the top of the regional list Sergei Mitin was a 'locomotive', who, like 64 other governors, were 'of more interest to the public than their less-known colleagues from further down the lists who ultimately end[ed] up as deputies in their places'.[52] As for

Table 10.4 Regional final list of candidates presented by United Russia for the Duma elections (in boldface the two candidates finally elected)

Name (year of birth) Place of residence	Functions and activities
1. Sergei Mitin (1951) Velikii Novgorod	Governor of Novgorod region
2. **Galina Izotova** (1960) Vologda	Deputy of the Plenipotentiary of the President[a] in the Northwestern Federal District
3. **Vladimir Golovnev** (1970) Moscow	Founder and president of 'Vostok-service' Co-Chairman of the association Delovaya Rossiya (Business Russia), partner of United Russia
4. Oleg Onishchenko (1957) Velikii Novgorod	Chief Federal Inspector for the Novgorod region
5. Elena Kirilova (1978) Velikii Novgorod	Sports teacher Member of the 'Young Guard' Regional winner, in June 2006, of the *Politzavod* contest

Note: [a] The creation in May 2000 of seven Federal Districts headed by plenipotentiaries appointed by the president is one of the first measures of the federalism reform.

Aleksander Filippov – the Duma deputy elected as an independent in the single-mandate district of Novgorod in 2003 who joined United Russia in 2005 – he was on the regional ten-name list established after the primaries. But, in September 2007, he accepted Sergei Mitin's proposal to become his deputy governor and did not even complete his term as a Duma deputy.

Among the 315 United Russia candidates who were elected, 52 (just under 17 per cent) had not been on the lists established by the party at the end of August, after the 'primaries'.[53] This does not mean that the other candidates who were on the lists established after the primaries were chosen by party members on a competitive basis – since this was not the declared aim of that procedure – but it allows us to understand the specificity of Novgorod and the fact that, there, these 'primaries' took place in a context of regional elite renewal. The example of the two deputies' selection demonstrates a trend in the choice of legislative representatives at the national level similar to the selection of the regional executive head: the new governor and the two Duma deputies were in fact not chosen by the region and had no previous associations with it. In addition, neither the former governor nor the former Duma deputy was able to complete their terms of office. In the same way, the anticipated elections that were held in the regional administrative centre – Velikii Novgorod – occasioned the renewal of the local political elite.

Local Elections in the Regional Administrative Centre

On 2 March 2008, the same day as the presidential elections, the electors of Velikii Novgorod voted at the same time to elect a new mayor and new local assembly deputies. These anticipated elections were held in a context of crisis after the resignation of Nikolai Grazhdankin – who had been the city mayor since 2002 and had joined United Russia in January 2006 – and the dissolution of the municipal assembly. Before seeing how the selection of the candidates allows us to understand the evolution of United Russia's conquest of the local level, it is necessary to explain the origins of this municipal crisis and how the role played by United Russia in its resolution reinforced its position.

'Abolishing Mayoral Election De Facto Without Abandoning Them': The Replacement of the Velikii Novgorod Mayor

According to the new city charter that was adopted by municipal deputies in April 2005, the mayor was no longer elected but rather chosen from among the municipal deputies and appointed by them.

As Cameron Ross writes, if the question of mayoral appointment has been on the political agenda for a long time, top United Russia officials such as Igor Shuvalov, deputy secretary of the presidium of the party's General Council, 'spoke out against the direct appointment of mayors'.[54] So did Mikhail Prusak and the regional section of United Russia, who firmly resisted the abolition of mayoral election. During the summer of 2007 the United Russia Novgorod regional branch organized a petition campaign. They gathered more than 9000 signatures and started calling for the dissolution of the municipal assembly in September 2007. The extent of the crisis between United Russia, the governor and the municipal duma was such that, on 12 September, 8 of the 25 municipal deputies resigned, saying: 'We do not want the Novgorod inhabitants to blame us for having deprived them of the right to elect their mayor. The adoption of the new city charter was one of the main resolutions of this legislature'.[55] Five days later, the remaining deputies and the governor signed a 'joint declaration' modifying the city charter, restoring the mayoral election and announcing the dissolution of the municipal Duma. On 10 December 2007, a week before the end of his term, Nikolai Grazhdankin, who had been suspected of embezzlement and abuse of power, resigned in favour of his first deputy, Yurii Bobryshev, who became interim mayor until the elections, then planned for 2 March 2008.

The resignation of Grazhdankin one week before the end of his term and the fact that Bobryshev became his deputy only one week before his resignation[56] suggests there is reason to question the modalities of the transfer of power between the two mayors since it allowed the future candidate supported by the ruling party to campaign while he was already in the mayor's office. It is also interesting to note that Bobryshev – while he was a member of United Russia and a United Russia deputy in the regional assembly – decided to run as an independent. This way of playing with the partisan label can be considered as a strategy that allowed Bobryshev to present himself as a consensus, not simply a United Russia, candidate since he said he had made this decision the day after he had met the governor and the leaders of the other parties, who had agreed not to run their own candidates against him.[57]

Last but not least, Bobryshev also declared himself in favour of the appointment of capital city mayors by governors: 'If the governor had not asked me to run for mayor, I would not have. I am for the consolidation of vertical power.'[58] By claiming a legitimacy that came more from the governor's invitation to run than from the votes of the electors,

Bobryshev presented direct elections as a weakening factor in the power vertical and then justified the top-down appointment of mayors. This last statement might seem paradoxical since he became mayor thanks to the action that had been taken by the governor and the regional section of United Russia to restore mayoral elections. Given that Bobryshev was finally elected with 75 per cent of the votes in the conditions described above – already in office, member of the party of power, supported by other political parties that did not present their own candidates – the Velikii Novgorod case illustrates what Ross[59] has described as United Russia's 'effort to abolish mayoral election de facto without abandoning them'. We can also wonder to what extent the United Russia mobilization against the elimination of mayoral elections was also aimed at discrediting the members of the municipal assembly and justifying its dissolution.

Political Parties at the Local Level: United Russia's Victory and a New Generation of Local Deputies

The 2008 municipal legislative elections in Velikii Novgorod can be seen as an important turning point in the political history of the city. For the first time, a political party had a landslide victory: not only did United Russia support 15 of the 25 elected deputies[60] but, as the ten others were independents, only one parliamentary group in the municipal assembly was finally created. This was very different from the situation in the previous legislature, since in the 2004 municipal elections United Russia had presented only two candidates, neither of whom was elected. More generally, it shows the long-term transformation of Russian local politics, characterized since the beginning of the 1990s by the weakness of political parties.[61]

As the example of the municipal elections in Velikii Novgorod shows (see Table 10.5), half the number of candidates were supported by a party in 2008 whereas this had been true of only a fifth of the candidates in 2004. Besides – as the 2004 and 2008 results demonstrate – party affiliation did not seem to play any role in the success of candidates, except for United Russia in 2008. The fact that United Russia was the only party that won seats in these elections – while, for example, none of the 19 candidates presented by the LDPR succeeded – shows that, except for the party of power, political parties at the local level remained as weak as they had been before.

If the organization of anticipated elections to the municipal assembly obviously permitted the first victory of United Russia at the local level, the consolidation of the power vertical at the local level seemed to imply

Table 10.5 Numbers of candidates and elected deputies supported by political parties in the municipal Duma elections of 2004 and 2008

	2004 Third Legislature	2008 Fourth Legislature
Number of candidates nominated by parties	**24 of 125** United Russia 2 LDPR 4 Communist Party 8 Yabloko 9 Party of Life 1	**48 of 95** United Russia 20 LDPR 19 CPRF 5 Just Russia 3 Patriots of Russia 1
Number of deputies elected nominated by parties	**1 of 25** Yabloko 1	**15 of 25** United Russia 15

at the same time the emergence of a new generation of local deputies. Of the 15 deputies that United Russia presented, only one – one of the three who resigned at the beginning of September 2007 – had been a deputy in the previous legislature. Two were on the ten-name list established after the regional primaries and belonged to the so-called Cadre Reserve, one of them the winner of the Politzavod project. Finally, it is interesting to note that only five were members of the party while the ten others were independents supported by the party.

The process of local elite renewal that permitted the first victory of United Russia in the city was part of a more general attempt to take back the region from the influence of two businessmen who were being pursued for fraud and criminal activity. The 'decriminalization' of the region – especially of the city duma, whose previous legislature was said to be under the control of these groups – was an important theme of the 2007–08 elections, including the replacement of Prusak, who was blamed for having been unable to prevent such a situation.[62] Regional elite renewal was then presented as a way to break away from the Yeltsin era, and the discredited '90 methods' of government[63] that had supposedly survived through practices and people.

Conclusion

A few days after his election, the new mayor of Velikii Novgorod, Yurii Bobryshev, stated: 'Things came full circle: a new president, a new governor, a new mayor and a new municipal duma. All these changes will allow us to work for the good of the city.'[64] If we add the two new Duma deputies, this sentence sums up the political elite renewal that had taken place in the region in the course of the 2007–08 parliamentary and presidential elections. This can in turn be considered as a second step in United Russia's construction after a period of 'privatization' that had been characterized by the continuity in office of people who had been elected before they joined the party. The quite abrupt and sometimes unexpected nature of these changes shows how this second step in the party of power's regional development resulted in the marginalization of former elected officials and the selection of new people, often elected for the first time – as was the case for the two new Duma deputies and for 14 of the 15 municipal deputies supported by the party – and, in the cases of the governor and Duma deputies, without any previous ties to the region. An analysis of the so-called primaries – which in fact deprived the region of the possibility of choosing its own Duma candidates – underlined the opacity and centralization of the political recruitment process to such an extent that there was no need to have the capital city mayor appointed by the governor since he was de facto vertically integrated into the party's structure.

What makes the Novgorod region particularly useful for observing centralizing processes is that it shows the importance of organizational change in United Russia itself. In Novgorod, the replacement of former political officials in 2007–08 reflected the centralization of the party's structure, which was no longer under the control of the former governor. The analysis of this transformation demonstrated how the role of United Russia in the strengthening of the power vertical meant not only that the party should have a quasi-monopoly in the selection of elected officials at all levels but that it should also have its current pyramidal structure. Finally, the case of the Novgorod region also showed the limits of the party's autonomy in spite of the creation of special procedures for political recruitment or 'cadre reserves' such as 'primaries', *Politzavod* and special quotas for young people. The first mandates held by the party were not won against the former regional and local elite but thanks to the governor, the State Duma deputy, and the city mayor, who had all joined the party. Afterwards, elite renewal was able to continue through the new procedure for the appointment and dismissal of governors while, at the local level, the party label was not of primary importance.

Notes

1. G. M. Hahn (2001), 'Putin's Federal Reforms: Reintegrating Russia's Legal Space or Upsetting the Metastability of Russia's Asymmetrical Federalism', *Demokratizatsiya*, Vol. 9, No. 4, Fall, pp. 498–530.

2. The text in English is available at http://www.un.int/russia/press-rel/2000/00_07_00.htm.

3. Ibid.

4. V. Gelman, 'Leviathan's Return: The Policy of Recentralization in Contemporary Russia' in C. Ross and A. Campbell (eds) (2009), *Federalism and Local Politics in Russia* (London and New York: Routledge), pp.1–25.

5. The texts of these laws are available in English on the website of the Central Election Commission of the Russian Federation: http://www.cikrf.ru/eng/law/. In particular since the 2004 amendments to the law, political parties must have at least 50,000 members: 500 in half the Federal Subjects, 250 in the others.

6. K. Wilson (2006), 'Party-system Development under Putin', *Post-Soviet Affairs*, Vol. 22, No. 4, October, pp. 314–48.

7. 'Russia needs parties that enjoy mass support and stable prestige. ... The time is ripe now for drafting a law on parties and party activity', said Vladimir Putin in his July 2000 *State of the Union Address*: see http://www.un.int/russia/pressrel/2000/00_07_00.htm.

8. V. Gelman (2006), 'Perspektivy dominiruyushchei partii v Rossii [The Perspectives of the Dominant Party in Russia], *Pro et Contra*, July, pp. 62–71.

9. R. Smyth (2002),'Building State Capacity from the Inside Out: Parties of Power and the Success of the President's Reform Agenda in Russia', *Politics & Society*, Vol. 30, No. 4, December, p. 556.

10. D. Slider (2010), 'How United is United Russia? Regional Sources of Intraparty Conflict', *Journal of Communist Studies and Transition Politics*, Vol. 26, No. 2, p. 272.

11. Vladislav Surkov is Deputy Chief of Staff of the President of the Russian Federation and is considered as one of the main ideologists of the Kremlin.

12. Vladislav Surkov (2006), 'Suverenitet – eto politicheskii sinonim konkurentosposobnosti', [Sovereignty is a Political Synonym of Competitiveness], Speech to United Russia cadres, 7 February, http://rumol.ru/files/library/articles/future/suverenitet_politicheskij_sinonim_konkurentosposobnosti.pdf.

13. B. Geddes (2003), *Paradigms and Sand Castles: Theory Building and Research Design in Comparative Politics* (Ann Arbor: University of Michigan Press), pp. 51–2.

14. V. Gelman (2006), 'Perspektivy dominiruyushchei partii v Rossii" [The Perspectives of the Dominant Party in Russia], *Pro et Contra*, July, pp. 62–71.

15. A. Konitzer (2005), *Voting for Russia's Governors Regional Elections and Accountability under Yeltsin and Putin* (Washington, DC: Woodrow Wilson Center Press), p. 219.

16. N. N. Petro (2004), *Crafting Democracy: How Novgorod has Coped with Rapid Social Change* (Ithaca, N.Y., London: Cornell University Press); and B. A. Ruble and N. E. Popson (1998), 'The Westernization of a Russian Province: The Case of Novgorod', *Post-Soviet Geography and Economics*, Vol. 39, No. 8, October, pp. 433–46.

17. Mikhail Prusak was born in 1960 in western Ukraine. His national political career started when he was elected to the USSR Supreme Soviet in 1989. For

a detailed biography see R. W. Orttung, D. N. Lussier and A. Paretskaya (eds) (2000), *The Republics and Regions of the Russian Federation: A Guide to Politics, Policies, and Leaders* (Armonk, NY: M.E. Sharpe) pp. 383–6.

18. O. Kryshtanovskaya (2004), *Anatomiya rossiiskoi elity* [The Anatomy of the Russian Elite] (Moscow: Zakharov), p. 140.
19. Kryshtanovskaya (note 342), p. 142.
20. B. A. Ruble and N. E. Popson (note 340), pp. 433–46.
21. Petro (2001), 'Creating Social Capital in Russia: The Novgorod Model', *World Development*, Vol. 29, No. 2, p. 232.
22. Petro (note 334), p. 88.
23. Petro (note 339), pp. 229–44.
24. V. Gelman, S. Ryzhenkov and M. Brie (eds) (2003), *Making and Breaking Democratic Transitions: The Comparative Politics of Russia's Regions* (Lanham: Rowman and Littlefield), p. 25.
25. Fatherland-All Russia and Unity were both 'parties of power' since they were led by representatives of central executive power: former Prime Minister Evgenii Primakov (1998–99) for Fatherland-All Russia, and Minister of Emergency Situations Sergei Shoigu (since 1994) for Unity. Unity was also supported by the new Prime Minister Vladimir Putin (appointed in August 1999).
26. H. Oversloot and R. Verheul (2006), 'Managing Democracy: Political Parties and the State in Russia', *Journal of Communist Studies and Transition Politics*, Vol. 22, No. 3, September, pp. 395–8.
27. R. W. (2000), *The Republics and Regions of the Russian Federation: A Guide to Politics, Policies, and Leaders* (Armonk, NY: M.E. Sharpe) pp. 384–5.
28. 'I vlast, i ekonomika, i prezident na 7 let. Tri gubernatora predlagayut Putinu reformirovat vse' [Power, Economy, and the President for 7 Years. Three Governors Propose Putin to Reform Everything], *Nezavisimaya Gazeta*, 25 February 2000, http://www.ng.ru/regions/2000–02–25/4_7years.html.
29. See Vladimir Putin's discourse: http://old.edinros.ru/news.html?rid=296&id=76950.
30. Vladimir Gelman defines 'satellites parties' as 'Kremlin-driven "projects" [that] served two basic – and not mutually exclusive – goals: first, to form a reserve or substitute to the party of power and avoid placing too many eggs in one basket (especially given the background of transitional uncertainty); and second, to weaken the oppositions of various colours by splitting their votes by spoiler parties', V. Gelman (2008), 'Party Politics in Russia: From Competition to Hierarchy', *Europe–Asia Studies*, Vol. 60, No. 6, August, p. 922.
31. According to *Nezavisimaya gazeta's* sources, Mikhail Prusak consulted the president before taking the decision to head the Democratic Party of Russia: Olga Tropkina (2001), 'U "Edinstva" poyavilsya novyi konkurent' ['Edinstvo' Got a New Rival], *Nezavisimaya gazeta*, 31 August, http://www.ng.ru/politics/2001–08–31/3_konkurent.html.
32. Valerii Tsygankov (2003), 'Lyublyu. Tseluyu. Prusak' [I Love, I Kiss, Prusak], *Nezavisimaya Gazeta*, 3 March, http://www.ng.ru/politics/2003–03–03/2_prusak.html.
33. Andrei Riskin (2003), 'Prusak "edinorossam" ne tovarishch' [To Members of "United Russia" is Prusak No Comrade], *Nezavisimaya gazeta*, 9 April, http://www.ng.ru/politics/2003–04–09/2_prusak.html.

34. A. Konitzer (2005), *Voting for Russia's Governors: Regional Elections and Accountability under Yeltsin and Putin* (Washington, DC: Woodrow Wilson Center Press), p. 222.

35. On the official website of the party's regional branch, the report on the meeting of the 5 August 2003 Regional Political Council states that 'United Russia members unanimously said that, amongst the candidates for Governor; the best one was Mikhail Prusak', '"Edinaya Rossiya" rasschityvaet na shirokuyu narodnuyu podderzhku' ["United Russia" Expects Wide Public Support], 5 August 2003, http://old.edinros.ru/news.html?rid=1836&id=4383

36. From 1993 to 2003, elections were held under a mixed electoral system: half the 450 Duma members were elected by a party-list system of proportional representation with a threshold of 5 per cent, and half were elected as individual representatives from single-member districts.

37. 'Predsedatel novgorodskogo regionalnogo otdeleniya partii "Edinaya Rossiya" Evgenii Zelenov o vyborakh', 9 December 2002 [The Chairman of the Novgorod Regional Section of the United Russia Party Evgenii Zelenov about the Elections] http://www.businesspress.ru/newspaper/article_mId_33_aId_137045.html.

38. Konitzer (note 352), p. 222.

39. Vladimir Lysenko (2005), 'Naznachenie gubernatorov – put k odnopartiinoi sisteme' [The Appointment of Governors – the Road to a One-Party System], *Nezavisimaya gazeta*, 24 March, http://www.ng.ru/politics/2005–03–24/2_er.html.

40. A. Kynev, 'Electoral Reforms and Democratization: Russian Regional Elections 2003–2006', in C. Ross and A. Campbell (2009), *Federalism and Local Politics in Russia* (New York: Routledge), p. 121.

41. E. Chebankova (2006), 'The Unintended Consequences of Gubernatorial Appointments in Russia: 2005–6', *Journal of Communist Studies and Transition Politics*, Vol. 22, No. 4, December, pp. 464–9.

42. 'Prusak ne nameren stavit vopros o doverii' [Prusak Does Not Intend to Ask for Confidence], *Kommersant*, 3 July 2007, http://www.kommersant.ru/news.aspx?NewsID=117269&NodesID=0.

43. D. Slider, 'Putin and the Election of Regional Governors', in C. Ross and A. Campbell (2009), *Federalism and Local Politics in Russia* (New York: Routledge), p. 114.

44. Mikhail Vinogradov (2007), 'Gubernatory na peredovom fronte izbiratelnoi kampanii' Governors at the Frontline of the Election Campaign], *Nezavisimaya Gazeta*, 14 August, http://www.ng.ru/politics/2007–08–14/3_kartblansh.html.

45. A. Pravda (ed.) (2005), *Leading Russia: Putin in Perspective* (Oxford and New York: Oxford University Press), p. 175.

46. United Russia was an exception since the federal troika was replaced by the sole name of Vladimir Putin after he decided to head the electoral list on 1 October.

47. The Young Guard (Molodaya Gvardiya), created in November 2005, is the youth wing of the party.

48. On the official site of the party: 'Stali izvestny imena pobeditelei " [The Names of the Victors Became Public], Politzavoda-2006, 28 June 2006, http://old.edinros.ru/news.html?id=114075%20.

49. The report is on the website of the think-tank: http://www.cscp.ru/clauses/52/c/2640/.
50. National Institute for the Development of Contemporary Ideology (2007), 'Cadre Reserve: Approaches and Methods', Material for the "Centre of Social and Conservative Policy" session', 7 April, http://www.cscp.ru/clauses/52/c/2640.
51. On the official site of the regional branch of United Russia in Novgorod: 'Idet podgotovka spiska kadrovogo rezerva' [A List of Cadre Reserve is Under Preparation], 24 August 2007, http://edinros.nov.ru/index.php?mmm=news&year=2007&month=08&id=136.
52. D. S. Hutcheson, 'Russia: electoral campaigning in a "managed democracy"', in D. W. Johnson (2008), *Routledge Handbook of Political Management* (New York: Routledge), p. 339.
53. From the comparison of the lists established after the 'primaries and published on the site of the party at http://old.edinros.ru/news.html?id=122163 and the definitive federal list established after the 8th Congress, which was held on 1–2 October 2007, http://old.edinros.ru/news.html?id=124494.
54. C. Ross (2009), *Local Politics and Democratization in Russia* (New York: Routledge), p. 182.
55. See the statement of Anna Filinkova, the only one among the resigning deputies who was reelected in March 2008, with the support of United Russia even though she was not a member of the party: 'Novgorodskii deputat: My ne khotim, chtoby na nas pokazyvali paltsem' [Deputy from Novgorod: We Do Not Want Them to Show Us the Finger], 12 September 2007, http://www.severinform.ru/index.php?page=newsfull&date=12–09–2007&pr=&rg=11&newsid=53490&col=2.
56. Yuri Bobryshev has been deputy in the regional duma since 1997. He is a member of United Russia and was appointed deputy mayor on 3 December 2007: http://www.zaks.ru/new/archive/view/37654.
57. All this was said during a press conference held on 28 January 2008. The report is available in: 'Kakaya demokratiya? O chem vy govorite? Nuzhno ukreplyat vertikal vlasti' [What Democracy? What Are You Talking About? It is Necessary to Strengthen the Power Vertical], 29 January 2008, http://www.velikiynovgorod.ru/interview/?id=87. The two parties that also supported him were The Liberal Democratic Party of Russia and Just Russia. None of the five others candidates against Yurii Bobryshev was supported by a political party.
58. Ibid.
59. Ross (note 373), p. 182.
60. The municipal duma deputies are elected under a single-member majoritarian system.
61. Ross (note 373), pp. 139–60.
62. M. Grigorev (2008), *Final novgorodskogo chikago* [Finale for the Novgorod Chicago] (Moscow: Fond issledovaniya problem demokratii).
63. Aleksei Gromskii (2007), 'Chto skazal Klebanov?' [What Did Klebanov Say?], *Novye Khroniki*, 5 July, http://novchronic.ru/716.htm.
64. 'Novyi mer Velikogo Novgoroda dovolen sostavom novoi gorodskoi dumy' [The New Mayor of Velikii Novgorod is Pleased with the New City Duma], 5 March 2008, http://www.severinform.ru/index.php?page=newsfull&date=11–032008&pr=0&rg=11&newsid=65183.

Part IV

Challenges and Risks of Modernization

11
Modernization and the Russian Regions

Nikolai Petrov

Introduction

To understand the nature of political processes in a huge country that still retains some federal elements, it is important to bear in mind that the regional and municipal levels are of no less importance than the federal one. A top-down view of the political system at the federal level needs to be combined with a view from below. Not only does a federal perspective alone give us an oversimplified picture of what is taking place nationally, but it also gives us a mistaken picture.

Although developments at the federal and regional levels are connected to each other, they are not necessarily connected directly and even if they are connected there is a substantial lag between them. Federal and regional politics can indeed be moving in different directions. Governors are a good example: their diminished powers in the early 2000s led to a weakening of their influence at the national level, but at the same time led to greater competition in the regions in which governors were no longer the dominant political figures.

So far as the regions themselves are concerned, two different processes began to take place as a result of the actions of the federal authorities: direct and intended results of the centre's efforts, such as unification and centralization; and indirect effects, including even some increase in political competition as a result of the weakening of the dominant position of the governors.

There is both good and bad news with regard to the regions' role in modernization. The bad news is that modernization in a huge and diversified country like Russia, with a high degree of centralization and without an active and autonomous role for the regions, is impossible. This means that full-scale modernization is impossible in present conditions.

The good news is that it seems that centralization has reached its maximum extent and that its continuation is impossible; indeed, there are some indications of movement in the opposite direction, with the partial re-emergence of political competition. For the moment, however, these are contained within the single dominant party, United Russia, and are not articulated as separate parties.[1]

As it proceeds with modernization, some genuine regional autonomy is not a luxury but a vitally important element in the Russian economy, social sphere and polity. This is because of the gap between an environment that is changing very fast and an archaic political system, a gap that is widening all the time. It is also because of the fact that in recent years economic, social and political development has been moving in the opposite direction, towards demodernization.

This chapter starts by looking at the ongoing demodernization of the regions in three major dimensions: political, economic and social. It considers the system of 'micromanaged democracy' at the regional level along with the way in which management as a whole is organized. It then examines the diversity of political systems across the regions and the main types of conflicts, and the various democracy and modernization ratings that have been suggested at the regional level. In conclusion it discusses the larger prospects for modernization.

The Results of Demodernization

The balance between modernization and demodernization for the country as a whole since 2008, when the slogan of modernization was first put forward by President Medvedev, is in favour of demodernization. At the regional level this is even more clearly the case. Interestingly enough, if in the 1990s ongoing regionalization from below was a way in which regional political elites could protect themselves from modernization,[2] in the 2000s it was demodernization from above that was used to fight against regionalization.

Demodernization in the Economy

The recovery economic growth model had exhausted itself even before the 2008 economic crisis. The strategy for economic development up to 2020 that was formulated to replace it appeared to be untenable and is currently being revised.[3] The existing Strategy 2020 places its emphasis on state corporations and industrial modernization of a 'Stalin–Beria' type, which is based on the direction of resources in what appear to be the most promising directions to provide a breakthrough of the kind that was achieved in the past in relation to nuclear energy and space exploration. Apart from the fact that this logic no longer makes sense in a post-industrial age, this is not a means of generating demand for innovation, which means that even existing innovations will not filter through to the real economy.

There is a further problem with small and medium-size business, which should be the most dynamic sector of economy. In the highly personalized Russian system, small and medium business is systematically neglected because it does not generate large tax revenues and has no institutional representation of its interests. Moreover, in a situation of crisis in which regional budgets had already lost much of their revenues, the pressure on small and medium business became even greater, for all the rhetoric.

Demodernization in Politics

Demodernization is proceeding along two major lines: primitivization/ oversimplification and unification. Primitivization of the entire political system, including a return to archaic forms of political organization, is most clearly seen in the North Caucasus. Political and managerial primitivization is connected above all with a weakening of the separation of powers along the horizontal and vertical axes, meaning executive branch hypertrophy in the first case and federal level hypertrophy in the second. Systemic modernization in such a huge and diversified country as Russia is absolutely impossible without restoring and developing real federalism.

The unification of political organization is taking place at the regional level. It has two major minuses. First, unification means levelling to the average, which means a decline for most advanced regions. Second, unification means not taking into account regional peculiarities or regional advantages, diminishing competition and leading to fewer innovations, and slowing down the development of the system even further.

The regions, as a result, lost their innovative role. They are no longer laboratories where very different innovations are invented, tested and, if the results are encouraging, copied and disseminated to other regions. This could be new forms of relationship between executives and legislatures, changes in the relations between the regions and local government, bicameral parliaments, modifications of the electoral system and so forth.[4] Now, it is the federal authorities that serve as the single innovator and unifier at the same time. Its innovations are implemented simultaneously and everywhere, not only without taking into account regional specificities but often without a preliminary check on the way in which they are likely to work in practice.

The ending of direct mayoral elections and further limitations on passive voting rights at the municipal level, where the proportional system is being introduced while at the same time public associations are losing the right to nominate candidates, can serve as examples of the most recent negative innovations. One can find positive examples as well, the most important of which is the deconstruction of local political machines in Kalmykiya, Bashkortostan, Tatarstan and Moscow.

Demodernization in the Social Sphere

This demodernization results from underinvestment over many years in such important sectors as education and health care. Young people were no longer taking positions in higher education in the same numbers, for instance, which led to a slowdown in renewal. There was a modest improvement in this respect before the international economic crisis, but it was not an enduring one. These spheres are chronically underfunded, and their human capital is in decline.

There is also an accumulated fatigue in the social infrastructure, whose results are not as evident as in the case of the technical infrastructure but are no less important. The Soviet heritage is coming to an end here as well, making a landslide effect inevitable. It can hardly be avoided although its negative consequences could be moderated.

Along with demodernization of the social sphere, a demodernization of society is going on. It is leading to a decline of social capital, with extremely low levels of trust both within society and between society and government, paternalism with regard to the state, and an outflow of the youngest and brightest. With a sharp decline in the space that is available for public politics as a result of the abolition of first gubernatorial and more recently mayoral elections, opportunities for positive collective action have diminished and social capital is not being generated.

It should be noted that demodernization has been uneven in its spatial dimension, with districts far away from Moscow experiencing it less than the capital city. It was demodernization of the polity and society that made possible the appearance of the present micromanaged democracy model.

Overmanaged Democracy at the Regional Level

The overmanaged democracy model at the federal level was outlined above. At the regional level it has a number of distinct features, which we can examine in terms of a series of paradoxes: hierarchical, geographical and structural–political.

Paradox 1 (hierarchical). Dismantling the system of checks and balances at national level and the suppression of political competition there can lead to growing competition at regional level. A micromanaged democracy (MMD) at the regional level has to be different from one at the national level. This is in part because of retarded development: it has just not been possible to construct MMDs in regions to the same extent as at the centre. Also, a regional MMD model, unlike the federal one, cannot be closed, which makes it more difficult to establish, much less complete without excessive control.

Paradox 2 (geographical): there still is some diversity in spite of ongoing unification. Levelling by average means that most autocratic regional regimes like Bashkortostan or Kalmykiya are moving in the direction of democratization, while among the most advanced regions, such as Perm, Sverdlovsk and St Petersburg, a reverse movement is taking place towards a weakening of democratic elements. Thus the process of micromanaged democratization in different regions can go in different directions. Reducing regional differentials, which in other circumstances might be desirable, means in this case holding leaders back artificially. Regional diversity in both the general character of political organization and in concrete forms and institutions has been diminishing. Advanced regions no longer serve as laboratories where new forms of political organization can be tested. These forms are now defined by the federal lawmaker according to the principle 'one size fits all'.

Paradox 3 (structural–political): along with the strengthening of monocentric institutions at the national level and the construction of power verticals, there is transition from mono- to polycentrism at the regional level. The paradoxical character of this transformation is connected with the fact that the head of a region, while not directly appointed by the centre, did formerly control the political situation in that region as well as contacts between it and the centre to a much greater extent than at present, when he has in effect become the senior federal official in that locality. Although governors have been incorporated into the power vertical that Putin began to establish after 2000, other members of the regional establishment have evidently become part of different organizational verticals that have become even stronger.

It would be too optimistic to speak of the fully fledged development of democracy in the regions, perhaps, although in many of them there has been an increase in political competition in recent years. Many regions have a much more developed system of checks and balances than the one at the centre, and it was the weakening of the federal system that led to the development of regional ones. Regional parliaments are much more autonomous vis-à-vis governors and executives in general than the federal one, and real business–political clan interests are represented within them. Although United Russia dominates there as well, first, it is not completely controlled by the governor; second, it is a strong form of organization that has been able to unite the major business–political players; and third, it is not homogeneous and reflects a complex balance of competing political and economic forces. The judiciary, moreover, although totally subordinated to the executive, is relatively independent of regional officials in most regions.

Politics in the regions is usually more transparent (and cynical) than at the federal level, even though it is not wholly public. It is more like a village – everybody is visible and everybody knows everything about everyone else. This applies to the major players and their interests, and to the connection between politics and business, and to personal relations between the players.

Regions are open systems. Power verticals there are managed from outside. The subordination of all branches of government to the executive is taking place at the supraregional level. But this allows for the possibility of real political competition at the regional level itself. Here, as in the ancient tragedies, a deus ex machina can appear at any time to put things in order.

The System of Power at the Regional Level

Figure 11.1 illustrates the organization of government at both the regional and federal levels. In 2000 the centre's power pyramid was oriented towards regional ones because of its wide base, while regional pyramids looking at it from their tops with governors who stayed there controlled all contacts between federal and regional levels and the federal level was represented by different uncoordinated players. Now things are very different. Not only is this because of a greater degree of coordination on the part of the centre. It also stems from a reduction in the ability of the governor to regulate external contacts. A whole range of figures within the regional establishment are no longer the governor's direct subordinates; their subordination to a minister, the prosecutor general or a presidential envoy has increased and at the same time they have become much more independent of the governor.

So-called power verticals now bypass governors, whose positions have become weaker with regard to both the peak of a federal vertical and its regional base. An appointed governor who may often come from outside the region as a 'Varangian' has no genetic and sometimes not even functional connection with the indigenous political elite (Table 11.1). Many

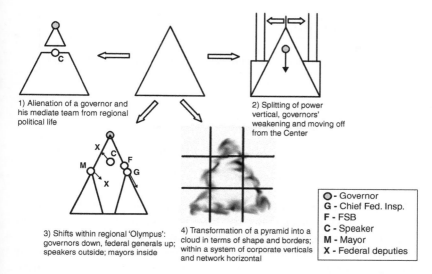

1) Alienation of a governor and his mediate team from regional political life

2) Splitting of power vertical, governors' weakening and moving off from the Center

3) Shifts within regional 'Olympus': governors down, federal generals up; speakers outside; mayors inside

4) Transformation of a pyramid into a cloud in terms of shape and borders; within a system of corporate verticals and network horizontal

○ - Governor
G - Chief Fed. Insp.
F - FSB
C - Speaker
M - Mayor
X - Federal deputies

Figure 11.1   The evolution of regional power pyramids, 2000–11

federal officials at the regional level and first of all the force-exercising and law enforcement agencies had broken out of a pyramid even earlier.

It is not by chance that it is the figure of a governor who attracts so much attention, as it is at this point that both the federal centre and regional elites seek to apply their influence. It was in this way that governors, wholly or in part, lost their control over the appointment of federal officials in their region. In most cases the governor became more distanced from local political elites; later he became even more removed from the centre of power because a new link appeared between them in the vertical chain of command, the presidential envoy.

Under these circumstances a governor becomes more or less the centre's governor-general (*namestnik*). It was the speaker of the regional assembly who started to play a leading role in coordinating and representing the interests of regional elites, until United Russia announced that it would be combining this position with the position of the United Russia regional council secretary.[5] Because of their inclusion in the Kremlin party vertical, speakers are also losing their role of representing the interests of regional elites. Overall, regional political systems are becoming less autonomous and are becoming less super-gubernatorial and more gubernatorial–parliamentary.

There is a difference between regions: some of them, especially the ethnic republics, maintain traditionally high levels of autonomy with a head

Table 11.1   Major players in the Russian regions by their level of connection
with regional political elites and term in office (as of January 2011)

	Regional head	CFI	UVD chief	Prosecutor	SKR	FSB	Judge	UR Secretary	Σ
Connection to region*	3.9	3.2	1.5	1.7	3. 6	1.3	3.8	4. 7	2.9
Term in office (years)	5.1	3.6	3.6	3.8	2.7	2.7	8.2	2.5	4.1

*Measured in points from 1 (the absence of any connection to a region before being appointed) to
5 (coming from a core of regional elites). CFI=chief federal inspector; UVD=Ministry of Interior
division.;

Source: Author's estimates and regional website.

whose power is close to absolute. However, even there regional heads have
had more success in blocking the implementation of central decisions
than in influencing the decisions that are taken in the first place.

If some of the functions of a former governor who was directly elected
and had governed the region for a long time with the ability to continue
to do so were somehow transferred to the speaker of the local parliament,
the governor in his turn in his new role of governor-general expanded
functionally at the expense of the chief federal inspector (CFI). The role
of the latter has indeed become somewhat obscure as it is the governor
who in fact is now the chief federal representative in a region.

The mayor of a regional capital can compete with a speaker for political influence in many regions. Until recently in almost all regions this
was an elected person well rooted in the local establishment. It was
mayors who were the centres of consolidation for the second biggest
business clan in a region after the one that surrounded the governor.
In this respect 2010 was a watershed, with the switch to the model of
an appointed city manager instead of a directly elected mayor in a large
proportion of the biggest regional centres.

Recently, due to ongoing municipal reform, competition has increased
between the governor's and mayor's clans for control over land plots
in the regional capital and over financial flows, a good proportion of
which go through that capital. In many cases there have been no clear
winners in this battle, with regional lawmakers usually strengthening
their positions at the regional level at the expense of municipal officials, but the uncertainty in the position of the governor has allowed
the power of the mayor to increase somewhat by way of compensation.
Table 11.2, based on the influence ratings of political elites in regions, is
helpful for evaluating these ongoing developments.

Table 11.2 Degree of influence of main status positions within the regional elite (based on ISANT data, 2003 and 2007)

Position	Total points	Average points	Average ranking	Spread of positions	No. of regions
Degree of influence by position in the regional elites in 2003					
Regional head	135	4.5	1.43	1 –5	30
Deputy regional head	118	3.8	4.29	2 –10	31
Chairman of the Legislative Assembly	104	3.7	5.4	1 –10	28
Deputy of the State Duma	86	3.6	5.25	1 –10	24
Region's capital head	84	3.8	4.77	1 –9	22
Deputy of the Legislative Assembly	70	3.5	6.8	3 –10	20
Mayor, District head	63	3.5	6.6	3 –9	18
Chief federal inspector	53	3.5	6.87	3 –10	15
Senator	46	3.5	6.8	2 –10	13
Head of the Department of Internal Affairs/ Ministry of Internal Affairs	39	3.5	7.5	4 –10	11
Head of the Federal Security Service Department	32	3.5	6	2 –10	9
Prosecutor	29	3.6	8	1 –10	8
Head of Electoral Committee	19	3.7	6	4 –9	5
Chairman of the Regional court	7	3.6	5	4 –6	2
Degree of influence by position in the regional elites in 2007					
Regional head	303	8.9	1.1	1 –3	34
Deputy regional head	264	5.5	6.5	2 –10	32
Chairman of the Legislative Assembly	195	6.3	3.9	2 –9	31
Regional capital head	168	6	5	2 –10	28
Deputy of the State Duma	74	5.3	6.6	3 –10	14
Chief federal inspector	53	5.3	6.5	2 –9	10
Deputy of the Legislative Assembly	53	4.8	7.7	4 –10	11
Head of the administration, of the office of the regional head	52	6.5	4.4	2 –8	8

Continued

Table 11.2   Continued

Position	Total points	Average points	Average ranking	Spread of positions	No. of regions
Head of Department of Internal Affairs/Ministry of Internal Affairs	41	4.6	8	5 –10	9
Chairman of the city council, Duma	31	5.2	6.7	5 –10	6
Mayor, District head	28	5.5	8.2	5 –10	5
Presidential representative, deputy presidential representative	24	6	3.7	2 –5	4
Senator	20	5.1	6.3	3 –10	4
Head of the Federal Security Service Department	20	5	6.8	6 –10	4
Prosecutor	20	4.9	7.3	4 –9	4
Chairman of the regional court	14	4.7	8.3	7 –10	3
Head of electoral committee	9	4.6	6.5	5 –8	2

Note: The 'spread of positions' shows the spread over the top entries of the regional lists.

Source: Based on 'Samye vliyatelnye lyudi v Rossii 2003', Moscow: ISANT, 2004, Expert, No. 12 (553), 26 March 2007. ISANT=Institute of Situational Analysis and New Technologies.

The top ten most influential politicians in a region usually include the governor, the speaker, the head of the regional government under the governor or the head of the governor's administration, and the mayor of the regional capital. In recent years the role of the speaker and the mayor became more important since the governor's role lost its monopolist position. In politics, the speaker and the United Russia Party's secretary challenged the governor's dominance while in the economic sphere big business–political clans formed around the mayor of the regional capital.

Increasingly often the *siloviki* and CFI representatives or even the presidential envoy were seen as the upper echelon of the regional political power structure. The greater role of those in law enforcement was a reflection of their independence from the governor's control both formally and informally and their transformation into more or less autonomous representatives of these corporate verticals. The split among the *siloviki* at the federal level was to a certain level also reproduced at the regional level. When the regional *siloviki* were capable of forming alliances, the prosecutor usually played the leading role as the 'natural integrator' and was able to convert the power resources of an alliance into business–political ones.

Shifts within the regional power pyramid reflected important general trends: a looser internal consolidation of the regional political elites along with a weakening of their relations with citizens, stronger subordination to the higher level, intensified internal political competition and declining accountability to the population.

Major Lines of Tension

The regional political construction consists not only of nodes but also of connections – cooperative in some instances, conflictual in others. We took into account 230 conflicts in 83 regions in 2010 – an average of nearly three conflicts per region. The number of conflicts varied from zero conflicts in depressed Mordoviya, the Jewish autonomous district, Chukotka, and Tambov oblast to 9 in the Irkutsk oblast – 112 conflicts. Half the number is an inner-authority conflict, with 48 of them along the vertical (including 2 with the Centre, 2 with the presidential envoy, 32 with the mayor of the regional capital and 12 with other mayors). There were few direct conflicts with society – 3 with authorities and 10 with business.

The major types of conflict were as follows:

the authorities vs the opposition (33);
the Governor vs the mayor of the regional capital (32);
Tthe authorities vs business (30);
officials from other regions vs the local elites (24);
business vs business (19);
within a municipality (14); and
the Governor vs the municipal head (12).

Let us evaluate recent political dynamics and ask the question whether there are political competition and autonomous centres of influence. On the one hand, the top–down verticals demolish the governor's power monopoly and restore a certain division of power at the regional level. The Centre's manipulations of the United Russia Party's structures promote a greater role for regional assemblies as a venue for presenting and coordinating various political, business and other interests, and for promoting regional politics. On the other hand, a region is no longer a self-regulatory system when conflict management and resolution move to the centre, to which players appeal instead of solving conflicts themselves. A lesser role for elections and referenda leads to removing citizens from influence over decisions: conflicts move from the public space to the non-public space, develop differently and have different results.

Although it could be expected that there would be more room for political competition at the regional level, this very competition weakens under the conditions of a sharp decline of public politics and as citizens are removed from the political process but it will continue on a different basis. The presence of conflicts is important, as are the character of their development, their resolution and the results. For example, competition in ideas and programmes in elections can lead not only to the selection of the best candidates but also to developing and enriching programmes and forming teams capable of realizing programme and mobilizing citizens.

In order to construct a typology of regional political regimes, two major axes represented levels of power and influence. One showed the main centres of political influence and one depicted competition within the party system. At one end there were regions with a single political centre and imitative party system: Mordoviya, Chechnya, Chukotka, Yamal-Nenets and Kemerovo. At the opposite end there were regions with numerous centres of political influence and a highly competitive party system: the Perm, Irkutsk, Sverdlovsk regions and St Petersburg. Most regions fell in the following categories: those with a one-and-a-half political centre and a weakly competitive party system (24 regions including Tatarstan and Moscow); regions with one and a half political centres but a rather competitive party system (14 regions, including Komi and Samara); and regions with several centres and a rather competitive party system (16 regions, including Kalmykiya and Murmansk).

Ratings of Democracy

At the regional level, quite paradoxically, political competition and a system of checks and balances can survive and even become strengthened despite being practically dismantled at the federal level. There are several reasons for this: the division of power following from the weakening of the governor's dominance, his weaker control over legislatures, courts and law enforcement agencies, provoked instability and political competition with regard to appointments by the governor, a strengthening of United Russia's regional branches as representative offices of a federal structure and competition between big corporate players. Inertia is an additional factor, and a time lag of the political development in regions with regard to the centre. When development at the centre goes in the direction of strengthening democratic institutions, regions look less democratic as a whole. When development at the centre starts to go in the opposite direction, regions look more democratic. In addition, the regular replacement of governors and ruling political elites in regions makes life in the regions more dynamic and less regulated by the centre.

The Carnegie Moscow Center rated the practice of democracy in Russia's regions. One rating was based on experts' estimations of numerous parameters, and another, instrumental, rating was based on elements of electoral behaviour. The level of democracy was seen as an integral expression of the overall political climate in the country and the state of society. It was assessed on the basis of a series of observations. The evaluations were relative in terms of both space (in relation to other regions/countries) and time (dynamics in one region/country).[6]

The data compiled by the Carnegie Moscow Center's programme on social-political monitoring of the regions from 1995 to 2010 offer an overview of the level of democratization in Russia's regions by region and over time along the lines of the Freedom House surveys of democracy in countries throughout the world.[7]

The rating of the level of democracy in a region was calculated on the basis of scores for ten distinct political spheres:

1. the region's political regime (the balance of power, including number of centres of decision making, the number of elected versus appointed officials, the independence of the judiciary and law enforcement agencies and the extent of citizens' rights);
2. the openness of political life (the extent of transparency and of public involvement in political life);
3. the level of democracy in federal, regional and local elections held in the regions (the existence of free and fair elections for posts at all levels, open competition, the use of so-called administrative resources, including direct interference by the authorities or courts, and the limitations to realizing political rights);
4. the extent of political pluralism (the existence of stable parties, factions in the legislative assembly, and coalitions during and after elections);
5. the degree of media freedom and independence;
6. the degree of corruption (the merging of political and economic elites and corruption scandals);

7. the extent of economic liberalization, including the situation with small and medium business, the investment climate, and conflicts and scandals regarding property rights;
8. the development of civil society (nongovernmental organizations and their role, various forms of public activity, demonstrations, pickets and strikes not sanctioned by the authorities);
9. the quality, perpetuation and turnover of political elites, varied nature of the elites and vitality of mechanisms for compromises between competing interests; and
10. the level of local self-administration (the existence of elected bodies of local government and their level of activity and influence).

Regions such as the Perm (#1) and Krasnoyarsk (#6–7) krai, Sverdlovsk (#2), the Irkutsk (#3–5), Novosibirsk (#3–5), Samara (#8–10), Archangelsk (#11), Nizhnii Novgorod (#8–10), and Yaroslavl (#7–9) oblast, St Petersburg (#6–7), and Kareliya (#3–5) are traditionally positioned among the top ten in democracy ratings (figures in brackets show the position in the 2004–09 rating). These regions – with their competitive environment in terms of both politics and economics, high human potential and social capital – should serve as locomotives for modernization.

The Regional Dimension of Modernization

The political and business elites at the federal level live in the hope of maintaining the raw-materials export model, but in most regions this is not possible. Many regions do not have such abundant resources and are not the main beneficiaries of resource sales. They are therefore forced to search for more suitable development models. Excessive centralism and unification in many areas limit their freedom of manoeuvre, while at the same time encouraging activeness and initiative in those few areas that are still open to them. Although many speak of modernization, the regions are in actual fact undergoing a process of de-modernization, so it would be more accurate to speak of a balance between these two processes.

We calculated three composite indexes in order to identify the various regions' modernization potential and evaluated progress made with regard to both purely technological modernization and broader social and political modernization. Figure 11.2 shows the potential for modernization calculated on the basis of data on the number and overall share of residents living in big cities (as of 1 January 2011), gross and per-capita total foreign investment received in recent years (2005–2009),

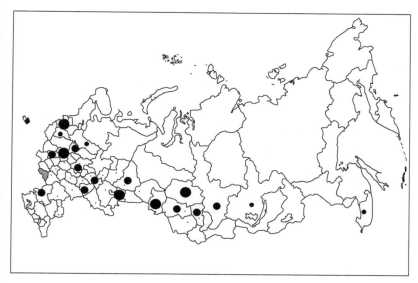

Figure 11.2 Leading regions in terms of their modernization potential

the human development index potential (2008), and Internet access. Moscow and St Petersburg lead here by a wide margin. The following top 20 regions are located in Siberia (Omsk, Tomsk, Krasnoyarsk, Kemerovo, Novosibirsk, Irkutsk) and adjoining Primore; the Volga area (Samara, Tatarstan, Nizhnii Novgorod); the north-west (Kaliningrad, Novgorod, Vologda); the Urals (Chelyabinsk, Sverdlovsk); the Central area (Yaroslavl, Kaluga) plus Rostov oblast in the south.

All the Caucasian regions were outsiders in this respect (Chechnya, Ingushetia, Karachai-Cherkessiya, Kabardino-Balkariya, Adygei, Dagestan, North Ossetia); southern Siberia (Altai, Tuva, Khakassiya, Buryatiya, the Jewish autonous region); northern Russia (Nenets, Khanty-Mansiisk, Yamal-Nenets, where investments in the oil and gas sector are not taken into account, and Magadan), some regions of central Russia (Vladimir, Orel), and the north-west (the Leningrad region and Pskov).

Figure 11.3 reflects the level of technological modernization and takes into account the presence in a region of national research centres, federal universities, and special economic zones for the introduction of technology as well as whether the region served as the venue for meetings of the Modernization Commission chaired by the president (which usually meets at innovative enterprises that have achieved successful

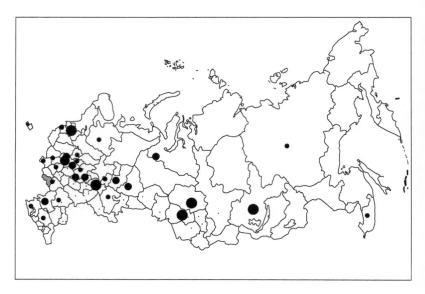

Figure 11.3   Leading regions in terms of technological modernization

results), is a member of the Association of Innovative Russian Regions, and receives Rusnano grants.

The space of technological modernization which we are considering is much narrower than the whole area within Russian borders – there are only 36 regions where our indicators differ from zero. Seventeen leading regions form four clusters: Central (Moscow and Moscow region, Vladimir, Kaluga), Volga (Tatarstan, Chuvashiya, Mordoviya, Nizhnii Novgorod), Urals (Perm, Sverdlovsk, Khanty-Mansiisk), and Southern Siberian (Tomsk, Irkutsk, Novosibirsk, Krasnoyarsk). There are also two separate regions – St Petersburg city and Rostov. The fact that seven of the twelve Russian cities with populations of more than a million are represented comes as no surprise. They are both capitals, Novosibirsk, Ekaterinburg, Kazan, Nizhnii Novgorod, Rostov (Perm, which left from the millionaires club in 2004, could be added).

Finally, Figure 11.4 reflects modernization in the broad sense. This index was calculated as a sum of evaluations of five parameters. Four of them are expert evaluations themselves and reflect the electoral, broadly political and business environment from the point of view of competiveness and conditions for competition. The fifth parameter – direct mayoral elections, one of the key characteristics of the political system – was measured directly. Evaluations regarding situations with

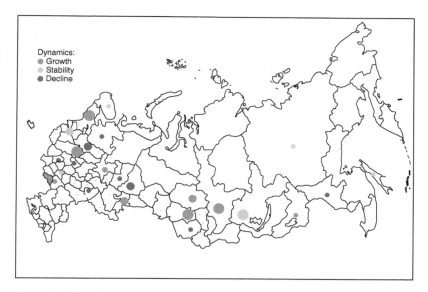

Figure 11.4 Leading regions in terms of modernization in the broad sense

elections and with corruption were made by experts when calculating democracy ratings for 2007–11. The evaluation of political system complexity was carried out by Aleksander Kynev at the end of 2010 and the evaluation of business environment by Aleksander Kynev and Natalya Zubarevich in early 2011.

The top 20 consist of big regions in the Urals (Sverdlovsk, Chelyabinsk, Perm) and Siberia (Irkutsk, Krasnoyarsk, Novosibirsk, Tomsk, Altai, Zabaikale), regions of the Centre (Yaroslavl, Vladimir, Voronezh, Kaluga, Lipetsk) and North-West (Kareliya, Vologda, Arkhangelsk, Leningrad). Closer to the end of the top 20 are Volgograd (No. 18) and Samara (No. 20) from other parts of the country.

The bottom 20 consist of republics in the Caucasus (Kabardino-Balkariya, Ingushetiya, Chechnya, North Ossetia, Karachai-Cherkessiya) and Urals-Volga (Mordoviya, Bashkiriya, Mari, Udmurtiya, Tatarstan) plus a couple of neighbour regions (Ulyanovsk, Saratov), regions of Southern Siberia (Tyumen, Kemerovo, Tuva), the South (Rostov, Kalmykiya) and Far North (Yamal-Nenets, Chukotka). Bryansk region stays alone. However, if it was added to Moscow and Moscow region and with Tambov a little higher in the list, there would be a territorial cluster of the centre.

A comparison of these three indexes reveals a significant degree of overlap when it comes to modernization potential and technological modernization (the leaders here are the capitals and big interregional centres), and a very different picture when it comes to broader modernization, where the leaders are regions far from the capital. The different pictures that emerge show that technological modernization and overall modernization are not closely linked, which means that technological modernization efforts alone will not be enough to resolve the country's main problems.

Conclusion

How should modernization look and who should be its driving force? In the narrowest sense, modernization is about technological improvements and that is what can be seen at present, and what is taking place under the auspices of the presidential commission on modernization and the premier's commission on innovation. Skolkovo in the Moscow region as a Russian Silicon Valley could serve as the official symbol of such a modernization. Special economic zones of a technical-implementing type in Moscow, Dubna, St Petersburg and Tomsk could serve this role to a lesser extent.

All of this is important, but it does not exhaust the notion of modernization. In a wider sense economic modernization includes a transition from an outmoded economic structure to a modern one based on sophisticated technologies.

In 2008 the 'Sigma' group, acting for the Institute for Contemporary Development (INSOR), developed a study of possible scenarios of Russian development, including the presence or otherwise of coalitions of serious actors interested in realizing this or that scenario. The modernization scenario was the one that attracted no serious coalition to back it in order to change the current paradigm of economic development. This underlines that there will be no serious economic modernization if it is to be led from above, initiated by very important players that are at the same time interested in maintaining the status quo such as Gazprom and the biggest state companies. The role of regions in this respect is becoming even more crucial.

Finally, socio-political modernization is a must for any deep changes in the economy. This means that there are regions which should become subjects of modernization rather than its objects. From a place where different projects are being developed and where the centre is carrying out modernization they should become active and independent players that initiate modernization changes by themselves.

Another problem is connected with the fact that it is exclusively the state that is leading the process. This makes the whole chain longer, the scheme not so effective, and the result problematic. Changes in the over-centralized taxation system are needed to promote modernization in the real sector. What we have now is the redistribution of financial resources from top to bottom, with the state budget determining how much money is needed in which sector and in which company and then allocating the money. It will be hard to speak about a real base for modernization at the regional and municipal levels until this extremely centralized and bureaucratized taxation system is revised and until the regional and municipal levels of government are more self-sufficient financially.

The common wisdom is that any modernization in Russia must be another 'revolution from above', that the government is the country's largest 'European' and accordingly its largest modernizer, and that it should promote modernization with an iron fist so as to lead its citizens to paradise. This is absolutely not the case. It was different in the past, it is different now and will be different in the future. Post-industrial modernization cannot be promoted by force. Thus the task of the federal authorities is not to carry out modernization according to a detailed plan, but to provide conditions in which modernization will develop by itself, to create stimuli for modernization, and to remove obstacles. There are three major real driving forces that should promote modernization, and one of them is more independent regions; the others are the cities and small and medium-size business, both sustained by political actors that have already made clear their commitment to this kind of objective.

Notes

1. The November 2010 amendment to the law on the Federation Council can serve as a good example. It stipulates that from 1 January 2011 representatives delegated to the Council of Federation by regions will receive the status of senators in two weeks without any approval procedures.
2. Thus mosaic demodernization appeared leading to what was called a federation of khanates.
3. At the beginning of 2011 a large-scale examination of Strategy-2020 with a view to its revision began on Putin's initiative, with the involvement of hundreds of experts and officials. This work should be completed by the end of 2011 and will in effect provide an economic programme for the new presidency.

4. The list of different innovations in the regions in the 1990s published in the Political Almanac of Russia was many pages long: Michael McFaul and Nikolay Petrov (1998) (eds), *Politicheskii almanakh Rossii 1997 g.* [Political Almanac of Russia ion 1997] (Moscow: Carnegie Moscow Center), Vol. 1, pp. 124–35). The top three leaders with the largest number of political innovations used to be Sverdlovsk region, Tatarstan and Primorskii territory. With the second raw innovative regions there used to be four compact cores: Ural, Tatar-Bashkiriya, Chechen-Ingushetiya, plus the two capitals and Primorye.

5. As of May 2011, 24 of 83 speakers were United Russia regional leaders

6. Subjectivity is inevitable here, but one way to reduce the effect is to ask a number of outside experts to contribute their evaluation. We did this in 1997 and 1999 in order to assess the extent of democracy in 57 oblasts and two federal cities (Moscow and St Petersburg). See Michael McFaul and Nikolay Petrov (eds), *Politicheskii Al'manakh Rossii 1989–1997* [Political Almanac of Russia, 1989–97], Moscow: Moscow Carnegie Center, 1998, Vol. 1, pp. 139–46. What complicates this approach is that experts do not have an equally well-informed understanding of all the relevant regions, particularly in the context of the stormy political life of post-Soviet Russia. A number of qualified experts recently visited a few of the regions and are informed of the situation in a number of other regions, but their opinions about most of the regions are based on indirect, secondary sources.

    This second approach can help avoid systemic mistakes conditioned by uneven knowledge about developments in regions and public stereotypes. The alternative approach lies in detailing the scores for levels of democracy and breaking them down into individual components. Such an approach is labour-intensive and requires examination of voluminous raw data from each of the regions. At the same time it is justified for two reasons. First, it ensures relative uniformity of the evaluation method in each region, and second because the grade is assessed not once but each year, highlighting the dynamics of the transition. Both diminish the significance of the inevitable imperfections of the methodology.

7. In its general programme of country freedom-rating evaluations, the Freedom House usually assigns numbers tothe state of democracy as reflected by both political and civil rights on a seven-point scale, with 1 indicating maximum freedom and 7 indicating minimum freedom. The resulting evaluation is presented in three grades – free, partly free and non-free. Since 2004 Russia has been rated as a non-free state. Freedom House applied a much more detailed grading to the post-Soviet and post-communist countries in transition under the aegis of a special Nations in Transit programme. Twelve ratings vary within the same range (1–7), but they are calculated more precisely – up to the second decimal digit: 1) the nature of the political process; 2) the development of civil society; 3) the extent of media freedom; 4) the system of administration; 5) the legislative and judicial systems; 6) the extent of corruption; 7) the degree of privatization; 8) the condition of macroeconomic policy; 9) the condition of microeconomic policy; 10) the extent of democratization; 11) the rule of law; and 12) the amount of economic liberalization. See www.freedomhouse.org/political.

12
Benefits and Risks of Political Modernization in Russia

Irina Busygina and Mikhail Filippov

Introduction

A government-proclaimed desire to promote technological innovation and boost economic growth in Russia implies the need for the state to take an active role in the economy and to provide the right stimuli and guarantees for investors. Since under its current political regime the Russian state lacks trust and credibility, and since the actions of the state to promote innovative economic development as well as its likelihood of succeeding depend on its type and characteristics, such an economic agenda would demand democratization. For entrepreneurs and investors, in its current form the Russian state is inefficient, riddled with corruption, lacking in accountability, and unpredictable. Most importantly, it cannot credibly commit to respect property rights and sustain the rules with which they are associated. Democratic reforms, ideally, could modernize the Russian state and make it simultaneously strong, limited, accountable, conducive to good governance and, thus, an effective agent of economic modernization. Yet the same Russian leadership that proclaims the vital importance of economic and technological innovation is reluctant to engage in political modernization, attempting instead to improve the existing model of governance by administrative methods.

This chapter explains such reluctance by the heightened political risks that would arise from democratic reform for the stability of the current political regime. It argues that (1) the increased degree of uncertainty and significant costs of the political reforms accrue before one could expect their positive effects on the economy, and (2) due to the specifics of the Russian political system, the transitional period may be expected to last longer and, therefore, be on the whole even riskier and costlier. Thus, we are quite pessimistic about the short- and medium-term perspectives of the economic innovations programme in Russia. On the one hand, the current political regime cannot provide 'good governance' and a credible commitment to form and sustain incentives for domestic and international businesses to invest in technological innovation. The existing political regime is more suitable for a status quo economy based on natural monopolies exporting raw materials, metals and energy. On the other hand, the anticipation of high costs and the risks of political reform make the choice to pursue them rather unlikely, even less so during the electoral cycle of 2011–12. In any case, political reforms would not have their desired effect on the economy for a number of years.

The chapter starts by introducing the theoretical assumptions behind our argument in the first section. The analysis is based on the main premise that any attempt to change existing institutions, such as the modernization of a political system or an economic structure, would lead to the redistribution of benefits from some groups to others. Groups who benefit from the political and economic system as it presently exists will prefer to block any changes to the status quo, and this includes the completion of reforms. The following section explains that in Russia today the state must necessarily play the role of the key promoter of economic modernization and technological innovation. Moreover, the state will probably need to remain the crucial actor in any future attempts to shift the prevailing equilibrium in the Russian economy – from the dominance of natural monopolies exporting resources and energy to a technologically oriented innovative economy. The third section argues that the efforts of the Russian state in its present form to influence the innovation climate in Russia will have very limited success unless the state itself is modernized. We claim that for successful innovative development, Russia needs *a different state* – modernized, more effective, less corrupt and – an essential requirement – better motivated to see innovative businesses succeed. Yet the Russian leadership is reluctant to engage in political reform, attempting instead to improve *governance* within the existing regime by administrative methods. The fourth section presents the argument that only a democratic political system could create effective governance and thus a state in which investors could trust. In the fifth section we discuss the period following the onset of any political modernization when both risks and efficiency are adversely affected. We show that the depth of this decline and the duration of the negative impact are contingent on a number of factors of an institutional and societal nature. In Russia, due to the importance of such factors, we can expect the period of instability and inefficiency caused by the initiation of political reforms to be particularly protracted and volatile. The sixth and final section concludes that, to succeed in democratization, Russia needs time and considerable economic and political resources to stay the course until the benefits of the reform begin to emerge. Moreover, the process of transformation of the political system will cause serious risks. Thus we expect that either the political reform essential for a climate of economic innovation will not be initiated, or that the effect of such reform will not yield positive economic results for an extended period of time.

Theoretical Premises

This section focuses on the benefits and risks associated with democratic reforms (now called political modernization) that arise from a number of distinctive characteristics of Russia's social, political and economic structure. We define political modernization as a process of institutional reform involving change in both the formal and informal rules of politics with a view to increasing democratic competitiveness and liberalism. Our main hypothesis is that there is a period following the onset of political modernization when both risks and efficiency are adversely affected. Furthermore, the depth of such a decline and the duration of any negative impact are contingent on a number of factors of an institutional and societal nature. The importance of such factors in Russia suggests that its transition to democracy will be particularly protracted, difficult and volatile. The indicators of possible decline (or later of improvement) that we use in lieu of the dependent variable are economic growth, attractiveness to foreign direct investment, the protection of property rights, levels of corruption in government, crime rates and threats to territorial integrity.

Our analysis is grounded in two main premises, focusing on the political economy aspects of economic modernization. First, there are always distributive conflicts among groups in society over the content of government policies. Second, because institutions (rules) matter and alternative rules yield different policy outcomes, politicians seeking support from dissimilar groups may be expected to prefer different institutional arrangements. In other words, there also exists a distributive conflict over the choice of institutions (rules). And under the pressure of having to compete for office, politicians are forced to demand institutional arrangements that are the most beneficial for their core support groups and constituencies. Thus any attempt to change existing institutions, such as the modernization of a political system, would lead to a redistribution of benefits from some groups to others. Those who gain advantages from the political system that presently exists may prefer to block such changes. The larger and the more diverse the state, the more likely will its various groups and constituencies have conflicting interests and, therefore, the more difficult it is to form the broad consensus that is necessary to continue to push through with institutional changes once the first redistributive outcomes are realized and interests are identified.

The propensity of different political groups to engage in distributive bargaining over the terms of alternative institutions (rules of the game) hinders the successful implementation and completion of political reform. We suggest that the initial consensus to *start* political reform (with media liberalization, a return to more competitive elections and federalism) is easier for the political elites to achieve, as it amounts to abolishing the status quo and any group can become a potential future winner. It is when the specifics are decided that future distributive outcomes become locked in and the identities of winners and losers are revealed. Thus it is harder to complete political reform than to start it. However, some rules for societal decision-making are always in place. And although they might be haphazard and inconsistent due to interruption of the reform sequence, this does not mean that they do not form expectations among players and direct behaviour.

An institutional system undergoing reform faces the danger of 'freezing' at whatever stage the new set of winners (who prefer to have a half-reformed political system) manages to interrupt it. In general, this problem has been identified as the problem of 'early winners'. Stabilization following an incomplete reform locks in the gains of the early winners, but interrupts the transformation at a low efficiency level for the society at large.

To take a hypothetical example, if looking ahead to a possible attempt to reintroduce political federalism in Russia, we might expect it to be broadly supported by the elites of many of the federal units that are seeking a greater degree of political autonomy. But at the same time we would expect elites in different regions to push for different approaches to renewed federal relations. We argue that any political modernization, once the initial changes are in place, would necessarily lead to the re-emergence of bargaining between Moscow and the regions over the rules of federalism. Until that bargaining ran its course and expectations in the federal process stabilized and became routine, inefficiencies and unpredictability would be unavoidable. Then, as was the case in the late 1990s, difficulties in federal relations would provide a justification for those who had reached their optimal level of gains to make a populist push to stop reforms on the grounds that they would be likely to weaken the Russian state and threaten its territorial integrity.

The Russian State as the Key Agent of Modernization and Innovative Development

Any political regime seeking to implement a socially important reform faces multiple obstacles and risks. The champions of the reform have to build a lasting coalition of various political, social and economic groups in support of the proposed change. Thus, the discussion of economic modernization in Russia inevitably focuses on which societal, political and economic groups might support or oppose it. Which actors could have enough interest in innovation to serve as agents of the modernization process in the short and medium term? And what role should the state play in creating conditions for innovative development?

There are two conflicting approaches with regard to the role of the state and the business community in creating an innovative economy. Proponents of the first approach argue that the Russian state is too clumsy, inefficient and conservative, while private business is the natural driving force of economic modernization. Their opponents, on the contrary, argue that in Russia the state has to perform the role of the driving force of modernization since the interests of business are short-sighted, motivated by quick profit maximization and cannot serve as a basis for a long-term strategy of economic modernization.

In the classic economic tradition, following Schumpeter, innovations are considered to be either new goods and services or modified technological processes and productive assets. In other words, innovations by definition occur in the natural course of business activity. For Schumpeter, the term 'innovation' applies to the utilization by the market of prior research and technological development, with business entrepreneurs, accordingly, being the key figures in the innovative paradigm of economic development.[1]

Thus, theoretically, one might expect businesses to introduce innovations ahead of the state sector, as they have the advantages of flexibility and the ability to react more quickly to changing market conditions as well as a genuine interest in achieving a competitive advantage. If that is the case, then the state could limit its role to its classic function: laying down clear rules of the game, enforcing contracts and protecting property rights. Extending this line of argument, since the state in

Russia is frequently seen as corrupt and a primary violator of property rights, limiting the role of government could improve both the governance and the functioning of markets. And the willingness of Russian businesses to invest in innovation should increase with the removal of artificial obstacles erected by the state and the bureaucracy. Indeed, in June 2010, 73 per cent of respondents from 'economically active groups' named corruption as the greatest obstacle to technological innovation. The second most frequently named problem was bureaucracy.[2]

On the other hand, Petr Aven has recently complained that in Russia 'there is still a very strong belief [that] the state can determine the best areas of investment'.[3] And leading Russian economists argue that the state not only can but must define the direction of economic development. They point out that the theory that businesses are motivated to lead in the innovation process contains no guarantees that contemporary businesses as they exist in Russia will have sufficient inclination to follow a path of innovative development. As business universally seeks to maximize the flow of profits, the best way to achieve those purposes under current Russian conditions is not to spend time and money on innovation with their inherent market risks. Left to their own inclinations, Russian entrepreneurs would most likely preserve the status quo: an economy dominated by large natural monopolies exporting raw materials and energy. Thus, Evgenii Yasin argues that just by following market signals and financial incentives, business in Russia will concentrate even further on resource exports since they yield the highest rates of profit.[4]

Incentives for foreign investors appear similarly problematic. Insofar as they operate in Russia, their calculations can hardly be fundamentally different from those of Russian companies. Of course, there might exist a separate possibility of designated funds in the form of investments or aid from the US and West European governments motivated at least in part by political goals.

Thus, the Russian state is both the main obstacle to economic competition and the necessary promoter of economic modernization and technological innovation. At the Global Policy Forum held in Yaroslavl in September 2010, a consensus emerged among the Russian specialists and officials who were present that an active role for the state should be recognized as imperative for the success of the modernization project. The specialists argued that the Russian state today had to be the main driving force of innovative processes; it must break the status quo of the raw material orientation of business and the economy as a whole. And these conclusions certainly make sense. However, it is not enough to proclaim what the state must do in order to hope that in its current form it is capable of promoting innovative economic development. It still lacks trust and credibility, and is inefficient, unaccountable and corrupt. Most importantly, it cannot credibly commit to respect and sustain the rules of the game which it itself promises to investors. Evidence of this reputational problem is that Russia loses in the competition for foreign direct investment in the most advanced sectors of economy. As Aven succinctly puts it, 'there are so many emerging economies where people believe there is huge potential for growth, and the problem is that Russia is not regarded as one of them by investors. That is mainly because of the lack of a competitive environment, corruption, and a legal system that is not completely adequate'.[5]

Does Russia Need a Different State?

As shown above, the Russian debate about the prospects of economic modernization centres on the role of the state in providing favourable conditions for innovative economic development. This section claims that different types of state would play different roles.

In order to form any expectations of the role that the state might play in the economy, one needs to assess how and on whose behalf that state articulates and protects what is often called the 'public interest'. It would be unhelpful to say that this is done on behalf of the society as a whole even in the best of democracies, since societies are customarily made up of opposing economic interests. Instead, the likely beneficiary of the state's efforts is a long-term winning coalition that maintains incumbents in power. The size and shape of that coalition are, of course, affected by the rules of elections and government that are in place in the country in question. In the Russian case, those mechanisms include elections but also business lobbies, special interest groups, and such routine and therefore expected institutional violations as campaign manipulation, disinformation, electoral fraud, media control and political corruption.

Ever since 1962, when Buchanan and Tullock published *The Calculus of Consent*,[6] economists have known that, while market mechanisms often lead to efficiency losses from the societal point of view, state intervention does not always guarantee an improvement. Whether it does so or not depends on the characteristics of the state and who controls it. A state focusing on the general provision of some unspecified public good is an abstraction, a theoretically unacceptable oversimplification. In practice, politicians and bureaucrats are motivated either by their own interests or by the interests of their constituencies. Thus, even if we could know what the true public interest might entail, they would be unlikely to champion it.

Countries such as Finland, Norway, Ireland, Canada, Austria, Switzerland, Singapore or France are often presented as examples of a state exerting a positive influence on the innovation climate. If it worked there, could it work in Russia? It could, if the Russian state bore enough similarities with theirs. But in reality it could hardly be more different. All the countries on the list have very low levels of political corruption. And economic theory makes clear that what a state can and should do in countries with the lowest corruption in the world (such as Singapore, Finland and Sweden) cannot be done in countries where the state is more corrupt and less effective. Instead, one could say that for each country there exists an optimal level of state intervention in the economy. A meta-regression analysis of a sample of 483 estimates derived from 84 studies on democracy and growth indicated that democracies might be associated with larger governments. At the same time, cross-national evidence indicates that in many cases state intervention in the economy has had negative results. Examples in which the state has managed to conduct effective economic modernization are rare – for every successful case there are numerous cases of failure.

The more effective and less corrupt the state, the higher is its optimal level of intervention in the economy. In certain countries the state is so weak, inefficient, corrupt and influenced by special interests that any attempt by political leaders to improve economic conditions would lead to wasting resources and even more corruption. So the message seems to be that attempts to influence the innovation climate in Russia are doomed to be of very limited effect unless the state itself is modernized. One could even say that in order to succeed in innovative development, Russia needs *a different state* – modernized, more efficient, less corrupt, and with a vested interest in the success of innovative businesses.

At the Global Policy Forum in Yaroslavl in 2010, Sberbank chairman German Gref argued that the most acute problem in present-day Russia was that the state was the instrument but at the same time the object of modernization. However, 'the instrument has to be appropriate. So the first priority is to modernize the state itself'.[7] Another participant in the session on 'The State as an Instrument of Technological Modernization', Anatolii Chubais, suggested that economic modernization without a political component could be launched but could not be completed, so, 'it is necessary to start with the economy and finish with politics'.

Unfortunately, any practical measures to modernize the Russian state would require considerable effort and time. Given the country's territorial make-up and economic asymmetries, political change is fraught with high risks for its territorial integrity and political stability. Heightened political risks would in turn inevitably depress investment and Russia's attractiveness for the purposes of innovation. In other words, although in the long run the innovation climate in Russia needs state modernization, and therefore political reform, in the short and medium terms modernization efforts would be likely to lead to a temporary decline in investment attractiveness. Thus it comes as no surprise that, although democratic political reform could ideally modernize the Russian state and make it an effective agent of economic modernization, the same Russian leadership that proclaims the vital importance of economic modernization is reluctant to engage in political reform, attempting instead to improve governance by administrative methods.

Since his election in 2008, President Dmitrii Medvedev repeatedly stressed the strategic role of technological innovation by listing it as one of his four priorities in economic policy, the others being infrastructure, investment and institutions. While there were similarities between the statements by Vladimir Putin and Dmitrii Medvedev on the subject, observers noted that 'Medvedev has struck a more liberal note, pointing out the need to create better incentives for innovation rather than just increasing the role of the state'.[8] More specifically, Medvedev pushed the idea that the modernization of Russian governance is needed in order to promote technological innovation and increase the global competiveness of the economy. It is important to note that Medvedev, like Putin and other key Russian officials, suggested improvements to current governance practices, not any change in the political system as a whole. It was suggested that the Russian political leadership should play a more active role in promoting effective, predictable, corruption-free and low-cost governance, which in turn would boost technological innovation and high-quality economic growth in the country. If we follow the public pronouncements of the Russian officials, we might start to believe that improvements in governance of this kind are feasible without undertaking the risk of significant political reforms.

In March 2009, Medvedev signed a decree to reform the civil service system as a part of his campaign against corruption. The decree aimed to introduce more effective technologies and modern methods of operation to increase the efficiency and professionalism of civil servants.[9] In late 2009, the gazeta.ru website published an open letter from President Medvedev to the Russian people under the headline 'Go, Russia!' in which he explained that the government had a plan to modernize the economy: 'In the coming decades Russia should become a country whose prosperity is ensured not so much thanks to commodities but by intellectual resources: a so-called intelligent economy, creating unique knowledge, exporting new technologies and innovative products... We have already developed detailed, step-by-step plans to move forward in these areas'.[10] According to Medvedev, economic modernization required improvements in governance by means of reducing corruption: 'We need to cultivate a taste for the rule of law, for abiding by the law, respect for the rights of others, including such important rights as that of property ownership. It is the job of the courts with broad public support to cleanse the country of corruption. This is a difficult task but it is doable.'

A year later, in his November 2010 presidential address, Medvedev hardly mentioned 'political reform'.[11] Kremlin commentators explained that the key milestones had already been reached and that the focus of presidential attention had shifted to social issues and the improvement of governance: 'Modernization produces a smart economy but it also requires smart policies that create the conditions for an extensive renewal of society. We need new standards in governance and public services, a higher quality of courts and law enforcement, modern ways for people to participate in the development of their city or village, and more involvement on the part of the people in the work of municipal authorities.'[12] By the end of 2010, government officials and politicians were saying that all was in place for economic growth and technological innovation apart from good governance. There were business incubators, centres for technology transfer, and so forth – all supposed to become elements of a national innovation infrastructure. The state spent the equivalent of billions of dollars to finance the Skolkovo research-intensive technology park in an attempt to replicate California's Silicon Valley in Russia. The Russian Venture Company was launched by the government to encourage Russia's own venture capital industry – with a starting capital valued at almost a billion dollars. The former privatization chief, Anatolii Chubais, was put at the head of Rosnano – a huge, state-controlled 'innovation company' intended to foster nanotechnologies throughout the national economy.[13] In 2010, according to then Finance Minister Aleksei Kudrin, state procurement orders totalled about $133 billion, and 15 per cent of those went to Russian technology companies. Kudrin said that the government ordered ministries and state companies to use more of their procurement budgets to buy products that qualified as 'innovative' and were made in Russia.[14] There were monthly televised meetings of the Presidential Commission for Economic Modernization and Technological Development of Russia's Economy (the 18th such meeting took place in November 2010). In March 2010, another commission, on High Technologies and Innovations, was established with Prime Minister Putin as its head.[15]

Yet despite all the financial and leadership efforts, the results remained modest. As Prime Minister Putin had to admit, the economy remained non-receptive to innovations: 'Our main economic shortcoming is resistance to innovation. *Everything we do seems to go to waste*. There is little progress (emphasis added).'[16] By 2010 both the state bureaucracy and the economy at large continued to treat the appeals of Russia's leadership for technological innovation and economic modernization as something alien and prescribed from above. The term 'coercive innovation' became popular in the Russian press. As had happened many times in Russian history, no one dared to contradict this pressure from above, waiting it out instead. A year after the publication of his modernization manifesto, President Medvedev thus assessed the results of the campaign: 'overall then, there is ideological consensus on this subject. I don't think the problem now is that there are forces that oppose modernization, but that a large number of civil servants, and part of the business community too, unfortunately, still see it as a passing thing. They see it as the slogan of the day, but nothing more.'[17]

Critics meanwhile repeatedly prophesied that modernization hopes would fail without a genuine political reform that would democratize the government. And they argued that only a democratic political system could create effective governance and establish a situation in which investors will be prepared to trust the Russian state.[18]

A Democratic State for Better Governance

Modern good governance is not just about the state. It is also about political parties, parliament, the judiciary, the media and civil society. Yet, although the practice of governance changes over time, the role of the state in the protection of property rights and providing the right stimuli for economic agents remains crucial. Whether the government is large or limited is, by itself, not a decisive factor in terms of guarantees of the protection of property rights and the enforcement of market rules. Rather, whether small or large, a government must be willing and able to be proactive in providing good governance and competent to set effective and attainable economic goals.

Neoliberal economists warn that in many countries 'politicians have insulated themselves from popular control, acting on behalf of special interests, including interests in their own power, privilege, and financial gain'.[19] When governments are guided by such private interests, state economic intervention generates economic inefficiencies even though it benefits the interests in question. This is why, argues Przeworski, 'improving economic performance requires political reform. But neoliberals wrongly conclude that improved performance – even measured by their own standard of efficiency – would be best achieved by reducing the economic role of government. To make the political economy work better, we need instead to ensure that government conduct is subject to vigilant oversight by citizens. We should, in short, reform our economy by improving our democracy, ensuring that citizens can effectively hold governments accountable for their economic activities'.[20] The key thing to remember is that 'only rarely are those in power accountable to no one, the issue is to whom they are accountable, how much, and for what'.[21] Thus, in practice the non-accountability of the state means only that it has become an instrument of some narrow groups and special interests, and it does not serve the interests of a broader public, so it is said that economic policies have been 'privatized'. The excessive role of special interests is problematic, because it causes distortion of both democratic accountability and policy objectives away from economic efficiency. States with effective economic policies have two important characteristics. They are decisive and have administrative capacity (state capability), and they are accountable to citizens and the private sector (state accountability). In other words, such states are both capable of and motivated to provide good governance.

The fundamental dilemma with regard to the state is that, if it is strong enough to protect property rights, it is also strong to enough to become unaccountable if it abuses its rights vis-à-vis citizens and businesses.[22] In theory, the necessary safeguards are provided by a balanced system of democratic rules and constraints to protect people from politicians' inclination to abuse their powers. Democratic constitutions, freedoms of speech and assembly, human rights and citizens' rights are all institutions that constrain politicians and state officials.

In this regard, a well-designed constitutional contract between citizens and the state creates a government that is strong but limited. Investing efforts in institution building is premised on the fact that the choice of democratic institutions matters for policy outcome and that institutions themselves are in turn variables that are subject to deliberate evaluation and to explicit choice.[23] The important parameters of institutional choice are the main constitutional principles, the form of government (presidential or parliamentary, federal or unitary), electoral rules, the level of taxation, independence of the judiciary and the central bank, and so forth. But, of course, institutional choice is not the only important factor influencing democratic performance: history, culture, levels of economic development, social fragmentation, the nature of civil society, and international influences also affect the enforcement of rules and the social outcomes that those rules produce. Moreover, economists readily admit that 'the chief problem may not be so much to identify good institutions as to implement them and keep them'.[24] Most often successful implementation depends on finding a harmonious and synergetic correspondence between institutional and non-institutional factors for a particular society.

For economic reform to succeed, declaring the 'right' policy is not enough – creating incentives that lead to the implementation of that policy is just as important. Organizational and administrative inefficiency in the state does not just happen because corrupt and unprofessional individuals find their way into its apparatus. Were this the case we could simply start looking for better officials. One systemic cause of bureaucratic inefficiency is that political incumbents allow it to be that way. Competition for political office either forces incumbents to properly supervise their bureaucrats and select them with care, or it does not. Competition for office, in turn, is structured by political institutions, and some institutions are better than others in making incumbents responsive and accountable to the preferences of the broader society.

Political incumbents in Russia both lack accountability and do not have a continuing means of sustaining state capacity. In principle, state capacity can have two sources: from above (where authoritarian regimes have a relative advantage because of their hierarchical structure and repressive resources) and from below, where democracies are more effective due to a combination of electoral and societal accountability, media freedom, as well as institutional checks and balances which create 'horizontal' or intrastate accountability. As far as state capacity is concerned, states in the middle, with weak democratic institutions, find themselves the most vulnerable. They do not have the tight top-down hierarchy due to the weakening of the authoritarian order, nor do the institutions of democratic control function at a sufficient level, being still underdeveloped.[25]

The J-Curve of Democratization Effects

According to North, Wallis and Weingast, in states based on 'limited political competition', regime stability is maintained by the efforts of a relatively narrow ruling coalition with privileged access to political and economic resources. The dominant status of the elite coalition is secured through control over such key assets as courts, military forces, regional governments, the mass media and the church. Limited access to economic and political resources creates rents for the ruling elites. Since conflict in the society or within the elite threatens those rents, there are powerful incentives to maintain a level of unity that will be sufficient to contain any conflicts of this kind, and so the ruling coalition binds itself with certain commitments for the sake of preserving the status quo.[26]

In an alternative model with open public competition and open access to the elite, political and economic rents do not play a similar role for political stability. Rent-seeking opportunities there are temporary and because of open competition are relatively limited. Properly designed competitive mechanisms serve to resolve societal conflicts and allocate political offices and economic resources – through elections and markets. As far as commitment mechanisms are concerned, the different branches of government balance and control each other, while the mass media and civil society provide additional independent oversight of incumbents and the state bureaucracy. In its developed stage, a competitive model of this kind can be considered almost a different political system, a democratic system with open access to public authority. According to North, Wallis and Weingast,[27] today there are approximately 25 Open Access Orders in the world, with no more than 15 per cent of the world's population living in them. The remaining 85 per cent reside in natural states with limited access to public authority, although their levels of openness of political competition vary widely.

Both models face a choice of methods and mechanisms for structuring the political process. In particular, for securing stability both non-competitive and competitive orders need mechanisms of implementation of political decisions, resolution of conflicts and the provision of public goods. Non-competitive stability hinges on the personalities of politicians and their ability to make 'right', effective decisions. Implementation in these cases requires a group of officials who are loyal to the leaders, which in turn requires a strict hierarchy of appointments and accountability. Competitive stability results as a by-product of the self-organization of political agents as it is induced by the common and clear rules of the political game. Each individual politician acts in accordance with institutionally provided incentives and pursues his own self-interest. Thus, as long as the rules make it to their personal advantage to do so, elected politicians as well as bureaucrats will act in support of the political system. In other words, in the second model, competition for power and resources is regulated through a set of formal and informal rules and can be directed to serve the ends of political stability and economic efficiency.

One could introduce these institutions anywhere, by law or decree, but putting them on paper does not automatically lead to agents' believing that they are indeed the rules to follow. If agents do not expect others to follow formal rules and do not follow rules themselves, the role of formal institutions becomes negligible. Thus, evaluating the results of Putin's presidency, Duma member Sergei Markov claimed that Putin's personality had became more important for Russian society than all political rules combined. For that reason Markov was sceptical about the role of political institutions in Russia as real constraints on political or economic behaviour.[28]

Difficulties in bridging this institutional gap and transforming authoritarian regimes in the direction of greater openness and democracy have been addressed by Ian Bremmer,[29] whose approach is reminiscent of the analyses of the transitional costs associated with economic reforms. In his book, which became a best-seller in America, Bremmer suggests applying the J-curve as a means of understanding why the political transformation of authoritarian regimes progresses with such difficulty. Bremmer's argument links early increases in democratic openness with the rise of political instability in a state that is undergoing transformation. His definition of political stability consists of two essential criteria: resilience in the face of political, economic, or social crises, and a general ability to prevent the circumstances that generate such crises in the first place. Increases in democratization are evaluated as increased openness, domestic and international. Domestic openness implies unrestricted flow of information within the country: whether people can interact freely, have access to accurate news about what is taking place elsewhere in the country, and can influence government decisions. International openness is a measure of how easily people, information, goods, services and ideas are allowed to flow across a country's borders.

Arguably, countries such as North Korea, Myanmar, Zimbabwe and Belarus retain stability precisely because of their non-democratic, non-open political regimes, which prevent political conflict escaping containment by the state. Others, such as the United States and European Union member countries, maintain stability in the opposite fashion – by relying on an open but well-developed political system, which is perhaps less suitable for suppressing conflict but much better adapted to preventing or resolving it. These countries possess elaborate institutional structures and well-balanced democratic political processes within which political and social problems can be articulated and arbitrated. Another important element is that both the process and the outcomes of dealing with the issues in question are accepted as legitimate by the majority of citizens. In these open high-functioning democracies, institutional mechanisms as well as the willingness of elites and voters to abide by well-codified rules of decision-making ensure high levels of political stability.

The horizontal axis of Bremmer's J-curve portrays openness, combining its domestic and international aspects. Its vertical axis indicates the level of political stability. Plotting the assessed values of these two variables for the countries of the world generates a pattern with a dip in the middle of the openness range before an eventual rise – the J-curve.

The graph shows that a country that enjoys stability due to its lack of openness can become stable due to openness only after it traverses a dangerous interval of political instability. Some states, such as post-apartheid South Africa and Spain after Franco, have managed to survive this period and achieve democratic consolidation. Yugoslavia and the Soviet Union, however, collapsed along the way. Then there are countries that lost parts of their territory while on this path, for example India, Indonesia, Malaysia and Ethiopia. A number of multi-ethnic states simply chose to turn their back on the idea of democratization.

If we were to imagine that progress in democratic reform moves a country from left to right along the curve, then as openness increases political stability initially declines, and the country enters a period of instability that lasts until a fairly high level of democratic functioning can be attained. Some interval is necessary for the political structures and various aspects of the democratic process to evolve and settle into place, so shortening this period may not be possible. However, the depth of the 'dip' may vary and we suggest that it is greater when the country undergoing this process is a federation, like Russia. In the logic of Bremmer's J-curve, the instability loop there lies lower on the vertical axis than in small homogeneous states. These observations regarding the political costs involved in democratization are pertinent to the

Russian case because of the link between economic modernization and the need to have a state that is credible and thus fully democratic.

As the theoretical reason for the intermittent decline in regime stability noted by Bremmer we posit the unravelling of the initial reform coalition as it is abandoned by the 'early winners' who opt at some point to stop the reform progress, thereby locking in their gains. Either the early winners manage to form an alternative coalition that becomes dominant, or they weaken the coalition in power. In any of these circumstances the clash over the direction of future reform negatively affects political stability due to its propensity to polarize not just political but also economic elites and ultimately the electorate at large. This explains political costs in terms of the decline in political stability. In a federal country, when regional incumbents are among the 'early winners', such a force not only generates resistance to further change but can also eventually reach a strength (both political and financial) sufficient to block future reforms or even reverse their direction. This explains the cases that linger in the middle range of Bremmer's horizontal axis for a protracted period of time – either just sitting there or moving back and forth. And extra time spent in the middle range means an increase in the total political costs associated with eventually crossing that territory.

The theory of 'early winners' banding together to block continuation of reform was first advanced in a frequently cited work by Joel Hellman where he explained the persistence of partial *economic* reforms in postcommunist countries.[30] Back in the 1990s Adam Przeworski offered the hypothesis that democratic mobilization would mean that the pain of market reforms would be translated into political success for populist and anti-reform forces that would halt the transitions.[31] Fearing the early success of anti-reform populism, some concluded that market reforms needed to be shielded from popular checks at least for some time and argued against conducting democratization concurrently with market reform – pro-reform governments needed to be protected from political pressures. Thus Haggard and Kaufman referred to the experience of 12 Latin American countries and argued that political insulation of the government from the opposition was of the greatest importance early in the process of effecting the transformation.[32] Hellman, however, was the first to argue that the dangerous opposition to continued reforms originated not with those who had already sustained economic losses and could look forward to improve their circumstances in the future as the reform reached fruition. Rather, the early winners became an impediment to further progress as they sought to lock in the partial reform outcome as a new status quo that maximized their personal advantage.

Russian politicians who are economists by education and are familiar with Hellman's work have failed to connect this theoretical mechanism with politics and overlooked the problem of transitional costs when discussing democratic reforms, assuming instead that movement towards democratization and federalization would automatically improve both the economic and political situation in the regions and in Russia as a whole. Thus former Finance Minister Egor Gaidar insisted that thorough and detailed debates on the course of political reform were superfluous: 'The important thing is to adopt the strategic course to democratic transformation, and then we can go on resolving specific political and technical related matters'.[33]

Conclusion

Russia is a rich country that lags behind in technological innovations. Anatolii Chubais reports that it was ranked 7th for its GDP level but 73rd for its innovation level in 2009–10.[34] It has significantly more researchers per thousand inhabitants than China, Brazil or India, but in the 2010 survey by Thomson Reuters it fell far behind China, Brazil and India in registered patents.[35] Two-thirds of R&D funding was from Russian government sources, compared with one-third from business, while in the United States the government provided only 27 per cent of total R&D funding.[36]

By the end of 2010 the evidence was abundant that Russian businesses were reluctant to invest in new technologies. According to a survey by the Higher School of Economics in 2010, natural resource extraction remained the most active area of investment. Most disturbingly, the survey revealed the tendency to put new investment not into buying new technologies but into the repair and maintenance of obsolete equipment. The equipment in use became so old that it was now necessary to divert much of the available investment just to keep it running. Almost 60 per cent of all businesses reported that their key technological equipment was more than ten years old, while almost 20 per cent reported that it was more than 20 years old.[37]

In June 2010 President Medvedev instructed the government to set up a 'special investment fund in which government funds will be complemented with private capital; say, we will try to attract 3 rubles of private investment for every one ruble of state money'.[38] No results of such a new investment strategy had been reported by January 2011. On the other hand, it became known that in 2009 the state nanotechnology corporation (Rosnano) spent only 10 billion rubles (about $330 million) of the 130 billion rubles allocated to it in the federal budget. The rest of the money the management held in bank deposits and almost half of all actual incurred expenses were administrative costs.[39] In a similar way, another state-owned corporation created to promote innovation, the Russian Venture Company, kept over 80 per cent of all its funds in bank deposits rather than invest in risky high-tech products.[40] Despite these facts, the chief Kremlin ideologist Surkov continued to argue that finding more money was the key to the problem of economic modernization: 'methodologically, modernization is a simple thing – one needs money to introduce new technologies'.[41]

This chapter shows that the current political regime of the Russian state lacks the key characteristic of 'good governance' – political accountability, yet the Russian leadership is reluctant to recognize the importance of democratic political reforms. It also pointed out some of the risks and costs associated with democratic reforms that could explain such reluctance. It follows from the analysis that, in order to succeed in democratization, Russia needs time and the investment of considerable economic and political resources to maintain its trajectory until the benefits of reforms begin to emerge. Moreover, the transformation process will entail considerable risks. Political reforms require patience – on the part of both the population and key political actors. And they require an initial consensus with regard to the long-term commitment to stay the course.

There is every reason to expect the period of instability and inefficiency caused by the initiation of reforms in Russia to be long and painful. Winning coalitions are likely to form at an intermediate stage in order to reverse the direction of institutional change. This suggests that several back-and-forth reversals may realistically be envisaged in the future.

Notes

1. J. Schumpeter (1992), *Capitalism, Socialism and Democracy* (New York: Routledge).
2. http://www.vedomosti.ru/newspaper/article/2010/07/27/241703.
3. 'Russia Investment Climate Worsening, Says Banker Peter Aven', *Financial Times*, 2 December 2010, http://www.ft.com/cms/s/0/318bf286-fe5d-11df-abac-00144feab49a.html#ixzz17ihu02eJ.
4. http://www.hse.ru/ic2/materials_2/yasin_8.htm.
5. 'Russia Investment Climate' (note 391).

6. J. Buchanan and G. Tullock (1962), *The Calculus of Consent: Logical Foundations of Constitutional Democracy* (Ann Arbor, Michigan: University of Michigan Press).

7. http://www.rian.ru/politics/20100909/274063494.html.

8. 'Innovation Seen as Crucial To Russian Economy', 18 April 2008 at http://www.forbes.com/2008/04/17/russia-innovation-economy-cx_0418oxford.html; see also Neil Buckley, 'Russia's Leaders Split on Pace of Reform', *Financial Times* online edn, 8 September 2010.

9. RIA Novosti, 10 March 2009.

10. http://www.gazeta.ru/comments/2009/09/10_a_3258568.shtml, 10September 2009; the official English translation is available at http://eng.kremlin.ru/news/298.

11. The president mentioned a proposal to introduce municipal party-list-based elections.

12. Presidential Address to the Federal Assembly of the Russian Federation, http://rt.com/politics/official-word/transcript-address-federal-assembly/.

13. Russian Federation's asset contributions in RUSNANO: $4.5 bn; state-guaranteed debt financing (bonds issuance): $6.2 bn.

14. http://www.nytimes.com/2010/02/04/business/global/04ruble.html.

15. Analysts say that Putin's move to take over his own hi-tech commission could be linked to presidential polls due in 2012: http://en.rian.ru/russia/20100310/158149449.html.

16. 'Prime Minister Vladimir Putin attends a joint meeting of the Ministry of Finance and Ministry of Economic Development Boards', 14 May 2010, http://premier.gov.ru/eng/events/news/10586/. In Russian: 'Ved v chem glavnaya problema nashei segodnyashnei ekonomiki – nevospriimchivost k innovatsiyam. Hy, kazalos by, chego ni delaem – vse ne v konya korm. Net rezkogo dvizheniya v etom napravlenii', http://premier.gov.ru/events/news/10586/.

17. President Dmitrii Medvedev, Meeting with leading Russian and foreign political analysts, 10 September 2010, http://eng.kremlin.ru/transcripts/919.

18. K. Rogov (2011), 'Rossiya i vyzovy desyatiletiya: politika' [Russia and the Challenges of the Decade], *Forbes* (Russian edn), January, p. 106.

19. A. Przeworski (1996), 'A Better Democracy, a Better Economy', *Boston Review*, No. 21, p. 9.

20. Przeworski (ibid), pp. 10–11.

21. J. Fox (2007), *Accountability Politics: Power and Voice in Rural Mexico* (Oxford: Oxford University Press), p. 8.

22. B. Weingast (1995), 'The Economic Role of Political Institutions: Market-Preserving Federalism and Economic Growth', *Journal of Law Economics and Organization*, No. 11, pp. 1–31.

23. J. Buchanan (1990), 'The Domain of Constitutional Economics', *Constitutional Political Economy*, No. 1, pp. 1–18.

24. G. Brennan and L. Lomasky (1993), *Politics and Process: New Essays in Democratic Thought* (Cambridge: Cambridge University Press), p. 225.

25. H. Bäck and A. Hadenius (2008), 'Democracy and State Capacity: Exploring a J-Shaped Relationship', *Governance*, No. 21, pp. 1–24.

26. D. North and R. Thomas (1973), *The Rise of the Western World: A New Economic History* (Cambridge: Cambridge University Press). See also M. Levi (1988), *Of Rule and Revenue* (Berkeley: University of California Press).

27. D. North, J. Wallis and B. Weingast (2009), *Violence and Social Orders: A Conceptual Framework for Interpreting Recorded Human History* (Cambridge: Cambridge University Press).
28. http://club.fom.ru/article.php?id=25.
29. I. Bremmer (2006), *The J Curve: A New Way to Understand Why Nations Rise and Fall* (New York: Simon and Schuster).
30. J. Hellman (1998), 'Winners Take All: The Politics of Partial Reform in Postcommunist Transitions', *World Politics,* No. 50, pp. 203–34.
31. A. Przeworski (1991), *Democracy and the Market* (Cambridge: Cambridge University Press).
32. S. Haggard and R. Kaufman (1995), *The Political Economy of Democratic Transitions* (Princeton, NJ: Princeton University Press).
33. E. Gaidar (2009), 'Krizis privedet k izmeneniyu sushchestvuyushei sistemy' [The Crisis Results in Changes of the Existing System], *Forbes* (Russian edn), 15 March.
34. USRBC's 18th Annual Meeting 'From Silicon Valley to Skolkovo: Forging Innovation Partnerships', San Francisco, 20–21 October 2010.
35. Compare data in J. Cooper (2010), 'The Innovative Potential of the Russian Economy', *Russian Analytical Digest,* Vol. 88, pp. 8–12; and http://www.nytimes.com/2010/02/04/business/global/04ruble.html.
36. J. Cooper (2010), 'The Innovative Potential of the Russian Economy', *Russian Analytical Digest,* Vol. 88, p. 9.
37. www.vedomosti.ru/newspaper/article/251692/ne_do_investicij.
38. Dmitrii Medvedev addressed the St Petersburg International Economic Forum's plenary session on 18 June 2010; see http://eng.kremlin.ru/news/454.
39. http://gazeta.ru/business/2010/12/14/3466065.shtml.
40. 'Auditoriyam ne khvatilo venchurnykh investitsii' http://www.vedomosti.ru/newspaper/article/243885/
41. http://er.ru/print.shtml?17/3597, 4 June 2011.

Part V
Reflections in Early 2012

13
Modernization and After

Stephen White and Lena Jonson

The uncertain progress of 'modernization' in Russia reached a new stage in late 2011 as Dmitrii Medvedev's term moved towards its conclusion and presidential elections became imminent.

Pre-Election Manoeuvring

The extended guessing game about the country's future leadership came to an end at a United Russia Party congress on 24 September when Putin suggested that Medvedev should head the party's list at the forthcoming Duma election (it had, he explained, become a tradition that the incumbent president should take on this role). Medvedev in turn proposed that if the party won the election they should nominate Putin as their candidate for the presidency. Putin made clear that if he was successful he would approach Medvedev to head a new government, and Medvedev replied that he would accept the position if he was invited to do so.[1] The tandem, in effect, would be continuing; all that would change was that the two leaders would reverse their positions.

It was a decision, in the end, that reflected public expectations, and one that had apparently been taken some time earlier – in fact 'four years earlier', as Putin told a national call-in programme shortly afterwards.[2] There had in any case been repeated assurances that the two leaders represented, as Medvedev put it, 'one and the same political force',[3] or (as Putin had put it earlier) that they were of the 'same blood' and would no more compete against each other in 2012 than they had competed against each other at the previous presidential election in 2008.[4] During one of his national 'direct lines' Putin was asked: Who ran the country when the two leaders were asleep? 'We sleep in turns', he told the caller.[5] But Putin, Medvedev conceded, was the 'most authoritative politician in our country', and his approval ratings were 'somewhat higher'; this made his nomination the more logical, although these could be no more than recommendations: the final decision would have to be left to the electorate.[6]

Putin, it could be assumed, would all the same be re-elected without any difficulty as president in March 2012. He would then be able to serve another two presidential terms, each of six years, taking him up to 2024 (the Russian constitution prohibits more than two consecutive presidential terms, but places no limit on the number of terms that may be served in a lifetime). There had even been suggestions that the presidential term might be extended to seven years, allowing Putin to serve until 2026, and that he could be succeeded again by Dmitrii Medvedev, who would still be in his late sixties.[7] That would represent four terms altogether; but, as Putin pointed out, Franklin Roosevelt had been elected four times in a row to the US presidency (it was after this experience, in 1951, that the US constitution was amended to limit the number of terms that could be served by the same individual in their entire lifetime), and German Chancellor Helmut Kohl had been in power for 16 years without a break.[8] As the humorists had already put it: 'Pushkin is our everything, and Tsereteli [the popular sculptor] is our everywhere. Putin is our always'.[9]

Medvedev was particularly associated with the concept of modernization that is the recurrent theme of this book, and it was sometimes suggested that he favoured a slightly different, more liberal policy agenda than his hard-line predecessor.[10] He had no background in the security services, and it was unclear if he had even been a member of the Communist Party, although his grandfather had been a district first secretary who had 'very much believed in socialist ideals' and his own father had considered a party career before choosing the life of science.[11] His early speeches placed a heavy emphasis on the problem of 'legal nihilism' and the rule of law (a speech to a Krasnoyarsk economic forum in 2008 set out these themes with particular clarity[12]); more daringly, there were suggestions in some of his later speeches, particularly a statement released on his presidential blog in 2010, that the political system itself might require reform and that there was a danger that the stability they all enjoyed might become a 'factor of stagnation'.[13]

The record, at the end of Medvedev's first and perhaps final presidential term, was decidedly patchy. The economy contracted sharply at the end of 2008 and in 2009, when gross domestic product fell nearly 8 per cent. Unemployment increased from 6.3 per cent (on official figures) in 2008 to 8.4 per cent in 2009; and inflation was over 13 per cent in 2008 and 8.8 per cent in 2009. But the two leaders were able to argue, apparently with some success, that their problems were essentially external,[14] and growth resumed in 2010 and 2011. Government sources projected a further increase in GDP of 3.5 per cent in 2012, 4.2 per cent in 2013 and 4.6 per cent in 2014;[15] the World Bank's figures were slightly more conservative, but also assumed a level of growth that would comfortably exceed the global average.[16] Apart from this, Putin was able to tell the United Russia congress that the birth rate that had been achieved between 2008 and 2011 was the highest for 20 years and that total population numbers were once again increasing.[17] And although corruption was still a problem, the Transparency International figures that were released in December 2011 at least showed a slight improvement.[18]

But not all had been improving their living standards at the same rate, and social problems of all kinds had been deepening. Income inequality was greater in Russia than in the United States, according to the 2011 United Nations *Human Development Report,* and much greater than in a typical European country. In early 2011, according to official statistics, more than 16 per cent of the population were living below the subsistence minimum, a proportion that had been steadily increasing. At the other extreme, there were more billionaires than ever before, according to Forbes' annual listing of the global super-rich – more, indeed, than anywhere else except the United States and China.[19] And there was little sign that the economy was shifting away from its heavy dependence on the exploitation of the country's enormous mineral resources, which left the state budget, and public policy as a whole, heavily dependent on the world price of oil. The government bureaucracy had been increasing, not diminishing;[20] capital flight was continuing or accelerating;[21] and increasing numbers of the younger and better educated were seeking their future in other countries.[22]

Public opinion remained supportive of Putin and Medvedev, although in autumn 2011 a long-term trend of falling support for the tandem and the United Russia party became more pronounced. It was expected, however, that in the last resort electoral support depended on economic performance rather than on a commitment to the leaders themselves.[23] Therefore the government sought to strengthen its position as the elections came closer by increasing public spending. It was announced that pensions would be increased in February and again in April 2012;[24] military pensions would increase by a substantial 50 per cent.[25] Speaking to the United Russia congress in November that agreed to nominate him to the presidency, Putin also promised that there would be a move towards a more progressive form of taxation that would ensure the wealthy paid more than the middle class.[26] In another populist gesture the Moscow mayor opened three new underground stations on the morning of 2 December, just a couple of days before polling.[27]

The position of the United Russia party had further weakened when an energetic blogger and anti-corruption campaigner, Aleksei Navalnyi, began to describe it as a 'party of crooks and thieves' in a phrase that rapidly gained a wide circulation. Navalnyi was both a cause and a symptom: a symptom, in particular, of the extent to which the ruling authorities had lost control of newer forms of social communication to independent and sometimes hostile voices. Russia, it was calculated, had Europe's largest Internet audience, of about 60 million.[28]

The Outcome of the December 2011 Parliamentary Elections

The ability to communicate independently of the authorities was of crucial significance in the immediate aftermath of the Duma election that took place on 4 December 2011. There was little indication, in the survey predictions, that it would become such a serious challenge to the Putin–Medvedev leadership. Yet, a reduced support was predicted and United Russia officials had in any case already accepted that their vote would be substantially lower than in 2007, when Vladimir Putin had agreed to head their national list of candidates. The official results came out a few days later, on 9 December.[29] Turnout, at 60.1 per cent, was slightly down on the 63.7 per cent that had been recorded in 2007; it might have been greater, the head of the Central Electoral Commission explained, but for snow-storms and blizzards on Sakhalin, and rain and snow in central Russia.[30] The ruling party, United Russia, took by far the largest share of the vote and enough to secure an overall majority (238 of the 450 seats) in the new Duma.

But its share of the vote had fallen sharply, from 64.3 per cent in 2007 to 49.3, and in much of the country its share was very much lower. Indeed, there was hardly a national result at all. In Chechnya, United Russia had 99.5 per cent of the vote; in Dagestan, 91.8 per cent; in Ingushetiya, 91 per cent. In Yaroslavl region, on the other hand, it had just 29 per cent, in Kareliya 32.3 per cent and in St Petersburg 32.5.[31] In a particular humiliation, United Russia took a smaller share of the vote than the Communist Party in Putin's own constituency, in Moscow's Gagarin district.[32] In the traditional manner, the worst-performing regional heads were called to the Kremlin a few days later to account for their shortcomings and 'organizational conclusions' (sackings) were expected to follow;[33] the Vologda governor took the hint immediately, resigning a week later (United Russia had won just 33.4 per cent in his region).[34]

All of this was a familiar pattern, not just in Russia but in the other post-Soviet republics. What was unexpected was the public reaction that began to develop after the election had taken place, particularly but not exclusively in Moscow. Small numbers appeared on the streets on the evening of polling day itself; the following day, 5 December 2011, as many as 7000 took part,[35] although little of this was reported by the mainstream television or newspaper outlets. The evening after that, 6 December, about 250 people were arrested in 'another night of violence'; interior ministry troops were called in to maintain order, 'truncheon-wielding police clashed with hundreds of protestors and firebombs were thrown at pro-Kremlin activists'.[36] The respected daily paper *Kommersant* sent its own reporter to the gathering, where he witnessed 'mass arrests and beatings'; indeed he was beaten himself.[37] About 200 were arrested in St Petersburg the same evening, and about 100 came out onto the streets in Ekaterinburg.[38]

An even larger demonstration took place on 10 December 2011, when as many as 50,000 attended a public rally just a few hundred metres from the Kremlin and many more took part in similar actions in 'dozens' of towns and cities across the country.[39] The Moscow demonstrators approved a five-point manifesto, at the top of which was a demand that the entire election be repeated, this time with genuine opposition parties; another was that the more than 1000 people arrested in earlier demonstrations should be released. One of them was Navalnyi, who had been detained on the evening of 5 December and given a 15-day jail sentence for supposedly obstructing a police officer in the performance of his duties (he was all the same able to pass out a message of resistance to his supporters).[40] Meetings calling for the election to be invalidated had been held in almost 100 different Russian towns by this time, and outside Russian embassies in other countries; as many as 80,000 demonstrators had taken part, in addition to those who had joined the street action in Moscow.[41] At least superficially, there were parallels with the 'coloured revolutions' that had taken place in other post-Soviet republics, and with the 'Arab spring' that had overthrown the autocratic rulers of Egypt and Tunisia, after election outcomes that had appeared to be fraudulent.

The election, like its predecessors, had been witnessed by outside observers: about 200 under the auspices of the Organization for Security and Co-operation in Europe (OSCE), and about 600 altogether.[42] In a preliminary statement the OSCE described the election as 'technically well-administered' but 'marked by the convergence of the State and the governing party'; the contest had also been 'slanted in favour of the ruling party as evidenced by the lack of independence of the election administration, the partiality of most media, and the undue interference of state authorities at different levels'.[43] But delegation leaders were unwilling to pronounce on whether the elections had, or had not, been 'free and fair' (those who wanted an answer would have to read the full report that would be released at a later date). Nor were they willing to say if the election had been an improvement, or a step backwards, as compared with the Duma election that had taken place in 2007 (they never compared any election with any other). Nor had the mission maintained any observers in the North Caucasus, where much of the most outrageous ballot-stuffing had taken place (the governments concerned refused to allow their personnel to work in such a dangerous environment).[44]

Some individual members of the mission were much less critical and, not surprisingly, their views were more eagerly sought out by the Kremlin-friendly media. A television discussion hosted by Vladimir Solovev on the evening after polling day, for instance, asked two members of the OSCE mission to offer their own opinions. Both were very complimentary, and one of them, the British MEP Nick Griffin (leader of the far-right British National Party), declared the Russian elections a substantial improvement on those he had experienced in the United Kingdom – where, for instance, the ballot paper had a number on it and was accordingly less than entirely secret.[45] The election mission sponsored by the Commonwealth of Independent States (CIS), as usual, declared itself entirely satisfied; the election process had been entirely transparent and the outcome an accurate reflection of the wishes of the electorate, with just a 'few shortcomings of a technical character'.[46] Another group of independent observers, from the European Centre for Geopolitical Analysis, also took the view that any shortcomings were of an 'entirely technical character' and could not have significantly affected the outcome.[47]

There was a much more critical commentary from Golos, an independent association that is supported by Western funding (they have applied, unsuccessfully, for support from the funds that the Russian government sets aside for 'civil society') and which itself came under heavy electronic and administrative attack over the period that immediately preceded polling day. For Golos, who also reported their preliminary conclusions at a press conference on the morning after polling day, there had been 'significant and massive violations of many key electoral procedures', including multiple voting, the improper use of absentee ballots, violations of procedure in the course of voting outside polling stations, forced participation, insufficient openness in the work of the electoral commissions, and 'crude violations' in the treatment of constituency returns by higher-level electoral commissions.[48] Reports had already been made available on YouTube that appeared to show obvious violations taking place,[49] and another independent body, Citizen Observer, was suggesting that United Russia might actually have won no more than 30 per cent of the vote, with the rest attributable to 'administrative resource' and other forms of falsification.[50]

Initially, the Kremlin appeared unsure about how to respond to the largest protests that had taken place at any time since the last years of the Soviet Union. United Russia would clearly be the largest faction in the new Duma and Putin stated that this was a result that would allow United Russia to continue the country's stable development.[51] There had been some losses, the prime minister conceded a day later, but they were 'inevitable for any political force, particularly for the one that has been carrying the burden of responsibility for the situation in the country'. It could even be called a 'good' result, and it compared well with the situation in countries with a more stable economy, where 'millions' had taken to the streets.[52] Medvedev argued in similar terms that the party had secured the result it had deserved, 'no more and no less'; and there would be a 'more energetic parliament' in the future, which was very much to be welcomed as 'no one has a monopoly on truth'.[53]

But there were also indications that the electoral system might once again be opened up for discussion. Perhaps, suggested the new Moscow mayor Sergei Sobyanin, the single-member districts that had been dropped in 2005 might be reinstated: ordinary citizens felt they could relate to an individual they had directly chosen, not to a party list that was handed down from above.[54] Medvedev was also of the view that the single-member constituencies might be reintroduced,[55] and he thought there might also be a case for restoring the 'against all' option that had been dropped in 2006.[56] It might, in fact, operate to the Kremlin's advantage, as it would siphon off a part of the oppositional vote that might otherwise be cast for a more or less oppositional party. Putin, in his call-in programme at the end of the year, thought that a case could also be made for web cameras in polling stations to ensure there were no violations of the election legislation, and three days later he issued a corresponding directive.[57]

It was clear from the outset that there would be no repeat election of the kind the opposition demanded. Nevertheless, on 11 December

Medvedev said that any violations of the law must be investigated, and ordered an investigation into the violations that had by now been widely reported.[58] He insisted, however, that there was 'nothing to be seen' in the video clips that had been made available on the Internet which, he said, could have been prepared at any time.[59] Kremlin spin-doctor Vladislav Surkov, for his part, insisted that the extent of any electoral violations had been wildly exaggerated by people who were either 'legal nihilists' or 'illiterate'.[60] The head of the Central Electoral Commission, Vladimir Churov, claimed that fake polling stations had been set up beforehand in private apartments in order to provide fabricated evidence,[61] and some footage had apparently been released on the Internet before the election itself had taken place.[62]

Putin was even less accommodating, apparently obsessed with the experience of the 'coloured revolutions' in which Western agents had (in his view) been able to use contested election results to overthrow Kremlin-friendly local leaderships. 'People in our country don't want the situation to develop like in Kyrgyzstan or Ukraine in the recent past', he told a group of his supporters. 'Nobody wants chaos'.[63] Some of the demonstrators, it appeared, had been funded by the US State Department. 'Pouring foreign money into electoral processes is particularly unacceptable', Putin went on. 'Hundreds of millions are being invested in this work. We need to work out ways to protect our sovereignty and to defend ourselves from outside interference'.[64] He had been too busy learning ice hockey, he explained later, to pay much attention to the demonstrators. Election losers always said they had been cheated, he claimed. And although some of his critics were sincere and must be heard and respected, others were 'pawns in the hands of foreign agents' who were part of a 'well-tested scheme to stabilize society'.[65]

As preparations intensified for a second demonstration against the falsification of the elections to take place on 24 December, the Putin–Medvedev leadership understood the seriousness of the situation. People were registering their participation in the upcoming demonstration over the Internet, and demonstrations were being planned in cities all over Russia. In the 24 December demonstration in Moscow up to 100, 000 people participated in the largest demonstration since 1991.

On 22 December two days before the demonstration, Medvedev in his yearly presidential Speech to the Union presented what he called a complex of measures to reform the political system. In their essence these measures meant a partial return to the situation before Putin in the mid 2000s changed regulation concerning elections and parties. Medvedev's proposals included direct elections of the heads of the federal subjects (regions and republics); relaxation with regard to registration of parties to a formal request by 500 people from at least 50 per cent of Russian regions; reduction of the number of signatures for registering a party candidate in presidential elections to 300,000, and to 100,000 for non-party candidates. Medvedev also proposed a return to proportional elections for half the number of seats in the State Duma, and to widen the composition of the regional election committees to include representatives from all parties represented in the assemblies at federal and regional level. He also promised a future decentralization that would bring more power to the regions.[66]

Challenges for the Future

Although these proposals by Medvedev were welcome, they would hardly be considered enough by the critics. They were piecemeal changes which would not reform the political system. And they were clearly insufficient to make the political system capable of solving the serious problems of the country. Medvedev declared that more reforms were to come. At the same time the new appointments within the top leadership that followed demonstrated that Putin had no intention of listening to the demonstrators. Putin is the defender of a system and he will not carry out far-reaching reforms which might risk his own position. Putin's dilemma was again to be illustrated.

There would be no significant improvement in the problem of corruption, for instance, until there was a more independent court system. But a genuinely independent court might hold the leadership itself to account, with unforeseeable consequences. A legislature which is able to closely scrutinize the government would be more effective, but it might also uncover spending scandals and reject ministerial proposals. A more independent media would keep an eye on corruption, but it might also begin to investigate the connection between officeholders and wealth of a kind that might prejudice their privileges and perhaps their liberty. A competitive political system that allows parties and presidents to renew their mandate, or be peacefully replaced, would secure a greater degree of public legitimacy, but it might as well turn down the government.

All this suggest in turn that the uncomfortable choices raised in the chapters of this book would find no resolution in the near future and that the 'wait for reform' might be an extended one. Indeed, 'modernization' could be placed within a much longer perspective – back to Peter the Great and the periodic attempts to carry out a 'revolution from above' that allow Russia to catch up with and even overtake the Western powers. 'Modernization', in this connection, could be seen as another version of the 'uskorenie' (acceleration) of the early years of Gorbachev:[67] a leadership project that could hardly be expected to succeed unless it had the direct support of ordinary people, but which at the same time refused to allow them the institutions through which that support could be expressed or, if necessary, withheld. The uneasy stalemate that developed in the aftermath of the 2011–12 elections suggested that the 'modernization' project had exhausted its top-down potential but that the wider society had not yet been given the opportunity to articulate an alternative.

Notes

1. Nikita Girin, 'Sezd pobeditelei' [Congress of Victors], *Novaya gazeta*, 26 September 2011.
2. Anastasiya Novikova, 'Putin podgotovil grazhdan k smene vlasti' [Putin Prepared Citizens for a Change of Government], *Izvestiya*, 18 October 2011.
3. Per Sibide, 'Prezident Medvedev poshel v efir vne ocheredi' [President Medvedev Went on Air Ahead of Turn], *Izvestiya*, 3 October 2011.
4. Aleksandr Latyshev, 'Vlast razdelyat po-bratski' [They Will Share Power Amicably], *Izvestiya*, 14 September 2009.
5. 'Kto upravlyaet stranoi, kogda Vy i prezident spite?' [Who Runs the Country When You and the President are Sleeping?], *Izvestiya*, 17 December 2010.
6. Per Sibide (note 3).
7. Natalya Galimova, 'Kak vybrali preemnika' [How They Chose a Successor], (2008), *Moskovskii komsomolets*, 21 January.
8. Anastasiya Novikova (note 2).
9. Sergei Mishin, 'Vot chto znachit khoroshii artist...' [That's What a Good Artist Means], *Trud*, 9 October 2007.
10. See e.g. Oksana Antonenko (2008), 'Medvedev's Choice', *Survival*, Vol. 50, No. 2, April/May, pp. 25–31.
11. Nikolai Svanidze and Marine Svanidze (2008), *Medvedev* (St Petersburg: Amfora).
12. 'Tochki nad "i"' [Dotting the 'i'], *Rossiiskaya gazeta*, 16 February 2008.
13. Aleksandra Beluza, 'Medvedev provel partsobranie' [Medvedev Conducted a Party Meeting], *Izvestiya*, 25 November 2010.
14. Valentina Feklyunina and Stephen White (2011), 'Discourses of "Krizis": Economic Crisis in Russia and Regime Legitimacy', *Journal of Communist Studies and Transition Politics*, Vol. 27, No. 3–4, September–December, pp. 385–406.
15. Anastasiya Savinykh, 'Na pensionerakh reshili ne ekonomit' [They Decided Not to Economize on Pensioners], *Izvestiya*, 22 April 2011.
16. *World Bank in Russia*, Russian Economic Report no. 26, September 2011, available at http://siteresources.worldbank.lrg/INTRUSSIANFEDERATION/

Resources/305499–124538520910/6238985–1316082024531/RER26_ENG. pdf.

17. Kira Latukhina, 'Dvizhenie tolko vpered!' [Forwards Only!], *Rossiiskaya gazeta*, 26 September 2011.

18. Russia was ranked 143 out of 182 countries in 2011, with a score of 2.4 (the higher the score on a scale of 0 to 10, the lower the level of perceived corruption), the same as i.a. Nigeria and Uganda. See http://cpi.transparency.org/cpi 2011. In 2010 Russia had been ranked at 154 out of 178 countries, with a score of 2.1.

19. Pavel Arabov, 'V Moskvu ponaekhali milliardery' [The Billionaires Have Arrived], *Izvestiya*, 11 March 2011.

20. 'Dom-2 dlya elity' [House-2 for the Elite], *Argumenty i fakty*, no. 21, 2011. *Argumenty i fakty*, no. 21, 2011, p. 4.

21. Evgenii Arsyukhin, 'Kapitaly prodolzhayut ubegat' [Capital Is Continuing to Flee], *Izvestiya*, 6 April 2011.

22. See e.g. http://www.euronews.net/2011/11/11/29/russian-brain-drain-as-young-people-look-west.

23. Ian McAllister and Stephen White (2008), '"It's the Economy, Comrade!" Parties and Voters in the 2007 Russian Duma Election', *Europe–Asia Studies*, Vol. 60, No. 6, August, pp. 931–57.

24. Per Sidibe, 'Pensionery rasskazali tandemu o nravstvennosti i velichii strany' [Pensioners Told the Tandem About Morality and the Greatness of the Country], *Izvestiya*, 18 November 2011.

25. Anastasiya Novikova, 'Putin poobeshchal voennym pensioneram 1.5 trln rublei' [Putin Promised Military Pensioners 1.5 Trillion Roubles], ibid., 3 November 2011.

26. Kira Latukhina, 'Dvizhenie tolko vpered!' (Forwards Only!), *Rossiiskaya gazeta*, 26 September 2011. Academic economists were already pressing for a change of this kind: see for instance Evgenii Ershov, 'Akademiki predlozhili Putinu progressivnyi podokhodnyi nalog' [The Academicians Suggested to Putin that He Should Introduce a Progressive Income Tax], *Izvestiya*, 2 August 2011.

27. See http://en.rian.ru/20111202/169247389.html, last accessed 19 December 2011.

28. Per Sidibe, 'Kreml nashel sposob vovlech grazhdan v upravlenie stranoi' [The Kremlin has Found a Way of Involving Citizens in Managing the Country], *Izvestiya*, 28 October 2011.

29. 'Postanovlenie Tsentral'noi izbiratel'noi komissii Rossiiskoi Federatsii ot 9 dekabrya 2011 g. N 70/576–6 g. Moskva "O rezultatakh vyborov deputatov Gosudarstvennoi Dumy Federalnogo Sobraniya Rossiiskoi Federatsii shestogo sozyva' [Resolution of the Central Electoral Commission of the Russian Federation] of 9 December 2011 No. 70/576–6 Moscow "On the Results of the Election of Deputies of the State Duma of the Federal Assembly of the Russian Federation of the Sixth Convocation], *Rossiiskaya gazeta*, 10 December 2011; the official communiqué also appears on the website of the Central Electoral Commission, http://www.cikrf.ru.

30. Konstantin Novikov, 'Pryaniki dlya izbrannykh' [Cakes for the Chosen], *Rossiiskaya gazeta*, 6 December 2011.

31. 'V novyi god s novoi Dumoi' [Into the New Year with a New Duma], *Argumenty i fakty*, no. 49, 2011 (these were preliminary but, as it turned out, accurate figures).
32. 'Observers Question Fairness of Vote', *Moscow Times*, 6 December 2011.
33. 'Vladislav Surkov proinstruktiroval otstayushchikh' [Vladislav Surkov Gave Instructions to the Underperformers], *Kommersant*, 10 December 2011.
34. 'Vologda Governor Steps Down', *Moscow Times*, 13 December 2011.
35. Alexander Bratersky, '5,000 Protest Duma Election Results', *Moscow Times*, 6 December 2011.
36. Andrew Osborn, 'Opposition Leader Held as Russia Beats Back Protests', *Daily Telegraph*, 7 December 2011.
37. Andrei Kozenko et al., 'Tsentralnyi izbiratelnyi uchastok' [Central Electoral District], *Kommersant*, 7 December 2011.
38. Andrei Kozenko et al., Ibid.
39. Andrew Osborn, 'Winter Dissent Fuels Hopes of Moscow Spring', *Sunday Telegraph*, 11 December 2011.
40. Ibid. Navalnyi was jailed on the evening of 5 December: Alexander Bratersky, 'Putin Bids for Kremlin Amid Protests', *Moscow Times*, 8 December 2011. For his message of 10 December see http://www.opendemocracy.net/od-russia/alexei-navalny/darkness-is-clearing.
41. Ivan Tyazhlov, 'Rossiya zasbyulletenilo' [They Bulletined Rossiya], *Kommersant*, 12 December 2011; a map 'Kak v Rossii protestovali protiv itogov vyborov' [How They Protested in Russia Against the Results of the Elections] showed the scale of the protest across the country and in other parts of the world.
42. Petr Kozlov, 'Na vybory ot OBSE priedut 200 nablyudatelei' [200 Observers from the OSCE Will Come to the Elections], *Izvestiya*, 5 October 2011.
43. OSCE, International Election Observation, Russian Federation, *State Duma Elections – 4 December 2011, Statement of Preliminary Findings and Conclusions, 5 December 2011*, p. 1, also available on the OSCE website at http://www.osce.org/odihr/85757.
44. Notes taken at the OSCE press conference, Moscow, 5 December 2011.
45. Rossiya-1 television, 5 December 2011.
46. Andrei Semenov, 'Chto vidno izdaleka i vblizi' (What Can Be Seen from Afar and Up Close), *Rossiiskaya gazeta*, 6 December 2011.
47. Ibid.
48. Pervoe zayavlenie assotsiatsii 'Golos' po rezultatam kratkosrochnogo nablyudeniya khoda vyborov deputatov Gosudarstvennoi dumy Rossii, nazachennykh na 4 dekabrya 2011 g. Den golosovaniya (First Statement of the 'Golos' Association on the Results of the Short-Term Observations of the Conduct of the Elections of the Deputies of the State Duma of Russia on Election Day 4 December 2011), Moscow, 5 December 2011. p. 1, available at http://golos.org/elections.
49. One of these reports showed young men at a Moscow polling station engaged in so-called carousel tactics and voting multiple times. In another, an activist of the Solidarity opposition uncovers a stash of ballots already cast for United Russia in the station's toilet. Nikolaus von Twickel and Alexey Eremenko, 'Observers Question Fairness of Vote', *Moscow Times*, 6 December 2011, p. 1.

50. Nikolaus von Twickel, Alexander Winning and Rina Soloveitchik, 'Monitors, Party: up to 25% of Vote Fabricated', *Moscow Times*, 8 December 2011.
51. Per Sidibe and Mikhail Rubin, 'Partiya vlasti gotova na koalitsiyu' [The Party of Power is Ready for a Coalition], *Izvestiya*, 5 December 2011.
52. Miriam Elder, 'Kremlin Crackdown on Election Protestors', *The Guardian*, 7 December 2011.
53. Per Sidibe, 'Storonniki Medvedeva pozdravili "Edinuyu Rossiyu" s pobedoi' [Medvedev's Supporters Congratulated United Russia on Its Victory], *Izvestiya*, 6 December 2011.
54. Irina Granik, 'Dmitrii Medvedev nashel v Dume povod dlya veselya' [Dmitrii Medvedev Found a Reason for Celebration in the Duma], *Kommersant*, 6 December 2011.
55. Ibid.
56. 'Kandidata "protiv vsekh" mogut vernut k zhizni' [They May Return Candidate "Against All" to Life], *Trud*, 7 December 2011.
57. 'Liniya Putina' [Putin's Line], *Rossiiskaya gazeta*, 16 December 2011; Kira Latukhina and Konstantin Novikov, 'Vybore v pryamom efire' [Elections on Air], ibid., 19 December 2011.
58. Kevin O'Flynn, 'Medvedev's Facebook Attack on Protestors Backfires', *Daily Telegraph*, 12 December 2011.
59. Nikolaus von Twickel and Alexey Eremenko (note 49).
60. Jonathan Earle, 'Surkov and Prokhorov in Election Spinoff', *Moscow Times*, 7 December 2011.
61. Nikolaus von Twickel, Alexander Winning and Rina Soloveitchik (note 479).
62. Irina Filatova and Alexey Eremenko, 'Putin Blames Clinton for Vote Unrest', *Moscow Times*, 9 December 2011.
63. Ibid.
64. Andrew Osborn, 'Putin Accuses Americans of Orchestrating Russia Unrest', *Daily Telegraph*, 9 December 2011.
65. Andrew Osborn, 'Protestors are Paid Agents of Western Plot, says Putin', *Daily Telegraph*, 16 December 2011.
66. Poslanie prezidenta Federalnomu sobraniyu [Speech to the Federal Assembly], 22 December 2011 http://kremlin.ru/news/14088
67. V. B. Pastukhov, '"Perestroika" – vtoroe dykhanie: Revolyutsiya i kontrrevolyutsiya v Rossii' [Perestroika – a Second Breathing: Revolution and Counter/Revolution in Russia], *Polis*, no. 1, 2011, pp. 7–28, at p. 24. Acknowledgements for their financial support are due to the UK Economic and Social Research Council (RES-062-23–1378) and the Carnegie Trust for the Universities of Scotland.

Index